SWIFT

Murder and Vengeance in a California Town

St. Martin's Press

Swift Justice

JUSTICE

Harry Farrell

New York

Design by Susan Hood

Library of Congress Cataloging-in-Publication Data

Farrell, Harry.
    Swift justice : murder and vengeance in a California town.
        p.   cm.
    ISBN 0-312-07086-1
    1. Lynching—California—San Jose—Case Studies. 2. Kidnapping—California—San Jose—Case studies. 3. Murder—California—San Jose—Case studies. 4. California—History—1850–1950. 5. Hart, Brooke Leopold. 6. Thurmond, Harold. 7. Holmes, Jack. I. Title.
HV6468.C2F37 1992   364.1′523′0979474—dc20   91-37939

10   9   8   7   6   5   4   3   2

For my wife
Betty Regan Farrell
with love

Contents

Preface

Early in the Great Depression of the 1930s, two service stations—one Shell and one independent—stood opposite each other on San Carlos Street in San Jose, California. The old man who owned the independent station was busy all day because his gasoline sold for a penny or two less per gallon than Shell. The young man at Shell would sit there twelve hours a day and sometimes only a couple of cars would come in.

It was probably during the last half of 1932 that the old man crossed the street and asked the young man, "How would you like to buy me out?" The young man was interested.

"How much would it take?"

"You can have the business for the cost of the inventory." A figure of a few hundred dollars was mentioned.

"I can get the money from my father."

"There is one other condition," the old man said. "You'll have to provide a job for my son."

The son was a slow-witted twenty-six-year-old who had just lost his job with a lumber company.

"OK, I'll put him on at night," the young man promised.

When the young man and the old shook hands on the deal, they set in motion a chain of events that would bring about three homicides, devastate three families, inflame San Jose and blacken its name, spawn an effort to impeach the governor, involve two presidents of the United States in a nationwide moral debate, set off a demonstration in the British House of Commons, and fuel Hitler's World War II propaganda machine.

The young man's name was Francis Wyatt. The old man was Thomas J. Thurmond, and his backward son was named Harold. While working for Wyatt, Harold Thurmond met Jack Holmes, an oil company salesman who came around twice a week, and the two men became fast friends. Little more than a year after their first meeting, both would pay the harsh penalty of lynch law as the confessed kidnappers and slayers of department store heir Brooke Leopold Hart.

The crime of Holmes and Thurmond, neither of whom had been in trouble before, was incredibly brutal and incredibly stupid. Their bumbling execution of the atrocity verged on the comic. And they could have chosen no victim whose popularity and place in the community would more surely guarantee the violent retribution that followed.

A lifetime of close-range fascination with the Hart case led me to write this book. I was nine years old when Brooke Hart was kidnapped. Our home in San Jose was not far from the Hart home, and I went to a school Brooke had attended. Virtually everyone in the city, population then 60,000, knew either the Harts, the Holmeses, or the Thurmonds, or all three, and my family was no exception. One of Brooke's cousins was a schoolmate of mine. My father and Jack Holmes were business acquaintances.

Later, as a San Jose newspaperman, I came to know many other persons connected with the case—police officers, attorneys, vigilantes, friends and families of the principals. I also had the privilege of working with reporters who had covered the story for several newspapers.

The Hart case presents a lurid vignette of lawlessness in the 1930s. In my efforts to tell this bit of history as an informal narrative—not a scholarly treatise—I have learned that the historian's problems in finding the truth often exceed those of the contemporary reporter.

For the fabric of my story, I have used the conventional wisdom about the case, based on the facts as aired publicly and taking at face value the Thurmond and Holmes confessions. Indeed, the preponderance of the evidence supports the long-accepted version of the events.

As an objective reporter, however, I have had to deal with certain evidential inconsistencies which cast at least a passing shadow on that scenario. Had the case gone to trial, these discrepancies might have been explored and perhaps explained, but amid the supercharged emotions of 1933 they were ignored or glossed over. I have tried to examine them fairly in my final chapter, "Lingering Doubts." Each reader must make his or her own judgment of the truth.

My sources are essentially of three kinds: official documents, contemporaneous news reports and commentary, and interviews with persons directly involved in the events or having special knowledge of them. The insights of such persons, who have given information never before publicly aired, shed important new light on much of what happened. With each year that passes, fewer such persons remain. Many who have talked to me over the past several years are already dead.

Long ago the San Jose Police Department cleared the Hart case records from its files, and the only surviving records in the Santa Clara County Sheriff's Department are the county jail booking sheets for Thurmond and Holmes. Under the Freedom of Information Act, however, I have obtained the FBI's 345-page file on the case, exceptional in its detail. Unfortunately, a large number of other FBI exhibits, including two statements in which Harold Thurmond enlarged upon his confession, were destroyed in 1946.

In telling the story, I have striven for literal truth. But where sources are in conflict, in obvious error, or incomplete, I have had to make educated guesses.

Problems have arisen with direct quotations. Certain matter appearing within quotation marks does not meet the same tests for exactness that one would expect in a contemporary news story. Freely I acknowledge taking some liberties here, in order to produce a narrative in human terms. Where direct quotations are invented, however, their purpose is to enhance the truth of what is happening rather than distort or dilute it. What is indeed surprising is the amount of solid documentation I was able to find for quoted matter. For example, the seemingly stilted telephone conversation between Thurmond and Alex Hart, during the final ransom call, is one of the most accurately reported dialogues in the book; it faithfully follows a verbatim transcript in the FBI file. The talk that passed between Holmes and Thurmond before and during their crime is documented in the kidnappers' confessions and follow-up statements. My reconstruction of what went on in the Hart household, and what was said there, is based on recollections of family members.

The timing and sequence of small events is another matter which I could not determine with 100 percent accuracy. I have tried to follow the action minute-by-minute, but time references in both the old newspaper accounts and the FBI reports are often ambiguous or contradictory. Occasionally, in the interest of brevity and clarity, I have grouped repetitive events together, though they may have been spread over considerable time periods. In no such case is the sense of the story changed.

All persons mentioned are real. In a few instances, all footnoted, the names of characters have been changed for considerations of privacy.

In the half century that has elapsed since the events herein related, our customs, values, institutions, and even our language have changed. A word about style and usage is therefore appropriate. In general I have tried to keep the narrative compatible with the time of which it tells, avoiding expressions that have since crept into our idiom. In a few cases, however, I have chosen newer forms purposely, and I would call attention to two of them:

In the journalistic usage of 1933, the combination forms of the word *kidnap* were almost universally spelled with a single "p," i.e., *kidnaped, kidnaper, kidnaping*. To the modern eye these forms appear strange, so I have used today's double-p spellings, even within quotation marks.

The agency name "Federal Bureau of Investigation" was not used until 1935, two years after the Hart kidnapping. Before that, federal agents listed their affiliation only as "U.S. Department of Justice." Because "FBI" is universally recognized, however, I use it throughout this book for ease of understanding, although it is at odds with the designation of the time.

San Jose, California
August 17, 1991

EXTRA

Exclusive News
The Post-Enquirer is the only paper in Oakland which prints the news furnished by International News and Universal Service.

NRA MEMBER U.S. WE DO OUR PART

THE POST ENQUIRER

Oakland — World-City Beautiful   *Industrial Capital of the West*

EXTRA

Vol. 12, No. 279—The Post-Enquirer   OAKLAND, CALIFORNIA, MONDAY, NOVEMBER 27, 1933   THREE CENTS

SAN JOSE VIGILANTES LYNCH 2 HART KILLERS

MOB STORMS JAIL, HANGS KIDNAPERS ON TREES IN PARK

By Ralph Jordan
(Staff Correspondent, International News)

SAN JOSE, Nov. 27 (INS). — Vigilantes today had ridden again in California!

In a fierce throwback to the tumultuous days of '49, they stormed the county jail here, seized two confessed kidnapers and murderers, stripped the clothes from their bodies, strung them to elm trees in the public square and then attempted to make a pyre out of the body of one of their victims!

They hanged Jack Holmes and Thomas A. Thurmond, who admitted the abduction and killing of Brooke L. Hart, 22, Santa Clara university graduate and son of a wealthy San Jose family Nov. 9.

They fought a terrific pitched battle with the combined forces of Sheriff William J. Emig, Chief of Police J. N. Black and the state highway patrol.

They battered down the doors of the jail, dragged the two accused men from the jail across the street from St. James park, the public square of San Jose, and strung them to two elm trees as 10,000 men and women looked on.

Thurmond Pleads for Life;

"Don't hang me, please don't hang me! . . . Thurmond, slender, pale youth, pleaded as the crowd at the jail, numbering about 500, took him from his cell.

Cheering madly, the lynchers dragged Thurmond out of the jail, an old red brick building of California's early days, and across the street to the park, which had filled with well-dressed men and women on their way home after the shows and with college students.

"A rope," a big, burly man in overalls, but with uncalloused hands, cried.

A noose fell over the limb of a tree as automobile spotlights lighted the scene like a ghastly episode of the stage.

"Up with him," cried the throng, and the youth swung in a slight breeze.

"He didn't give, Brooke Hart a chance," cried the burly man as he tugged on the rope.

Sheriff Battles in Vain

Cheers went up again.

A few minutes later Holmes, fighting feverishly against his captors, followed his confederate to eternity.

"You can't do it," he shouted, as he lashed out.

Many fists beat him to the ground.

He was raised.

"What do you say now?" the leader of his group of captors asked as a noose was fitted around his neck.

"Nothing," he answered, sagging to his knees.

Fifty pairs of hands hauled out on his rope and he went up, the crowd stripping him of all his clothing and leaving his

[Turn to page 11, col. 4]

[Turn to page 11, col. 4]

VIGILANTE JUSTICE FOR BROOKE HART SLAYERS

THOMAS THURMOND, one of the slayers of Brooke Hart, is pictured hanged to elm tree in St. James park by vigilantes who seized him and his companion at San Jose.

JACK HOLMES, pictured at rope's end, following San Jose jail attack and lynching. More than 500 vigilantes took part.— Post-Enquirer photos.

BATTLE TOLD BY DEPUTY

By Deputy Sheriff John Moore

What the mob boiled into the jail, I was on guard with Under-sheriff Earl Hamilton, Jailer Howard Buffington and Deputy Sheriff Paul Arterich.

Arterich met the spearhead of the mob. He tried to stop them. He argued. He told them that Justice

[Turn to page 8, col. 8]

[Turn to page 8, col. 8]

GOV. ROLPH HAILS LYNCHING AS 'LESSON'

SACRAMENTO, Nov. 27 (INS).—"This is the best lesson California has ever given the nation!"

Governor Rolph was made here early today by Gov. James Rolph Jr., when informed by International News Service that a San Jose mob had lynched Jack Holmes and Thomas H. Thurmond.

country that California will not tolerate kidnaping," the governor added.

Governor Rolph was scheduled to leave by plane for Boise, Ida., last night but delayed the trip in order to be available in the event of further emergency.

The governor several days ago declined to call out the state militia to protect the two arrangers.

KILLERS NEAR VICTIM'S BODY

SAN JOSE, Nov. 27—The bodies of Harold Thurmond and Jack Holmes, kidnapers hanged by a mob, lay today in the undertaking establishment of Amos Williams, county coroner, close to the body of their victim, Brooke L. Hart.

The bodies of the killers were cut down from the elm trees in St. James park a half hour after the lynching and removed to the morgue.

Mother Begs Mob to Spare Thurmond Life

SAN JOSE, Nov. 27 (INS).—A woman who said she was Thomas Thurmond's mother pleaded with the crowd which begged him to cut him down after he was lynched.

Posse Too Late to Prevent Lynching

SAN FRANCISCO, Nov. 27 (INS).—A delay of 10 minutes more in bastling down the iron doors of the Santa Clara county jail would have allowed time for San Francisco police to arrive there with sufficient gas bombs and guns to stand off the lynching mob. It was revealed by officers here today.

Two machine loaded with officers, carrying with them five dozen of the latest army type of gas bombs, arrived 15 minutes after Jack Holmes and Thomas H. Thurmond were hanged.

SHERIFF HURT IN JAIL FIGHT

SAN JOSE, Nov. 27 (INS).—The official San Jose hospital casualty list of the fight preceding the Hart kidnaping case lynching was as follows today:

Sheriff William J. Emig, hit on head with brick, possible concussion of the brain.

Under-Sheriff Early Hamilton, badly bruised, possible internal injuries.

Jailer Howard Buffington, severely beaten about head and body.

State Highway Patrolman Nick Leader, shot in arm with tear gas gun.

Earl Johnson, druggist, gas poisoning.

Charles Hannah, truck driver, gas poisoning.

The list does not include the scores of citizens and officers who were treated for less serious injuries in physicians' offices and their own homes.

MOB RUSH INSPIRED BY TOTS

By H. R. Hill

SAN JOSE, Nov. 27.—From a small two blows spread the whirlwind of death.

And when Harold Thurmond and Jack Holmes were lynched from the elms in St. James park across from the courthouse, 10,000 citizens cheered and clapped.

"How do you like that, Cecky" Holmes?"

"What do you think of kidnaping and murder now, Harry?"

They stood there, these sober, church-going citizens on eve of the week's foremost religious commotion, and jeered.

It was a spectacle such as California has never witnessed before. Not even the Santa Rosa lynchings were comparable. For here, it seemed, the entire city of San Jose participated.

Cheered and jeered and fainted. Fell like tan pins as the rude figure of Holmes swayed ghostly in the light of a dozen torchlights, as the stilled Thurmond swung more soberly.

POLICE HELPLESS

They banged Thurmond first. They turned from him as vertebrae tore from a jam well done. Then finished Holmes.

A lone policeman watched, helpless, white-faced.

From a small rostrum, we said, spread the whirlwind of death, and then as far as we were in the center of it, listening.

The mobbing of the San Jose county jail can be traced to three tiny, childish. They stood, with rounded eyes, in the foremost rank of the crowd that surged against the south barrier of the court yard. Beside them their father and mother.

CHILDREN REMOVED

"Get them kids out of there," warned a deputy. "Suppose something should happen. No place for kids."

The father complied reluctantly. With the mother the children

[Turn to page 3, col. 1]

[Turn to page 3, col. 1]

The front page of the *Oakland Post-Enquirer*, November 27, 1933. The only paper to carry photos of the lynching in San Jose, it was seized by the city's police department as "indecent."

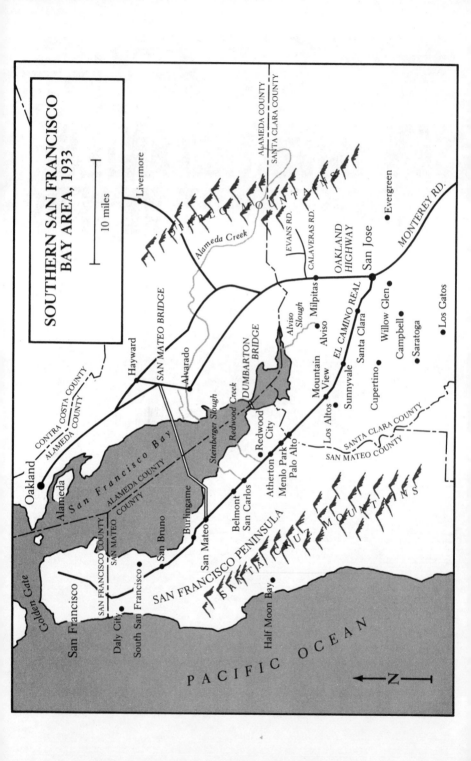

SOUTHERN SAN FRANCISCO
BAY AREA, 1933

10 miles

PINE MOUNTAINS

Livermore

Alameda Creek

ALAMEDA COUNTY
SANTA CLARA COUNTY

EVANS RD.

CALAVERAS RD.

OAKLAND HIGHWAY

MONTEREY RD.

San Jose

Evergreen

Milpitas

Alviso Slough

Alviso

Los Gatos

Willow Glen

Campbell

Saratoga

Santa Clara

EL CAMINO REAL

Sunnyvale

Cupertino

Mountain View

Los Altos

SANTA CLARA COUNTY
SAN MATEO COUNTY

Los Altos

Palo Alto

Menlo Park

Atherton

Redwood City

DUMBARTON BRIDGE

Redwood Creek

Steinberger Slough

SAN MATEO BRIDGE

Alvarado

Hayward

CONTRA COSTA COUNTY
ALAMEDA COUNTY

San Francisco Bay

ALAMEDA COUNTY
SAN MATEO COUNTY

Belmont

San Carlos

SAN FRANCISCO PENINSULA

SANTA CRUZ MOUNTAINS

Burlingame

San Bruno

San Mateo

Oakland

Alameda

Golden Gate

SAN FRANCISCO COUNTY
SAN MATEO COUNTY

San Francisco

Daly City

South San Francisco

Half Moon Bay

PACIFIC OCEAN

N

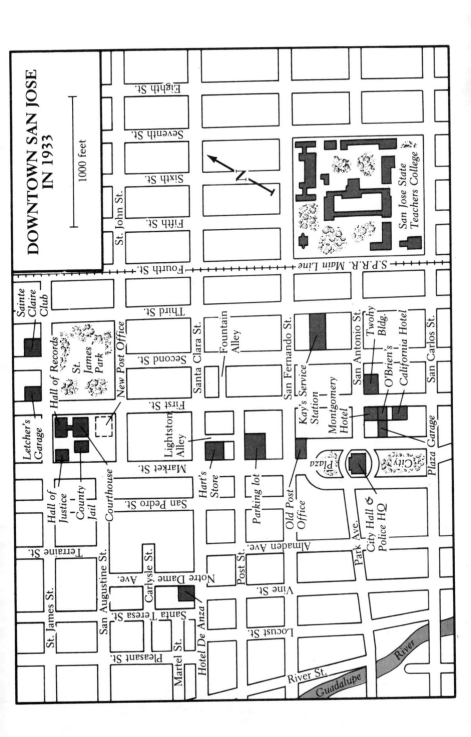

DOWNTOWN SAN JOSE
IN 1933

1000 feet

N

San Jose State Teachers College

Sainte Claire Club

Hall of Records

St. James Park

New Post Office

Letcher's Garage

Hall of Justice

County Jail

Courthouse

Lightston Alley

Hart's Store

Parking lot

Old Post Office

Kay's Service Station

Montgomery Hotel

Twohy Bldg.

O'Brien's

California Hotel

Plaza Garage

Plaza

City Hall & Police HQ

City

Fountain Alley

Eighth St.

Seventh St.

Sixth St.

Fifth St.

St. John St.

Fourth St.

S.P.R.R. Main Line

Third St.

Second St.

Santa Clara St.

First St.

San Fernando St.

San Antonio St.

San Carlos St.

Market St.

San Pedro St.

Terraine St.

St. James St.

San Augustine St.

Carlysle St.

Notre Dame Ave.

Santa Teresa St.

Pleasant St.

Martel St.

Hotel De Anza

San Augustine St.

Almaden Ave.

Post St.

Vine St.

Locust St.

Park Ave.

River St.

Guadalupe River

I

SHOCK AND AFTERSHOCK

1

The Vanishing

It was five minutes before quitting time when Brooke Hart strode out of his family's department store and vanished into the November dusk.

In the days following, the police would be able to trace his movements step by step, up to the instant of his disappearance. There was no scarcity of witnesses. Louis Rossi, the men's wear buyer, was the last to see him in the store.

"Hurry up, there, Curly. Don't keep your father waiting," Rossi called as the youth passed him a few minutes before six o'clock.

"That for you, Baldy," the twenty-two-year-old heir apparent retorted with a grin and a flippant gesture, as he left through the employees' door. From the warm fragrance of the department store, he passed into the chill evening air of Lightston Alley, a drab little side street barely wide enough for the delivery trucks that used it. At this hour it lay deep in the shadows of the buildings crowding each side.

Turning right, Brooke walked a short half-block south to the lot where he kept his car, a light-green 1933 Studebaker President roadster with yellow wire wheels, including two spares mounted on the fenders. His parents had given it to him upon his graduation from Santa Clara University the past summer, and some thought it the most gorgeous car in town.

The distance to the parking lot was about sixty yards. On the way, Brooke smiled and waved across the narrow street to Louise Hartz, a coed at San Jose State Teachers College. He recognized her as a friend of his sister, Aleese. Louise was waiting for her father, who worked for a real estate firm nearby.

"Going to the dance?" Brooke called. Louise knew he meant Kappa

Eta Rho's semiformal dance set for Saturday, two nights away. Brooke's cousin Miriam Fowler, a member of the sorority, was in charge of the arrangements. Louise waved back and made a noncommital reply. Brooke kept going without breaking stride.

He entered the parking lot on the stroke of six and passed three or four minutes in small talk with Henry Kuehn, the attendant, before proceeding to his automobile. He seemed in good spirits. The Studebaker was parked about fifteen yards from where they conversed, and Kuehn watched as Brooke started it up and eased it into the lot's only driveway, heading for the exit on South Market Street. As the car paused at the curb, awaiting a chance to enter the traffic, Kuehn's attention was distracted, but as far as he knew, Brooke had kept going, turning north on Market. The well-lit street was busy with homeward-bound automobiles.

Alex J. Hart, Sr., the father of Brooke and head of the store, waited impatiently with his daughter Aleese in the gathering twilight of the alley, outside the door by which Brooke had exited some ten minutes earlier. At age sixty-four the short, stocky merchant was balding above a round, pleasant face. What little hair he had left was painstakingly combed from one side of his scalp to the other. He was the soul of dignity, a man seldom seen without a three-piece suit. In San Jose's mercantile hierarchy he moved on a special plane of respect as an honest dealer, community leader, and philanthropist. On this evening—Thursday, November 9, 1933—he was slated to attend a dinner meeting of chamber of commerce directors at the San Jose Country Club in the foothills east of town.

Alex Hart had owned automobiles since horseless carriage times, but as a man accustomed to servants, he had never taken the trouble to learn to drive; it did not seem important. He employed a chauffeur, but tonight he was depending on Brooke to drive him. As the minutes ticked by without his son's return, he grew fidgety.

For eighteen-year-old Aleese, the fun-loving younger Hart girl, being the daughter of a department store family was a happy circumstance. With fair skin, blue eyes, and gold-flecked brown hair, she had many suitors, and her social calendar required a formidable wardrobe. This afternoon she had gone "shopping" in her father's stock, and her arms were full of garments from the alteration department. She too was counting on Brooke for transportation. She had meant to walk with him to get the car, but her father, seeing her laden down, had said, "That's ridiculous. Wait here with me." Later she would ponder whether, had she accompanied her brother as she intended, she would have shared his fate. Or would her presence have derailed the whole train of events that followed?

There could be no question about Brooke's understanding that his father and sister were depending on him. They had all gone over the plan together within the hour. At 6:30 that evening Brooke was to attend a public speaking class at the Hotel De Anza, down the street from the store, so he would be on a tight schedule. It had been decided he would leave the store five minutes early, get his car, and return to pick up Alex and Aleese at the Lightston Alley door. He would not have enough time to drive all the way to the country club and back—an eleven-mile round trip—so another arrangement was settled upon: Brooke would take his father just to the Sainte Claire Club, a genteel retreat for the city's monied male gentry, only a couple of blocks from the store. There, in the cocktail hour crowd, Alex could surely catch a ride with someone else headed for the chamber of commerce dinner. After dropping his father off, Brooke could run Aleese home, a quick two-mile ride, and still get back to the hotel for the speaking class.

But now, as 6:15 neared, it became obvious the agreed logistics had gone awry. Alex dispatched an employee to walk down the alley and check the parking lot for Brooke's car. In less than a minute the man returned, saying the roadster was gone.

Brooke's failure to appear was unsettling because it was out of character. The bond between father and son was close, and there was no reason that the lad would willfully leave Alex waiting. More puzzled than alarmed, Alex started inventing what Aleese thought were "silly excuses," one after another, for Brooke's tardiness.

"Maybe he didn't understand we were going to wait for him."

"That's ridiculous, Dad. We just talked about it."

"Maybe he's had an accident."

"Wouldn't we know it by now?"

Perhaps, the father said, Brooke had gone to pick up Charlie O'Brien, his best friend, who was also enrolled in the public-speaking course. Charlie worked at his family's restaurant and candy store a couple of blocks away.

Alex sent Aleese back inside to phone around. The department store was empty now, its vastness dimly lit. From the gift-wrapping room she called home and talked to her sister Miriam. No, nobody there had heard from Brooke. Aleese also tried to call Charlie O'Brien, but someone at the candy store said he had left for the day. Next she placed a call to Jane Hammond, Brooke's steady girl friend—very likely fiancée, though the engagement was not official. A small, classically beautiful brunette from Sacramento, cheerful and intelligent, Jane was a senior at the teachers college and lived in a rooming house near the campus. She and Brooke had been going together for a year and were seeing each other four or five evenings a week, but she had no idea where he might be now. Darkness was thickening in the dingy alley as Aleese rejoined her father.

"I don't know whether I should go to that meeting or not," Alex said tentatively, but instantly he overcame his wavering: "No, I've got to go. I've got to show up."

Deciding he could wait no longer, he asked Jack Foley, a trusted, long-time employee, to drive him to the meeting. Aleese remained at the store until almost seven o'clock, continuing lucklessly to call everyone she could think of who might have heard from her brother. Finally she accepted a ride home with Dale Range, head of the drapery department. He was a favorite of the Hart family and often drove Alex home, his reward being an invitation into the butler's pantry for a nip with the boss.

Charlie O'Brien may have been the last person to talk to Brooke Hart on the telephone. Brooke had called him at five o'clock to remind him of their speaking lesson. The two young men were inseparable. Not only had they chased the same girls and frequented the same beer joints as Delta Sigma brothers at Santa Clara, but now, each having graduated with a business degree the previous summer, they moved in the same circles. Each was the third-generation son of an old San Jose family, being groomed to take over a dynastic business that was a household word. O'Brien's was not your everyday soda fountain, but a California showplace, an elegant restaurant of palatial proportions, paneled in oak and rose-colored marble, aromatic of chocolates, ice cream, and pastries made on the premises.

A little before six, Charlie left the restaurant and strolled over to Hart's, intending to join Brooke there and go on with him to the elocution class, which was designed to develop the forensic skills of young executives. Someone at the department store told him Brooke had already left, so he walked on alone to the De Anza, three blocks west.

The big white house that Alex Hart had built for his family in 1920 was considered by many to be the loveliest residence in San Jose. His wife, Nettie, had admired the Petit Trianon at Versailles, and Alex's architect had adapted its design, producing a two-story mansion with much the same feeling. A pair of slim Ionic columns flanked the front door, which opened onto a broad, balustered veranda that ran the width of the house.

Set back from the street by a deep lawn, the house occupied one of the finest lots on The Alameda, a boulevard much favored by the wealthy of the town. It was a willow-shaded thoroughfare rich in history, being a section of El Camino Real, the mission trail of the Franciscan padres who had Christianized California in the eighteenth century.

Miriam Hart was not alarmed when her sister called home from the store saying that Brooke could not be found. Any number of easy explanations came to mind. Foul play was not one of them.

At twenty, Miriam was midway between Brooke and Aleese in age. She was a slender girl with large, dark eyes, and like her sister was a student at San Jose State. She was supposed to attend a class in life drawing that evening, and a little before seven she climbed into her car to drive to the campus. When she was barely out of the driveway, her engine stalled.

An "act of God," she called it later. She managed to restart the machine and get it back into the garage. As she re-entered the house, the telephone was ringing. She picked it up and heard Charlie O'Brien's voice:

"Did Brooke come home sick, Miriam?"

"No, isn't he with you?" Suddenly Miriam experienced her first pang of visceral fear that something was terribly wrong.

"He didn't show up for the speaking class. I was wondering. . . ."

"Charlie, we don't know where he is. He left Dad and Aleese standing on the street down at the store."

"I'm coming over," Charlie said. "I'll be there right away."

The short trip took him only five or six minutes.

Viewed from the San Jose Country Club on its lofty hillside, the darkened floor of the Santa Clara Valley was a black ocean dotted with flickering flecks of light. Alex Hart saw each light as a home where people bought their clothing, shoes, hats, furniture, appliances, sheets, blankets, towels, yardage, pots, pans, dishes, silverware, can openers, groceries, soap, and playing cards from L. Hart & Son Company. As much as any man, Alex could claim this valley as his domain.

Tonight's dinner, inducting a new slate of chamber of commerce directors, was going to be a changing of the guard in troubled times. The Great Depression, entering its fifth year, suffocated the land. In San Jose as everywhere men were idle, business was off, hoboes poured into town on every freight. The fittest of the town's shopkeepers were surviving, but for others it was a time of quiet despair. This evening there was little consensus about what should be done. President Roosevelt's New Deal, now in its ninth month, was anathema to most of those present—Republicans for whom laissez-faire was an article of faith. If anything set Alex apart from his peers in the room, it was that he did not hate Franklin Delano Roosevelt. Although a Republican, he had voted for FDR in 1932. His advertisements prominently displayed the Blue Eagle of the National Recovery Administration, and he had told his employees, "I have absolute confidence in the NRA program. I think we are on the verge of better times." Some of those attending thought the repeal of Prohibition, predictably less than a month away, would help business. Others, teetotalers, looked upon repeal as the devil's work.

Alex had barely arrived at the country club and was sipping a soon-to-be-legal cocktail when Perry Belshaw, the club manager, gently tapped him on the shoulder.

"You're wanted on the telephone, Mr. Hart," he said. "You may take it at my desk."

Miriam's voice, betraying her fear, greeted Alex when he picked up the phone: "Charlie O'Brien just got here, Dad. He says Brooke didn't show up at the speaking class tonight."

Belshaw saw a deep frown crease Alex's face.

"I must come home right away," he told his daughter, speaking softly. "Ask Charlie to please come and get me." After a moment's reflection he added, "And Miriam, call Chief Black immediately."

John Newton Black, San Jose's chief of police, was a crusty old-time cop with a beaked nose that gave him the look of an angry buzzard. He had been a policeman for forty-four of his sixty-two years, and chief since 1917. Well before the turn of the century he had responded to murder calls in a horse and buggy. His longevity in office was due at least as much to political resilience as to professional competence. He was well-connected fraternally—Masons, Scottish Rite, Shrine, Native Sons, Foresters. A gut-fighter in politics, he was the wily survivor of three decades of treacherous city hall infighting. He had seen a dozen regimes rise and fall, and he understood the wisdom of accommodating whatever regime was running the town at any given moment.

Alex Hart and Chief Black were longtime friends. Alex had once served on the city police and fire commission, and the chief counted on him to drum up merchant support for the sporadic drives to clean up the joints along Market and Post streets. But tonight Black infuriated Miriam when she reached him by phone to report Brooke's disappearance.

"What do you want me to do?" was his brusque response—probably more brusque than he intended. It was likely that his seeming unconcern reflected nothing more than his recognition that most missing-persons cases solved themselves. But it gained him the lasting enmity of Brooke Hart's oldest sister.

Dale Range's car, bearing Aleese, rolled into the porte cochère of the Hart residence, and she entered to find Miriam and Charlie by the phone in the little corridor that led from the side door into the spacious entrance hall. Miriam, who had just hung up after talking to Black, was still fuming about his callousness. It was decided that Miriam, using the family car, would go to pick up Alex, and Aleese would remain to care for their mother, Nettie, who was ill in her upstairs bedroom, unaware of the consternation below. Charlie was dispatched to bring Jane Hammond from her rooming house.

Nettie Hart, a one-time Baltimore beauty, was forty-one—almost twenty-three years younger than her husband. A goiter sufferer, she had undergone a thyroidectomy in late October, and her convalescence had been difficult. Her doctors still deemed her condition precarious. After Miriam and Charlie had departed on their respective errands, Aleese went upstairs and quietly entered her mother's darkened room.

"Want something to eat, Mom?"

"No, I'm not hungry."

Nettie knew that her husband was supposed to be at the chamber of commerce dinner, but she had questions about everyone else:

"What's Miriam doing? What about Brookie?"

Aleese responded evasively. She was determined not to alarm her mother without good cause. And anyway, she had no good answers.

Alex Hart was waiting at the country club door when Miriam drove up; he climbed in with her quickly. As she headed down the road back to town, she told him of the brush-off—or such she deemed it—that the chief of police had given her. When they arrived home, after eight o'clock, Alex and both his daughters held an impromptu conference, reviewing all that had happened in the past two hours. Then the father turned back to Miriam.

"Drive me to the police station," he said. "I'd better talk to John Black myself."

The San Jose police headquarters, along with the city jail, occupied the basement of the city hall, a ponderous, ivy-clad, brick Victorian structure in the center of the City Plaza, two blocks south of Hart's Department Store. A curious tunnel, big enough to drive a patrol wagon through, bisected the basement east to west, with the jail's main cell block on the south side and the drunk tank, reeking of boozy sweat, vomit, urine, and Lysol, on the north. Alex and Miriam easily found the chief's office, which opened off the tunnel on the drunk tank side. Black was still at his desk despite the lateness of the hour. He listened to all that Alex could tell him, but to Miriam he still seemed standoffish, reinforcing her feeling that he wanted no part of the case and was washing his hands of it.

Time dragged in the mansion on The Alameda. Several times Aleese was in and out of Nettie's room, making small talk at her bedside. Thirteen-year-old Alex Hart, Jr., the baby of the family, sensed the tragedy that was unfolding. Brooke was his hero.

Presently Billy Morris showed up unannounced at the door. He and Brooke, close in age, were fast companions as well as cousins. The Morrises—Alex, Sr.'s sister and her husband—lived not far away, and Billy came by often. Tonight he had no inkling of what he was walking into.

Ray Renwick, the scoutmaster of the troop at Westminster Presbyterian Church near the Hart home, worked in the boys' department at the store and was also, unofficially, Brooke's brother-in-law. He was married to the third Hart "sister," Jeannette, who was really the daughter of Ernest Sauliere, the family's chauffeur at the time of World War I. After her natural mother had died, Jeannette and her stepmother had not gotten along, so the Harts had raised the girl as their own, and she had taken their name.

On this night Renwick was attending a Boy Scout court of honor in the Eagles Hall downtown, where several members of his troop were to be awarded merit badges. Midway through the ceremony the door opened, and a deputy sheriff entered, quickly locating Renwick in the crowd.

"I've come to take you to the Hart home," he whispered. "Something has happened."

"What is it?"

"Not here. I'll tell you when we're in the car."

Once they were underway, the deputy said, "Brooke Hart has been kidnapped."

Kidnapping had never entered the family's thoughts until the phone had rung in the mansion at 9:30. Aleese, still awaiting the return of her father and Miriam, had answered:

"Hello."

The soft, unhurried, well-modulated voice of a male stranger inquired, "Is your brother missing?"

"Yes, who is this?"

"Is your father there?"

"No, but he should be here any minute." Even as she spoke, Aleese heard the car with Alex and Miriam arriving in the porte cochère.

"Your brother has been kidnapped," the caller said matter-of-factly. "You'll be hearing from us."

"Please! Hold the line a minute. I hear a car outside now." Terror-stricken, Aleese lay down the phone and ran to meet her father. "Quick, Dad," she called. "A man on the phone says Brooke has been kidnapped."

By the time Alex got to the telephone, the caller had hung up. Now, for the first time, the Harts understood what they were up against.

"We've got to go back downtown and tell Chief Black, right now," Alex announced decisively.

"Can't we phone him?" Miriam asked.

"No, I'm afraid to use the telephone." Alex was adamant. At all costs, they must keep the story out of the papers, lest they alarm or anger Brooke's captors. If they phoned, who knew what reporters might be snooping around in Chief Black's office at the other end of the line?

Alex and Miriam set out once more on the round trip to the police station. On arrival, they learned that Alex's concern for confidentiality was well-founded but too late. Outside the chief's office Miriam ran into *San Jose Evening News* reporter Jim Chesnutt. He already knew Brooke was missing.

"Please don't ask questions," Miriam begged. "This is very serious."

"You might as well level with me," Chesnutt prodded. "The story's coming out. I'm a newspaperman and I'm going to print it. I'd print it if it were about my own mother."

The encounter would sour Miriam on the press throughout the ordeal ahead. Alex Hart, of course, had been naive from the outset in his belief that Brooke's disappearance could be kept under wraps. Too many now knew about it. Fifteen of his employees, who had witnessed his consternation in the alley, had already fanned out across the county in their own cars, combing the back roads for Brooke's roadster. And Chief Black had not been so idle as Miriam supposed. His first move had been to call the chief operator at the San Jose telephone office to request tracing on all calls to the Hart residence. Then he had called Charles Dullea, the captain of detectives in San Francisco, reasoning that if this was a kidnapping, the big city fifty miles to the north was a likely place for Brooke's captors to hide out.

Black's department had just put into service its first four radio cars, 1933 Pontiacs with bulletproof windshields. The chief ordered them to watch for the green Studebaker. He also called Sheriff William Emig, who put a description of the car on the state teletype.

By a little past ten o'clock all of the Harts, plus Charlie O'Brien and Jane Hammond, were back in the family home, beginning a vigil whose duration and outcome they could neither perceive nor guess. Of all those gathered, Ray Renwick was the least worried; he didn't think Brooke had been kidnapped at all. Renwick was from Sacramento, and Brooke had often bunked in his home there while pursuing girls other than Jane. Renwick thought it highly likely that he had run off with one of them and was using a kidnapping ruse to cover his elopement, but kept these thoughts to himself. Now there was nothing to do but wait.

An hour had passed since the frightening call that Aleese had received. Now, at 10:30, the telephone jangled again. Billy Morris, who was close to the upstairs extension, picked it up.

"Mr. Hart?" It was the same voice, menacing in its serenity, that Aleese had heard—the voice of a young man:

"This is your son that you missed tonight."

"Is that you, Brooke?" Morris asked, at the same time realizing it wasn't.

"Is this Mr. Hart?" the caller asked.

"No, I'll get him."

Before Alex Hart could take the receiver, however, Miriam picked up the phone in the downstairs hall and said hello.

"Is this Miriam?"

"Yes."

"Is your brother missing?"

"Yes, do you know where he is?"

Upstairs Alex quietly took the phone from Morris and listened but did not announce himself on the line.

"We have your brother," the caller said calmly. "He is safe, but it will cost you $40,000 to get him back. If you ever want to see him alive again, keep away from the police. We will phone further instructions tomorrow."

Miriam and Alex, like Aleese an hour earlier, were sure they had never heard the voice before.

"Oh, please don't hurt him," Miriam implored.

Her plea was answered by a sharp click.

Black's arrangements with the telephone company quickly bore fruit. Within an hour he had a report that the kidnappers' first call at 9:30— the one Aleese had taken—had originated from an unlisted phone in a speakeasy run by Dan Dwyer in the 1000 block of Market Street in San Francisco. After hanging up, the caller had evidently left the bar and killed an hour before placing the 10:30 call from a pay booth in the Whitcomb Hotel.

It was midnight now. One by one, the fifteen volunteer employees of Hart's store who had scoured the countryside in their cars looking for Brooke's Studebaker were straggling in. No one had seen anything suspicious.

Up at the San Jose Country Club, Alex Hart's troubled departure had put a damper on the chamber of commerce dinner, but it lasted late. Perry Belshaw, the club manager, didn't lock up until after midnight.

A small, neat man with plentiful black hair, Belshaw was thirty-eight years old, a member of Santa Clara County's considerable Portuguese community. He faced a lonely ride to his ranch in the rolling country behind Milpitas, a homely village about six miles north of San Jose on the highway to Oakland. At this hour the roads through the hills were always deserted, so Belshaw was startled when a headlight beam caught his eye as he topped a gentle rise within sight of his house on Evans Road.

As Belshaw approached, he saw that the light came from an automobile parked on the shoulder at a crazy angle. A petting party, he thought, but he dismissed that idea almost at once. Kids who drove to this deserted road to make out did not leave their lights ablaze.

"Need help?" Belshaw called as he braked to a stop. There was no response. He got out of his car, walked over to the strange vehicle, and looked inside. It was empty, but nothing seemed amiss. He circled the car, a convertible, checking the Studebaker nameplate, and then drove the few remaining yards to his house. His wife, Anne, was awake.

"There's an abandoned car across the road, with the lights on," he said.

"My God, Perry," Anne replied. "It's a wonder the battery isn't dead. That car has been there since seven o'clock."

Instantly, Alex Hart's anguish came rushing back to Belshaw, and he picked up the telephone.

"Number please?"

"Operator, get me the sheriff's office."

A sheriff's car arrived twenty minutes later. From newspaper pictures, Belshaw recognized the man who alit from it, wearing a gray suit and a felt hat, as the sheriff himself, Bill Emig. Deputy Felix Cordray was driving. Belshaw led the officers back to the road where the Studebaker was parked, its lights dimming now. Cordray beamed his flashlight at the license plate:

"Yeah, it's the Hart boy's car all right," he said.

2

Players and Manipulators

Louis Oneal, the silver-haired political boss of Santa Clara County, had plucked Traffic Captain William J. Emig out of the San Jose Police Department and made him sheriff for the noblest of reasons.

It had happened three years before Brooke Hart vanished. One of the best trial attorneys in Oneal's law office was destroying himself with drink, and the patriarchal boss wanted to rescue him. Prohibition was in force, so Oneal called the man's bootlegger and asked that his booze be cut off. The bootlegger, more bellicose than wise, told Oneal to mind his own business.

A teetotaler himself, Oneal did not take the suggestion kindly. He next asked George Lyle, the sheriff, to clamp down on the bootlegger, but again he got a brush-off. So in the 1930 elections he supported Emig with his money, wisdom, work, and endorsement, with inevitable result: Lyle was out, and new Sheriff Emig expended much energy knocking over bootleggers' stills.

Oneal had been tightening his grip on the county courthouse for three decades. Before 1900 he had served a term in the state senate, as its youngest member, and returned from Sacramento with the blueprint for his political barony. In every California county there was a law firm that tended the interests of the Southern Pacific Railroad—Frank Norris's "Octopus"—which always ran the state, regardless of which party was nominally in power. Oneal became the "S.P." lawyer in Santa Clara County. Part of the job was snuffing out the lawsuits of grade crossing accident victims, but more important was keeping the local government friendly. So over the years Oneal had backed many candidates and filled the seats of authority with his own people. He had also served as eyes and ears for a series of governors, and the present governor, James Rolph, Jr., was his crony, chum, and neighbor.

In 1930, casting about for a candidate to oppose rebellious Sheriff Lyle, Oneal had seen in Emig what would later be called charisma. At age forty-two, Emig was a family man, ruggedly handsome with blue eyes and prematurely gray hair, outgoing and gregarious with a ready smile. As a San Jose cop, he had acquired what Oneal recognized as a formidable political constituency. A few years earlier, a child leaving school had been hit by a car and killed on a San Jose street, and in the ensuing surge of community grief, Captain Emig had formed the "school traffic patrol," a pioneering venture now emulated across the land. He went from school to school giving safety talks and recruiting the brightest boys for patrol duty. To them he symbolized safety, citizenship, patriotism, law, order, and self-reliance. To their parents he was a homespun hero—the cop who was keeping their kids from getting killed on the way home from school.

Oneal had reason to be pleased with his investment in Bill Emig. The sheriff regularly turned to him for counsel on matters of importance, and moreover, he was achieving a spectacular record as a crimefighter. He had had remarkable success catching killers. Under way in the courthouse at this moment was the trial of one murder suspect Emig had captured, a Portuguese youth named Ray Sousa,* whom we will meet again as our story nears its climax.

Emig's election as sheriff had elevated him to roughly the same plane of community recognition as his former superior, San Jose's Chief Black. The chief maintained correct relations with his ex-underling, but there was no love lost between them. There were those in the SJPD who looked on Emig, for all his recent success, as a poseur and less than a first-rate cop. Although the chief and the sheriff enforced the same criminal laws on their respective sides of the city limits line, their mandates differed. Emig held his job at the sufferance of the voters and Louis Oneal. Black, whose office was appointive, held it at the sufferance of the city manager, the city council, and a man named Charlie Bigley.

The conventional political wisdom was that Oneal owned the courthouse but Bigley owned city hall. It was an oversimplification but not devoid of truth. Bigley was a barrel-chested, forty-four-year-old garage owner and ambulance operator who now, with the end of Prohibition, was about to enter the liquor business as well. These were his licit

*Fictitious name.

enterprises; he also owned and collected the take from slot machines all over town. He had started building his political base while driving a bakery route early in the century by doing favors, especially for the Italians who lived in Goosetown on the south side. Along with the bread, he gave gratefully accepted advice on how to vote. Eventually he influenced so many votes that at any given time at least four of the seven city council seats were occupied by his minions. A benevolent man, Bigley coexisted comfortably with Clarence Goodwin, a sober Presbyterian elder who was the city manager. As long as Bigley could put his people in the police and fire departments—a not inconsiderable advantage for a man who derived his income from ambulances and slot machines—he let Goodwin run the rest of the city more or less by the book. They were an odd couple, but even their foes admitted they ran a taut ship. By and large, municipal services were good and taxes were low.

Governor "Sunny Jim" Rolph was a dandy, bon vivant, and womanizer—the man for whom the word "flamboyant" might have been coined. A buttonhole gardenia was his trademark and polished cowboy boots his customary footwear. He was a beaming, balding man, a little corpulent with advancing age but nonetheless handsome, with blue, laughing eyes, a fringe of white hair, and a finely trimmed white moustache accenting a round, florid face.

Rolph loved to entertain, donning an apron to barbecue steaks for his friends at his Alpine Ranch, high above Los Altos on the wooded western rim of the Santa Clara Valley. But he had to be careful about his own food and drink nowadays because his sixty-four-year-old arteries had begun to harden. He had purchased the ranch because the hunting was good there and because it adjoined the O and O Ranch of Louis Oneal. Like Oneal, the governor was an avid horseman who loved to ride in any rodeo or parade.

Growing up in the last century, "south of the slot" in the workingman's Mission District of San Francisco, Rolph had been a hustler. As a messenger boy for a shipping firm, he had become enthralled with the dispatch of vessels to exotic ports, so in 1900, when he was thirty, he had formed his own shipping company. In 1903 he had founded the Mission Bank.

Wednesday, April 18, 1906, was a turning point for him. A forty-two-second earthquake followed by fire leveled the old, frontier-flavored San Francisco, and Rolph built his public career around its resurrection. Elected mayor in 1911, he ruled city hall for nineteen years, rebuilding San Francisco as a metropolis of grace and splendor. His political creed was simple: make no enemies.

When he ran for governor in 1930, with Prohibition in force, the issue was wet versus dry, and Rolph was a wet. Campaigning in frock coat and silk hat, he romped to victory over the opposition of the Anti-Saloon League. Like other California governors before and since, Rolph took office with one eye on the presidency, but in January 1931, the governorship was a slippery stepping-stone for anyone with White House ambitions. Fourteen months into the Great Depression, meanness and despair were abroad in the state. In his inaugural message he promised "bright days ahead," but now after three harsh, grinding years, that vision had faded, both for the state and for Rolph, who found himself under attack from every side. His straitlaced lieutenant governor, Frank Merriam, was undercutting him; the unions were up in arms because he would not pardon labor martyr Tom Mooney; a legislative committee was investigating corruption charges; and the Grange was mounting a recall-Rolph campaign. And—unseen and unsuspected over the horizon—the Hart case was soon to haunt the rest of Rolph's days, which were fewer than he probably supposed.

The discovery of Brooke Hart's deserted roadster materially affected the police jurisdiction of the case. The remoteness of the spot where the car was found raised the strong possibility that whatever had happened to Brooke had happened outside the San Jose city limits. Clearly, the case had now grown onto Sheriff Emig's turf. If it was as serious as seemed likely, the way he handled it could make or break him in the 1934 elections.

In these first hours after midnight, another officer was also wading into the case. Thirty-year-old Reed E. Vetterli had just taken up residence in San Francisco, as special agent in charge for the FBI. Unlike Emig and Black, he had to please only one man, the bureau's demanding, prudish, egocentric director, J. Edgar Hoover. Vetterli was a stern officer from Mormon country, whose square, brooding face made him look ten years older than he was. He cultivated the grim image. Once when a news photographer commanded, "Smile, Mr. Vetterli," he refused, grunting, "I never smile."

Five months before the Hart kidnapping, Vetterli had joined the FBI's hero ranks by surviving one of the era's bloodiest shootouts, the Kansas City Massacre. On the morning of June 17, 1933, a prisoner-transportation detail had been ambushed at Kansas City's Union Station by three gangsters who opened up with machine guns. When the shooting stopped, four officers and the hapless prisoner that the outlaws were trying to liberate, Frank Nash, were dead; another FBI man had a back injury; and Vetterli an arm wound. The gunmen, including Charles Arthur "Pretty Boy" Floyd, made a clean getaway.

Twenty months had passed since the infant son of Charles Lindbergh had been snatched from his crib in Hopewell, New Jersey. A ransom of $50,000 had been paid, but the baby had been found dead, and no suspect was yet in custody. Across the land, the cowardly felony of kidnap-for-ransom had become big business. Fear gripped the wealthy and the well-known, who had begun hiring bodyguards. Reacting to public outrage, Congress had passed the so-called "Lindbergh Act," establishing clear federal jurisdiction in any kidnapping where the victim was taken across a state line, where extortion was attempted, or where the mails were used.

On the day Brooke Hart vanished, Vetterli had arrived back in San Francisco after a conference in Washington. Fatigued from the train trip, he had retired early. At midnight the phone startled him out of deep slumber.

"Hello. Vetterli here."

The telephone voice was raspy and metallic: "This is Chief Black in San Jose. We have what looks like a ransom kidnap down here, Reed, a bad one. We need all the help we can get."

Flipping his bedside lamp on, Vetterli rolled out of bed and grabbed a pencil and writing tablet from the nightstand. He jotted notes while Black told him everything known so far about Brooke Hart's disappearance. The ransom call at 10:30 from the Whitcomb Hotel meant that at least one kidnapper had been in San Francisco only ninety minutes earlier. Was he still in the city? Was Brooke Hart there too? After the chief hung up, Vetterli's first act was to call Western Union and file a fifty-word summary to J. Edgar Hoover. Next he headed for San Francisco police headquarters.

Bordered on three sides by water at the northern tip of its own peninsula, San Francisco was accessible by car from only the south in 1933. Vetterli quickly arranged for roadblocks on all highways leading down the peninsula, over which all San Jose traffic must pass. Guards were posted on the ferries which—with the Golden Gate and San Francisco-Oakland bridges unfinished—were still the city's only links to the north and east.

Working with Captain Dullea, Vetterli reinforced the San Francisco telephone surveillance that had already traced the ransom calls. Two radio cars were dispatched to lay low in the Market Street strip between the Whitcomb Hotel and Dan Dwyer's bar. In a curious investigative lapse—two hours now having passed since the calls from the hotel and speakeasy—no detective had yet visited either place.

A stroke of luck was at work in Vetterli's favor. One of the brightest young agents in his office, Bill Ramsey, was already in San Jose on another case, and Vetterli put through a call to him at the Sainte Claire Hotel. When he answered, Vetterli briefed him tersely and said, "Get going, Bill, fast."

Ramsey dressed quickly. From the hotel it was only a block's walk to the police station in the city hall tunnel, where a desk sergeant and Black confirmed much of what Vetterli had said.

"What do you know about the victim, Chief?" Ramsey inquired.

"Brookie Hart? A fine young fellow as far as I know. He's in line to take over the store when the old man quits. Good reputation, no bad companions we know about. I don't think he's in any gambling trouble."

The gratuitous remark about gambling stuck in Ramsey's mind. Strange, he thought. His next stop was at Emig's headquarters in the county jail, a grim, boxlike, three-floor bastille that had been erected behind the courthouse in 1871. There he learned that the sheriff had left to check out Perry Belshaw's report of the strange, deserted car on Evans Road.

Ramsey returned to the hotel, retrieved his car, and proceeded to the Hart home on The Alameda, where he rang the bell at 2:30 A.M. Alex Hart answered. Silhouetted in the doorway's dim light, he seemed old and drawn.

"William Ramsey, FBI," the agent announced, offering the leather case that displayed his I.D. Alex beckoned him in, and Ramsey stepped across the threshhold to enter the mansion where, it turned out, he would be secretly staked out for the next six days.

3

The Harts and Their Town

Three days before he vanished, Brooke Hart had served as a pallbearer for his friend Jerome Downing. To the detectives now sifting the events of Brooke's life, Jerome's funeral stood out as a morbid beacon.

The Downing ranch covered a couple of thousand acres of mountainous grazing land northeast of San Jose. Two years earlier, at age eighteen, Jerome had become the man of the establishment when his father, a pioneer in that part of the county, had died of a heart attack.

On the last afternoon of October, with the sun breaking through after the season's first rain, Jerome and his new bride, Marie, had taken Brooke riding across their open range. At this season the hillsides were brown, with the canyons sheltering blue-green thickets of scrub oak.

Jerome was a fine horseman, and when the riders came upon some cattle, he set upon demonstrating his skill by lassoing a steer. Suddenly the creature slipped on the muddy sidehill and fell, pulling Jerome's horse down on top of it and catching him between. As Brooke and Marie watched, the steer's horn punctured Jerome's belly. He never regained consciousness.

After the funeral, close friends gathered at the Downing ranch for lunch, trying to make it lighthearted as they supposed Jerome would have wanted. When Brooke returned home, he told his family he would want that too, when his time came. By itself the remark was unexceptional, but Jane Hammond told the investigators that Brooke had been subject to moody spells lately, and C. R. Hunter, the second-floor manager at Hart's store, said the youth had seemed "quiet and worried" during his last afternoon at work. Taken together, these reports suggested something ominous. The remote spot where Brooke's car had been found was a stone's throw off Calaveras Road, which led to the Downing ranch. A picture began to form in the minds of the investigators: a sensitive young man, overcome by grief, heading into the dark mountains to seek solace—by what means?—on the bleak terrain where his friend had died.

To be sure, this scenario did not explain the ransom call from the Whitcomb Hotel, but that could be anything—a diversion, a hoax, a shakedown. It was a flimsy hypothesis, but one that could not yet be written off. The newspapers were quick to pick up the Downing angle.

"Do you think Brooke may have lost his equilibrium? Could he be acting out of despondency?" a *San Jose Mercury Herald* reporter asked Alex Hart.

The father flinched as if struck in the face.

"It is *impossible* that my son has suffered a nervous breakdown," he responded. "He is in excellent health."

Indeed, at the time he vanished Brooke Leopold Hart was to all appearances a young man for whom every good thing was within reach. He was popular, financially privileged, and, as Louis Rossi would say half a century later, "as smart as they make 'em."

"I emulated Brookie because I rather liked everything that I saw," his younger brother, Alex, Jr., would recall. "He was extremely handsome. He was affable; he had a great smile; he was warm; he was kind to people. He was long-legged, lean, athletic, and he walked like a pony. He had a marvelous gait to him. To me, he was a thoroughbred race horse."

The description circulated by the police, after Brooke vanished, noted his "wavy, ash-blond" hair and "bright blue" eyes. His slender, 5-feet-11 frame carried only 138 pounds when he was stripped, but he was well-muscled. His body was not without blemish; there was a red birthmark the size of a strawberry on his shoulder blade and a mole on his left ring finger. He suffered from flat feet and a protrusion of the fifth metatarsal bone of his right foot.

Not surprisingly for the scion of a garment-business family, Brooke was a natty and meticulous dresser. When he strode out of the department store for the last time, he was a study in gray: His Oxford-gray suit, with a diagonal weave, was flecked with white. His shirt, lighter gray with a narrow stripe, had a fairly high collar whose points were anchored with a collar pin. His tightly knotted four-in-hand tie, which no one could quite describe later, might have been lavender. He wore a double-breasted gray camel's hair overcoat and a pearl gray, snap-brim hat. His pointed-toed, wing-tip shoes, size 10AAA, were of bluish-black calf. His suit coat, topcoat, and hat all bore the store's Brookhart label which, like his own name, combined the surnames of his mother and father.

He was wearing a gold Waltham wristwatch engraved "B.L.H.," with a square band. He carried a yellow Parker pen-and-pencil set, similarly engraved, and he wore a Santa Clara University ring. In his coat pocket was a pair of rimless glasses with tinted lenses in a gold-filled mounting and matching sidepieces that bore his initial in silver. His wallet, by his father's estimate, contained no more than $20 in cash.

On September 1, 1933, ten weeks before he disappeared, Santa Clara University had awarded Brooke Hart a bachelor of science degree in commerce. Then on September 18 there had been a festive banquet at the Hotel De Anza where, in the presence of sixty-three family members and store employees, Alex Hart had conferred on his son the vice-presidency of L. Hart & Son Company. The next morning the *Mercury Herald* had chronicled the event in a full-column story with two photographs. One was a stiffly posed shot of the father handing the son his letter of appointment, in front of a backdrop reading "FUTURE BOSS." The picture was destined to be rerun two months later with the grimmer caption, "Kidnap Victim and Father."

Brooke's new position was no sinecure for a rich man's son. Since childhood he had been groomed to take over the store—a job for which he had demonstrated exceptional aptitude. He had put in his time as a stock boy, run cash between departments, manned the soda fountain, put up grocery orders (to be delivered anywhere in the city for a dime), accompanied his father east on buying trips, and mastered the office routine. Early on, he had shown a genuine dedication to the business, combining a deep sense of duty with a creative imagination. He used Louis Rossi as a sounding board for ideas like replacing the store's homely two-story building with a six-floor edifice outshining The Emporium in San Francisco.

"We could even land airplanes on the roof," he enthused.

Alex Hart was much pleased. From the conviction that he would some day pass the company into capable and compassionate hands, he drew an abiding inner peace. He would remember the September banquet as "a high moment" of his life.

*   *   *

If the *Mercury Herald*'s extravagant coverage of the Hart banquet was essentially a sop to a big advertiser, it probably could have been defended nonetheless on the basis of news interest. Thousands of San Joseans knew Brooke Hart. Housewives saw him two or three times a week when they shopped. They had watched him grow up.

In San Jose Hart's store was more of an institution than the city hall. It was a gathering place and a club. On "Dollar Days" people swarmed there for bargains like women's and misses' knit dresses for one dollar, overalls for fifty-nine cents, work shirts for fifty cents, men's two-trouser suits for $24.95, coal and wood ranges for $59.50, two-piece chesterfield sets for $39.75, playing cards for nineteen cents a deck, and Lifebuoy soap at five cakes for twenty-nine cents. On all these items Hart's gave S&H Green Stamps; on certain days double stamps.

The store had been at the same location, the southeast corner of Santa Clara and Market streets, since Leopold Hart founded it in 1866, buying out an earlier establishment called the Corner Cash Store. Leopold, an honest, industrious immigrant from Alsace, was by nature a booster and a joiner. He belonged to the Odd Fellows and B'nai B'rith, became a community leader, and generously supported the local synagogue.

Alexander J. Hart, Sr., was born July 23, 1869, the only son among Leopold's six children. He went to work at the store as a teenager—as all his own children would later—and in 1902 gained official recognition when Leopold reorganized the firm as L. Hart & Son Company. Two years after that, Leopold died, leaving Alex in command. A gentle, soft-voiced man of great natural courtesy, Alex inherited his father's merchandising knack, civic spirit, and dedication to the community. He was the organizer of the San Jose Merchants Association and became president of the chamber of commerce.

Although ordinarily a man of careful, considered action, Alex Hart had a streak of impulsiveness. He was a never-married, forty-year-old bachelor when, during a 1910 buying trip to New York, he was introduced to Nettie Brooke at a rich friend's Long Island estate. At age seventeen, this dark-eyed beauty from Baltimore was so newly out of finishing school that she had never put her hair up or worn high heels. The Jewish man from California wooed the Catholic girl from Maryland ardently for ten days, until she accepted his proposal, and he married her twenty days after that. Their difference of religion never became a problem. Not only did the marriage succeed, but

Alex also hired Nettie's father, James French Brooke, and brought him to San Jose as superintendent of the store. He was his father-in-law's boss thereafter.

The original Corner Cash Store that Leopold Hart had purchased was small, occupying one of the few brick structures in a modest village built mainly of adobe and redwood. In the ensuing years the store expanded piecemeal into adjoining properties, absorbing four saloons. By 1933, after many facelifts, this structural hodgepodge had evolved into a nondescript edifice occupying two thirds of its block. The company had 200 employees and grossed about $3 million a year.

The town in which Leopold Hart had entered business in 1866 was the oldest civil settlement in California, founded by the Spanish in 1777 to grow food and fiber for the army outpost to the north at Yerba Buena, which would become San Francisco. For the first seven decades of its existence, the pueblo remained somnolent as it passed from Spanish to Mexican to American rule. Then suddenly, in 1848, gold was discovered in California, which two years later became the thirty-first state of the Union with San Jose as its capital. The motley band of pistol-packing, knife-toting legislators who converged there for their first session are memorialized in state lore as "The Legislature of a Thousand Drinks." In primitive San Jose, a dreary village of muddy streets, they found little but alcohol for diversion. Within two years the lawmakers moved out and took the capital with them.

By 1933, however, San Jose belied its Wild West origins and was a town of solid respectability. "The Garden City," it fancied itself, with its miles of shaded streets, municipal rose garden, and seven parks. The 1930 census had enumerated 57,651 persons within the city limits.

The city rose from the plain of the Santa Clara Valley, a rich alluvial deposit up to fifteen miles wide, stretching south sixty miles from the southern extremity of San Francisco Bay and flanked by the 4,000-foot peaks of the Santa Cruz Mountains and the Diablos. Later this terrain would be known as Silicon Valley, crammed with high-technology electronics industry. But in 1933, in the chamber of commerce brochures, it was still "The Valley of Heart's Delight." The valley floor was a carpet of fields, vineyards, and orchards that were pink and white in springtime bloom, green in summer, purple and gold at the harvest. What wealth the city enjoyed was derived from prunes, apricots, pears, strawberries, and grapes. San Jose was the largest fruit and vegetable canning center in the nation, with thirty-three canneries and twenty-one dried fruit packing houses.

By and large the townspeople were stable and industrious. Except for the migrants who came each summer to work in the crops, they seldom moved. The city had 19,000 single-family homes and only 400 apartments. Close to the center of town, the old families lived in ornate, roomy Victorians. On the outskirts, a mile away in most directions, were rows of neat stucco tract homes erected since World War I.

San Jose's Hispanic heritage was in eclipse in 1933. Long ago the Anglo-Saxons and Irish had captured the bases of political power. The chamber of commerce, which cared much about such matters, publicized 1930 census figures showing that almost five sixths of the population was native-born. Among those born elsewhere were 4,321 Italians, 887 Mexicans, 463 Japanese, 273 Chinese, 795 Canadians, 691 English, 136 Scots, 356 Irish, 641 Germans, 310 French, 361 Swedes, 200 Danes, 210 Swiss, and 436 Portuguese. There were 254 Negroes in the San Jose Township.

Probably few San Joseans in 1933 could have precisely defined the word bigotry, and those few would have denied practicing it. Their prejudices, which came with the territory and were uncritically accepted, were not severely malevolent. Most often, discrimination took the form of snobbishness based mainly on economic status.

Racial bias was institutionalized in the Caucasians-only deed restrictions of most preferred residential subdivisions and in laws barring Orientals from citizenship and land ownership. Ever since coolie labor had been imported to work the mines in the 1850s, the "Yellow Peril" had been decried in California. Well into the twentieth century the state constitution had contained a full article titled "Chinese," declaring them "dangerous to the well-being and peace of the state," forbidding corporations to hire them, barring them from public employment "except in punishment for crime," and authorizing cities to exclude them or confine them to ghettos.

San Jose was the seat of Herbert Hoover's home county (the newly deposed president still brooding in his hilltop residence at Stanford), and almost twice as many Republicans as Democrats were registered to vote, but in this first year of the New Deal the city's Republicanism was slipping a bit. Party loyalty was a discounted commodity in the freewheeling, undisciplined California politics of the troubled times. Voting for "the man, not the party" was a growing habit.

The courthouse, where Louis Oneal held sway, was a testimonial to the mind-set of the city, which suffered from a gnawing inferiority complex. After the loss of state capital status in 1852, an obsession to regain it had gripped the town for the rest of the nineteenth century; in 1866 the courthouse had been overbuilt with the idea that it might some day become the statehouse. It was a noble edifice, originally surmounted by a dome worthy of Sir Christopher Wren, but this had been replaced by an incongruous tile roof when the structure had been restored after a fire in 1931. The building's Corinthian portico fronted on St. James Park, a green square shaded with elms, syca-mores, and mulberry trees. Benches along the park's pathways were occupied mostly by old men and drifters.

San Francisco was another focus of San Jose's inferiority complex. In the mid-1800s, when San Francisco was important mainly as the lusty gateway to the mines, San Joseans could afford to be supercil-ious (if a little envious) about its forty-six gambling joints, forty-eight whorehouses, and 537 saloons. But Sunny Jim Rolph's new San Francisco, risen from the rubble and ashes of the 1906 earthquake, was a place of broad boulevards and handsome parks, the mercantile hub of the West, a cultural mecca with museums, galleries, theater, opera, and symphony. San Joseans, reacting to the splendid rebirth of the Golden Gate metropolis, were afflicted with a compulsion to disprove what they secretly feared—that they were, hopelessly, coun-try cousins. They therefore jealously cherished the symbols they per-ceived as confirmation of their own culture: their twenty-nine schools, their forty-six churches, the ivied tower and arcaded quad-rangle of the teachers college, and the Spanish-tiled buildings of nearby Santa Clara University (the latter regarded by red-neck WASPs, however, as a rowdy Catholic football school). Other sources of local satisfaction were the cottage where Edwin Markham had written "The Man with the Hoe," the places Jack London had slept, and the silvered domes of Lick Observatory atop Mt. Hamilton fifteen miles to the east.

For a city with a catch-up mentality, tall buildings were extremely important in the 1930s. San Joseans took inordinate pride in their six puny "skyscrapers," ranging from seven to twelve stories. One of these, a short block east of Hart's, was the squarish, gray brick First National Bank Building where Louis Oneal had his office. Another, three blocks in the other direction, was the cream-colored art deco spire of the ten-story Hotel De Anza, for which Brooke had been bound the night he disappeared. Named for a Spanish explorer, it had been built for $500,000 in 1930 by a syndicate of which Alex Hart was president.

* * *

Agent Bill Ramsey of the FBI, at age thirty, was a small, soft-spoken man with a round face, plentiful dark hair, a prominent lower lip, and dark, piercing eyes that at first scared the life out of Aleese Hart.

Because she had taken the first phone call from the supposed kidnapper, Ramsey began with Aleese when, within minutes after his post-midnight arrival in the Hart home, he undertook a painstaking interrogation of the entire family. She could not imagine why he asked so many questions that had nothing to do with the present trouble. Many of them she resented: Did Brooke drink? Did he chase girls? Did he gamble? Did he tell the truth? Did he lose his temper often?

Ramsey insisted on interviewing everyone in the house. Even Brooke's ailing mother, Nettie, pulled herself together and came downstairs in a robe to submit to his questions. Nettie had been told sometime around midnight that her son was gone. For Aleese, breaking the news to her mother would forever remain among the most painful memories of the whole episode.

Even as the interrogation continued, however, Ramsey's organized, unobtrusive, and tactful approach helped stabilize the anguished household, of which he now became a clandestine member. In the next six days he would become friend, confidant, comforter, and protector of the Harts. He began by giving the bounce to a *San Francisco Examiner* reporter who infiltrated their privacy and stripped photographs from their family album. In the end, Ramsey would play a key role in cracking the case.

Servants had always been a part of the Hart household, which employed a butler-chauffeur, a cook-housekeeper, an upstairs maid, a caretaker, and a gardener with as many helpers as needed. In designing the residence, Alex had made ample provision for the help, reserving a suite of rooms for them in the rear upstairs. Now he invited Ramsey to move into a maid's room which happened to be empty, a commodious one with its own bath. It became the FBI's frontline command post and communications center. Before daybreak the telephone company ran in a private line on which Ramsey could be alerted before any call to the residence was put through. Another special line gave him instant contact with the sheriff's office.

* * *

The investigators trying to get a handle on young Hart began by tracing his life's path from birth—as much of it as they could discern.

Brooke Leopold Hart was born in San Jose on June 7, 1911. His education, as the first son of a wealthy Jewish father and a Catholic mother, combined the democracy of the public school system, the exclusiveness of a private boys' school, and the discipline of the Society of Jesus. For a time he was enrolled in the fashionable William Warren School in Menlo Park. In San Jose he attended public elementary and junior high schools and Bellarmine Prep, a Jesuit institution for boys destined for Santa Clara University, which he entered in 1929.

At college he did well scholastically, made many friends, and plunged into fraternity life. SCU was a small school then, with some 450 students, two thirds of whom boarded on campus. Brooke, who lived only a mile and a half away, often brought his boarding friends to the house to enjoy home cooking. Among them was SCU's most famous undergraduate, former child actor Jackie Coogan.

On campus and off, Brooke became immersed in participatory and spectator sports. He exercised daily, played tennis on a private court, loved horseback riding, enjoyed camping, swam well, and was a hard-hitting boxer.

"He used to knock the hell out of me," recalled Ray Renwick, his usual sparring partner, long afterward.

Another friend who sometimes dined at the Hart table was Joseph Karesh, the rabbi of San Jose's Temple Bickur Cholim, to which Alex contributed generously, as his father had. At age twenty-five Karesh was the youngest rabbi on the West Coast, only three years Brooke's senior. Brooke and Renwick enjoyed arguing religion with him. From time to time Brooke pondered choosing between the Catholicism of his mother and the Judaism of his father. Although the family honored both faiths, he had neither been baptized nor had his bar mitzvah. Any choice he might make would risk hurting the feelings of one parent or the other, and he had not yet made one by November of 1933.

As the detectives canvassed the missing man's friends, relatives, and business associates, they grew skeptical and weary of hearing the same laudatory adjectives employed repeatedly to describe him: "gentle," "tender," "considerate," "temperate," "moderate," "affable," "likeable," "truthful." Charlie O'Brien called Brooke a "natural businessman," serious about his career but with a sense of humor and the knack of "kidding somebody and getting away with it." To another friend on the Santa Clara campus, Brooke was "just a helluva guy, one of the best . . . soft-spoken, wouldn't hurt anybody."

But occasionally a jarring note reverberated through the favorable chorus. On Friday, the day after the disappearance, the nervous young son of a San Francisco merchant appeared at police headquarters in that city and identified himself as Clark Burnham,* a friend of Brooke's. He was turned over to Vetterli, who had not yet departed for San Jose. After beating around the bush for a time, he came to the point.

"Mr. Vetterli, there's a man Brooke is afraid of."

"Tell me about it."

"His name is Jack Steele.* Brooke and I picked him up three or four years ago in San Diego. We had never met him before."

"Go on." Vetterli stared impassively at the young man.

"Steele has been following Brooke around ever since. He even came to Brooke's home a year or two ago and spent a couple of nights there."

The merchant's son fidgeted and stammered before continuing. Later Vetterli recorded, in stiff wooden FBI prose, "Burnham after close questioning intimated that Steele, Burnham and possibly the Victim [Brooke] had possibly indulged in some degenerate parties. However, this took place several years ago."

Burnham said Steele could be traced through a certain store on Pine Street in Long Beach, California, and Vetterli took the tip seriously enough to query the Los Angeles FBI office. The story had a grain of truth, but the facts were garbled. Several years earlier the Long Beach storekeeper had known Steele for a few weeks and had met both Brooke Hart and Burnham in Steele's apartment, but he had seen neither of them since.

Basking in the glow of official attention, Burnham would become a prolific tipster as the investigation continued. On his own, he journeyed from San Francisco to San Jose to be reinterviewed, and he sent the FBI agents letters about other "suspicious" characters in Brooke's life.

Joining Ramsey in San Jose, Vetterli hoped Brooke's diary would produce some clues. It was a precise record kept in great detail, but it only deepened the mystery. On the last page of the 1932 volume Brooke had written, "Continued to 1933 in next book," but all efforts

* Fictitious name.

to find the 1933 diary failed. Hart family members recalled seeing it around the house but could not account for its disappearance.

Whenever the agents ran out of others to interrogate, they returned to the victim's best friend, Charlie O'Brien. In one session they discreetly questioned him about Brooke's sex life and learned that sometime in 1931 or 1932, before his relationship with Jane Hammond, the missing youth had had a heavy fling, lasting a year, with a Sacramento girl named Marie.* The episode produced a revealing note in Vetterli's next report to J. Edgar Hoover: "It was ascertained that during the time Hart had associated with Marie, he had intercourse with her on at least one occasion."

If Brooke was mildly what would be later be called a swinger, he nonetheless had a strong puritanical streak. He screened his sisters' dates or arranged to double-date with them as a chaperone, and he monitored their behavior. He would not tolerate profanity, obscenity, or crude language.

"We couldn't even use the word 'darn!' " Miriam would remember.

Vetterli was much impressed by Jane Hammond, who remained at the Hart residence for the duration of the family's ordeal. One of his reports described her as "a very intelligent young lady [who] probably knows Victim better than anyone else." Jane was outgoing and forthright when Vetterli took her aside for questioning.

"When was the last time you saw Brooke?"

"Wednesday night." She named a popular San Jose speakeasy where they had gone for "a couple of drinks." When they parted later, she said, "He told me he'd call me at five o'clock Thursday afternoon. I was disappointed when he didn't; it wasn't like him to forget."

Vetterli paused, trying to fit this information into the time frame of the case. It did not seem to have great significance; the time at which Brooke had failed to call Jane was an hour before he had walked out of the store. Still, Brooke's default on the call was worth remembering.

"You say you went to a speakeasy. Does Brooke drink a lot?"

"Not a lot. He knows when to stop. He never gets sloppy."

"Does he gamble?"

"Not to excess."

Here was another affirmation of Brooke's moderation. Jane's words jibed with what others had said, trivializing Brooke's encounters with

* Fictitious name.

The Bottle and Lady Luck. (Alex: "He was never drunk in his life. I've seen him take one or two cocktails, perhaps; he always rejected a third cocktail." And Burnham: "He didn't gamble over fifty cents at a time.") Yet the frequent mention of alcohol and gambling fell uncomfortably on the Mormon ear of Reed Vetterli. The picture taking shape in his mind seemed to be that of a rich kid moving with a fast crowd in shady circles. Prohibition was still the law of the land— for a few weeks yet, anyway.

Vetterli got hold of Bill Emig. Most of San Jose's speakeasies were outside the city limits and thus in the sheriff's lenient jurisdiction. The two men made the rounds together, stopping first at the Portulupis' place.

Yes, said Mary Portulupi, Brooke Hart came in often to buy liquor, a pint at a time in a hip flask, usually to take to a dance or somewhere. He was always with Jane Hammond. As a matter of fact, they had been there just last Tuesday night, two days before Brooke disappeared.

"Brooke always conducted himself like a gentleman," Mary said. "We trade at Hart's store, and we're very fond of him."

The next stop was the Robin Hood Inn.

"The Hart boy? Sure, he comes in," said Ted Dorias, who ran the place. "He drinks a little, gambles a little, and probably plays around a little. Pretty normal. He was in here Thursday night with his regular girl. They drank for a while, and hey, Brooke got to feeling pretty good. He winked at me and said the girl was a real good sport if she got a couple of drinks in her."

"What night did you say that was?"

"Thursday, around nine or nine-thirty."

"You're sure about that?" Vetterli pressed.

"Positive, why?"

"By then, Brooke had been missing for three hours."

Vetterli and Emig went on to Frank Carnese's place where, according to rumors, Brooke had put out several bad checks and IOUs. Carnese was out of town and no one else could talk, so the two officers went to examine Hart's checking account at the First National Bank. It was the only bank account Brooke had, and hardly the account of a spendthrift playboy. The average balance over five years had been $200. On November 1 it had been down to $133, but one day before he vanished Brooke had deposited $55, so the current balance was $188. There had been no bounced checks or overdrafts.

The officers also checked with Western Union and Postal Telegraph, determining that Brooke had neither received nor sent any telegrams or money orders in the period immediately preceding his disappearance. And the telephone company said no long distance calls had been placed from the Hart residence since the beginning of the month.

Like images seen through a slowly turning lens, the events of Brooke's last days before the kidnapping gradually sharpened into focus for the detectives. Football had been much on his mind; he had been getting up a party to attend the Santa Clara–St. Mary's game on Sunday, November 19. He had invited Joe Karesh, the rabbi, who was a great sports fan. Miriam wanted to go, and Jerome Downing and his wife would be in the group. When these plans had been laid, in late October, who would have guessed that by the date of the game, Downing would be dead and Brooke feared so?

In October's last week there had been an incident that was unsettling at the time and now puzzling to the investigators. As Brooke had been parking his car not far from the store, three hard-looking men in another machine had cut in on him, attempting to pin him to the curb. With his engine still running, he had quickly shot away, out of the trap. Brooke had belatedly told his father about the episode, just the day before he disappeared.

From the time of Brooke's date with Jane Hammond on Wednesday evening, November 8, the investigators were almost able to trace his actions minute by minute during his last twenty-four hours on the scene.

On the way to work Thursday morning, driving his Studebaker, he had stopped to fill up with gas. This was significant because later, when the car was hauled back to San Jose from its place of abandonment, the tank was still only a little below full. Between Brooke's disappearance and the discovery of his automobile, it appeared to have been driven little more than the ten miles or so between the store and the spot where it was found.

Brooke had used part of his Thursday noon break visiting the office of Dr. W. H. Heuschele, to obtain relief from soreness caused by his foot deformity. The doctor had covered the protruded metatarsal bone with a felt pad, held in place with two-inch adhesive tape.

Most of Thursday afternoon Brooke had spent on the second floor at the store. About 2:30 he had been visited by a man wearing a salt-and-pepper suit, a gray hat with black band, and gold-rimmed glasses. The visitor was about five-feet-nine, weighing 155 pounds, and about thirty-five years of age, with a ruddy complexion. Brooke had conversed with him in ordinary tones.

It became clear to the investigators that dependability was prime among Brooke Hart's virtues. He kept his word; he was a creature of habit. Alex Hart told Ramsey that his son had been at the store every business day since he had become vice-president, usually remaining until closing time. What neither of them knew was that Brooke's regularity had been noted by others, and that when he had left the store on Wednesday of that week—as well as on Thursday—distant eyes had been watching.

4

A Sailor's Clue

The dry telephonic ultimatum of the kidnapper—"If you ever want to see him alive again, keep away from the police"—had chilled Alex Hart to his marrow, as intended. The admonition had been given too late, of course; by that time the police had been on the case for more than two hours. The *Mercury Herald* was all over the story already and would have it on the streets by morning.

Still, Alex felt compelled to make some show of good faith to his boy's captors, so with the concurrence of the police he issued a request to all news media to withhold specific mention of the kidnapper's phone calls and ransom demand. The *San Francisco Chronicle* and the Associated Press honored the plea; the *Mercury Herald*, which was ordinarily solicitous of Alex Hart's every wish, did not. The headline blazed across four columns of its front page on Friday morning:

Brooke Hart, Son Of Wealthy
Merchant, Kidnapped, $40,000
Ransom Demand Is Received

As the events became known, people in San Jose and across the land reacted. Driven by motives noble or base—desire to help, lure of the limelight, hope of reward, outrage, compassion, spite, or self-interest—they came forward with their hunches, suspicions, guesses, and observations. As the tips poured in, none seemed more important than one from Gertrude Van Arsdale, whose husband ran Hart's groceteria.

"I saw Brooke at twenty minutes past six last night," she reported. "He was alone in his car, and I waved at him." She had been outside her home at Fourteenth and Santa Clara streets when Brooke had driven by, eastbound on Santa Clara.

"Are you sure it was Brooke?" agent Vetterli asked her. The time she mentioned was at least fifteen minutes later than the last previous sighting.

"Oh, yes, I'd know that roadster anywhere."

John Sepulveda, who grew apricots in the hills east of Milpitas, was another who came forward. A neighbor of the Belshaws, he too had spotted Brooke's Studebaker on the east side of Evans Road at seven o'clock Thursday evening, about the same time Anne Belshaw had. He had been driving north, on his way to a dairy farm to buy milk cheap for his children. He said the car's lights were on, and he thought a man matching Hart's description stood in the shadows alongside. When he returned twenty minutes later, the car was still there but the man was gone.

The investigators now had three witnesses—Mrs. Van Arsdale, Sepulveda, and Ted Dorias of the Robin Hood Inn—who ostensibly had observed Brooke Hart, free of duress, during the first three or four hours of his absence. But these observations, not fitting into any neat pattern, raised more questions than they answered.

If Mrs. Van Arsdale was right, then Brooke had been fifteen blocks to the east of the department store a quarter hour after he left the parking lot, alone and headed in the general direction of the spot where his car was later found. But the street that naturally led to that lonely spot was North Thirteenth Street, and if Brooke was traveling east at Fourteenth and Santa Clara, he had already overshot it.

Sepulveda's sighting deepened the enigma. The shadowy man he had glimpsed beside the Studebaker had seemed to be tinkering with the motor. But when recovered, the car had been full of gas and in perfect running order. If indeed Brooke had been standing alongside it on dark, desolate Evans Road, he could have been keeping a rendezvous—but with whom?

Dorias's emphatic declaration that Brooke had been tipsy in his speakeasy about nine o'clock Thursday night likewise presented problems. Dorias insisted that Brooke was accompanied by "the same girl he always brought with him," and by all testimony that had to be Jane Hammond. Yet at the hour in question Jane had already arrived at the Hart residence with Charlie O'Brien.

Still, Dorias could be right. Had Brooke Hart, Jane's supposedly faithful swain, been stepping out with another girl on the sneak? Stranger things had happened.

On the night of the disappearance, Louis Rossi had left Hart's store as soon as the door closed, scarcely five minutes behind Brooke, and hurried home to a family observance of his thirty-fifth birthday. A tall, balding man with heavy black brows and a salesman's plastic smile, he could count himself fortunate in this autumn of 1933. Many men his age were queued up at soup kitchens, riding the rails, or pounding the pavement in search of jobs that did not exist.

Rossi was earning an adequate if not princely salary as manager of six departments at the store, and his future was as bright as his present was secure. He was married and had a comfortable home on Iris Court in the desirable and slightly snooty Willow Glen district. His little girl, Beverly, was a kindergartener at Willow Glen Elementary School.

Few among the store's 200 employees were closer to the Harts. In old age, Rossi would recall, "Alex Hart practically raised me, you might say. He was as close to me as my father." Rossi had begun working for the Harts when he was fourteen, as an office boy after school, and he had been with the store ever since, with time out for an Army stint during World War I and for college. Driven by ambition, he smilingly shouldered every burden Alex placed upon him, performing capably as he rose through the ranks. By his midtwenties he was president of the Hart's Welfare Association, organizing "pep parties" before every sale. He was a big-brother figure to Brooke and a favorite of Nettie. It was Louis to whom Alex had entrusted the arrangements for the banquet marking Brooke's elevation to the store's vice-presidency.

Rossi was a comer in the community as well as at the store. He was going through the chairs of the American Legion's Willow Glen Post and was on the committee for every patriotic parade. The political string pullers were beginning to mention him as a likely candidate for public office.

After his birthday party, he retired early. He was still asleep when the phone rang early Friday morning. He groped for the receiver.

"Hello."

"Louis, this is Mrs. Hart. Something has happened. Can you come to our house right away?"

Still unaware of the night's events, Rossi was unprepared for the desolation that engulfed him as he crossed the Hart threshhold. "Terrible, just terrible," he remembered much later. He was taken to the FBI command post upstairs, where Ramsey sized him up and decided to trust him.

"We have no idea where Brooke is or what's going to happen," the agent said. "But we think the kidnappers may send some sort of note, either to the house here or to the store. For the time being, all the mail that comes in at the store will be turned over to you."

"Yes, sir." Rossi regarded Ramsey with awe.

"You'll recognize most of the mail right away, of course, but keep your eye out for anything that looks strange and bring it to us. OK?"

Rossi nodded. Ramsey gave him detailed instructions about handling suspect letters only with tweezers and covering them with cellophane.

"Yes, sir. Is that all?"

"Not quite. It's pretty well known, isn't it Mr. Rossi, that you are a close friend of Brooke and the Harts?"

"Yes sir, everybody knows it."

"Then the kidnappers may try to make contact through you. We've already put a tap on your home phone."

As the mystery of Brooke's whereabouts deepened, opportunists all over the country began clambering aboard the publicity bandwagon. In Chicago, an assistant state's attorney named Mal Coghlan told newsmen he was sure that "Handsome Jack" Klutas had a hand in the California abduction. Klutas was an elitist underworld figure, a college graduate with his own gang, sought at this time for a string of ransom kidnappings in Illinois.

"All the gang members are well-educated and use three- and four-syllable words with facility," Coghlan solemnly explained to the reporters. He was certain Klutas was behind the Hart kidnapping because he had recently been in California and was known to hang out in Tijuana. Although Tijuana was 500 miles south of San Jose in another country, Coghlan's straight-faced declaration was enough to get his name on the national newswires.

Pretty Boy Floyd, Vetterli's gun-wielding antagonist in the Kansas City Massacre, also cropped up on a growing list of Hart case suspects. A tipster told police of seeing Floyd at the old New Almaden quicksilver mine south of San Jose, but searchers who combed miles of deserted shafts and tunnels found nothing.

One officer snorted at the "Chicago gangster" theory. To Chief of Police Black, the talk about Klutas and Floyd was nonsense.

"This is local talent," he told the newspapers. The kidnappers obviously knew too much about Brooke's habits, his family, and his friends to be outsiders. The ransom caller had used Miriam's name as a friend or acquaintance would. And only someone familiar with the lay of the land around San Jose would have picked remote Evans Road as the spot to abandon Brooke's car.

Of all who worked at Hart's store, none was more acutely attuned to the family's agony than Jack Foley, who had finally driven Alex to the chamber of commerce meeting when Brooke failed to appear. Afterward Jack had headed for the home of his brother Bill, knowing that if Brooke had fallen victim to a local hoodlum, Bill could find it out quicker than anybody—certainly quicker than the police. William E. Foley was San Jose's best known criminal lawyer, with unmatched contacts in the underworld. He was the mouthpiece for virtually all the seedy gamblers, speakeasy owners, racketeers, gunfighters, punks, pimps, and petty grafters.

The Foleys and the Harts were neighbors on The Alameda and good friends. The friendship had been reinforced during recent years when Brooke and Foley's son, Jim, had gone through Bellarmine Prep and Santa Clara University in the same class.

Upon hearing his brother's report of Brooke's disappearance, and after talking to Alex by phone, Bill Foley had started working his sources. With son Jim at his side, he spent all Thursday night on the phone to his outlaw clients and friends. What about Brooke Hart? What did they know? Had they heard anything? If recognized hoods had anything to do with Brooke's disappearance, Foley knew he would soon have a line on it.

Hours later he came up dry. No one had even a theory about what had happened to Brooke, let alone a rumor or a fact.

"Sightings" of Brooke Hart from one end of the state to the other, after his description went out over the wires and his picture appeared in the papers, compounded the investigators' bafflement.

Seventy miles north of San Jose in the Marin County village of Ross, a tall young man with blond curly hair, hatless, and wearing a gray suit was seen by three women and a twelve-year-old girl about three o'clock Friday afternoon. He appeared disoriented, asked directions to the business district, and then stumbled off in the wrong direction.

At about the same hour, Brooke or someone much like him was also reported more than a hundred miles farther north, in the tiny village of Orland. The chief of police there said the young man had lunch in a restaurant with two Italians.

In Los Angeles, 600 miles south of Orland, District Attorney Buron Fitts came forward with a strangely similar report. Fitts, an ambitious politician who had served a term as California's lieutenant governor, announced that Brooke had been positively identified in Los Angeles early Saturday morning, when two burly men had brought him into a cafe. The owner of the place said one of the men stayed with the youth, holding onto his coat, even when he went to the men's room. The two men ordered whiskey and offered a drink to their captive, who refused it. Later, the three got into a car and drove away.

Almost lost amid the publicity given these contradictory sightings was an inconspicuous paragraph far down in a *Chronicle* story:

> Police last night were investigating a report that a young man answering Hart's description, accompanied by two men, had crossed the San Mateo Bridge Thursday night in a closed sedan.

The San Mateo Bridge, linking the San Francisco Peninsula town of that name with Hayward south of Oakland, was about twenty-five miles north of San Jose, spanning the southern arm of San Francisco Bay.

Finally, sometime Friday, the San Francisco police paid a belated visit to the Whitcomb Hotel, where the ransom call to Miriam had originated Thursday night. It had been placed from a pay booth in the lobby, around the corner from the cigar stand. The man behind the counter could not remember anyone or anything unusual.

"Mister, just about everybody uses that phone," he said.

Nor could anybody at Dan Dwyer's speakeasy, from which the earlier call to Aleese had been placed, remember anyone who might have placed it.

In Washington, Vetterli's midnight telegram awaited J. Edgar Hoover when he arrived at his desk Friday morning. Scanning it, the FBI director sensed at once the importance and publicity potential of the Hart case. He wired back, ordering Vetterli to submit summary reports each night. Especially he wanted to know the attitudes of the Hart family and the local police. Over the next two days, Vetterli repeatedly reassured Hoover on both counts. Alex Hart's attitude, he reported, was "wonderful," and police cooperation was "100 per cent." Nowhere was the cooperation better than inside the Hart mansion. By Friday afternoon Ramsey had been joined in the back room upstairs by Deputy Sheriff Ray Hicks, a spare, angular, cigar-chewing man with a thin face and a prominent nose. Hicks's long suit was common sense. He empathized in the suffering of the Harts but remained cheerful and matter-of-fact in their midst. Ramsey quickly sized him up as a capable officer. From the outset, the two men were a happy team.

Friday passed with no further word from the kidnappers. Alex Hart was therefore dismayed when he was handed an early edition of Saturday's *Examiner*. A bold headline jumped out at him from the front page:

Hart Kidnappers Send Three Warnings;
Girls Deliver $40,000 Mystery Notes;
'We Mean Business,' Gang Declares

The story, which bore no byline, said Brooke's abductors had made three new contacts with the Harts on Friday, the first by a young woman who had rung the family's front doorbell and handed Alex an envelope addressed "in an educated hand." The reporter had drawn on a vivid imagination to compose the fictitious communication:

THIS IS TO VERIFY OUR TELEPHONE CALL LAST NIGHT. WE HAVE BROOKE AND ARE TREATING HIM RIGHT. NO HARM WILL COME TO HIM: 1. IF YOU WILL PAY OVER THE MONEY AS WE WILL DIRECT YOU TO, AND 2. IF YOU STAY AWAY FROM THE COPS . . . WE WILL GET IN TOUCH WITH YOU LATER AND TELL YOU WHERE TO LEAVE THE MONEY.

The girl who had delivered the message, according to the *Examiner*'s account, said it had been handed to her "by a well dressed man of 25 who gave no appearance of being a foreigner." After requesting her to take it to the Hart home, he had "tipped his hat and rapidly walked away."

One hour later, the story went on, had come the second contact, a phone call in which a voice of unspecified gender but "with a trace of accent" had renewed the warning, "Don't call in the cops!"

The third supposed contact had come at 6:30 Friday evening. The newspaper said a different young woman had shown up on the Hart doorstep with another note, saying she had been asked to deliver it by a man who had stopped her on the street:

WE UNDERSTAND THAT YOU ARE PLANNING TO USE LOUIS ONEAL AS YOUR INTERMEDIARY. ONEAL IS NOT ACCEPTABLE TO US AND WE DO NOT TRUST HIM. WE INSIST THAT YOU ACCEPT AN INTERMEDIARY OF OUR CHOICE THAT WE CAN TRUST.

There was not a scintilla of truth in the *Examiner*'s account. Alex showed the offending newspaper to Vetterli.

"Damn!" the agent said softly.

At this point, everything depended on coaxing Brooke's kidnappers to reopen communication. Whoever and wherever they were, Vetterli knew they were tense, uncertain, perhaps even irrational, probably perusing every newspaper that came off the presses for clues to what the Harts and the police were doing. A story like this, despite its patent falsity, could only confound them and scare them off.

The reported "third contact" with the kidnapper told something about the origin of the spurious story. The yarn had been concocted or planted by someone conversant with the politics and professional dynamics of San Jose—someone who understood boss Oneal's role in the town. There had been no thought at all about using Oneal as a go-between. But whoever had dreamed up the story probably knew that Alex Hart and Oneal sat together on the board of the First National Bank, that Sheriff Emig had been elected with Oneal money, and that Oneal was the sheriff's mentor.

"What can we do about stuff like this, Mr. Vetterli?" Alex asked.

"We can make them wish they'd never printed it."

"How?"

"I'll put out a denial. And if you're up to it, why don't you give an exclusive interview to the *Chronicle*? They'll love to catch the *Examiner* lying. You can set the record straight."

"I'll do it," the father nodded.

A few minutes later Vetterli emerged from the front door of the Hart residence and crossed the lawn to where a knot of newsmen stood.

"Anything new, Mr. Vetterli?" called the *Examiner*'s man.

"If I told you the truth, you wouldn't print it."

By this time all the reporters were bunched around the FBI man, pencils poised.

"Gentlemen," he continued, "I do have a statement, and I want to make it as emphatic as I can. There has been no further contact of any kind with the kidnappers since the first phone calls Thursday night. No notes, additional telephone calls, or other communications of any kind have been received by the family or its representatives, or by any law enforcement agency. In fact, there has not been a single solid development in this case in the past twenty-four hours. It stands exactly where it did at this time yesterday."

Now came Vetterli's turn to deceive.

"I should tell you," he went on, "that the federal government, respecting the wishes of Mr. Hart, is withdrawing all agents from the house here. All the local officers have also left. We want to give Mr. Hart and the family a free hand in dealing with the kidnappers. We will not take any further action in this matter until Brooke Hart has been safely returned."

The reporters had already noted the departure of police cars from around the residence. What Vetterli was telling them now, however, was a deliberate, calculated lie, a ruse to make the kidnappers lower their guard. Ramsey and Deputy Ray Hicks were still at their upstairs command post, with every intention of staying.

The next day, still fuming, Alex let it be known that he would be amenable to an exclusive interview with a reporter from the *Chronicle*. Soft-spoken, bespectacled reporter Leo Raridan soon appeared at his front door and was admitted without delay.

Inside, the tension was palpable. Raridan sized up Alex Hart, who greeted him with calm courtesy, as a man running on his last reserves, thinking well but drained of vitality. Alex spoke softly, choosing his words with care to reinforce what Vetterli had said.

"In the first place," Alex declared, "I want to nail as an absolute fabrication—a damned lie if you please—the statement published in the *San Francisco Examiner* or any other statement that the kidnappers of my son have contacted me by phone and letter since I received the first $40,000 ransom demand. The kidnappers have made absolutely no contact of any kind since Thursday night's anonymous telephone calls from San Francisco."

At Pier 32 on the San Francisco waterfront, merchant seaman Michael Redinger of the tanker *Midway* went topside late Friday afternoon for some air. The ship was riding high in the water now, having pumped its oil Thursday night into the liner *Lurline*, alongside. The liner had since sailed for Los Angeles en route to Honolulu.

Redinger's attention was drawn to an object resting on the guard rail of the tanker's previously submerged deck; inspection showed it to be a wallet. At first the seaman was disappointed, for it contained no money. But then, riffling through the contents, he decided his find might be salable. He went ashore, made his way to the *Examiner* office, and dumped the wallet's contents on an editor's desk. They included, along with four snapshots, a California driver's license, an Associated Oil Company credit card, a Western Union identification card, a San Jose Free Public Library card, a membership card of the California State Automobile Association, and eighteen personal and business cards.

All were in the name of Brooke L. Hart.

5

Manhunt

Babe Ruth, on vacation with his family, awoke to an insistent knocking on his *Lurline* stateroom door. It was early Saturday morning, November 11, and the liner was off Southern California, two hours from docking at Los Angeles. The Home Run King stumbled out of bed and across the cabin and opened the door a crack, confronting the ship's purser, J. C. Fishbeck.

"What the hell is going on?"

Fishbeck's face was a mask of mortification. "Sorry, Mr. Ruth, we have to come in. A boy has been kidnapped, and they think he might be aboard. We've been ordered to search every cabin."

"Wait a minute." Ruth pulled on a bathrobe, aroused his wife and daughter, and then admitted the embarrassed purser. Fishbeck was in and out of the stateroom in less than a minute.

The search order had been radioed to the *Lurline* at 6:00 A.M., along with word that the 188 passengers aboard would be detained after docking until police combed the ship a second time. Fishbeck hoped they would make fast work of it. The passenger list was heavy with football fans from the Bay Area, sailing south to watch Stanford play the University of Southern California that afternoon. With too much delay, they might miss the kickoff. The grumbling had already started.

Two other liners now on the high seas had also received search orders by wireless. Like the *Lurline*, both had been berthed Thursday night near the tanker *Midway* at Pier 32. The *Santa Paula* was en route to New York via the Panama Canal, and the *President Van Buren* had cast off for Honolulu on the first leg of a world tour.

Amid all the fears, suspicions, guesses, and "sightings" since Brooke Hart's disappearance, only two clues had real substance so far: his car and his wallet, found fifty or sixty miles apart. Detectives were at a loss to explain how either had arrived at its point of discovery. The FBI men, who wanted to grill seaman Redinger, were furious because he had slipped out of sight after surrendering the billfold to the *Examiner*, for what reward they could only guess. The *Examiner* was a Hearst paper, and at least one of the federal agents, H. R. Philbrick, was inclined to view the whole episode as a bit of Hearstian skulduggery. He was aware of Ramsey's earlier action ejecting a snoopy *Examiner* reporter from the Hart home; had the newsman filched the billfold, from Brooke Hart's bedroom perhaps, and planted it on the tanker to give his paper a scoop?

A better hypothesis, most investigators decided, was that the wallet had landed on the *Midway* after being tossed from a *Lurline* porthole while the two ships were alongside each other. The tanker, so heavy with oil that its guardrail was submerged, had tied up next to the liner at 5:00 P.M. Thursday—about an hour before Brooke Hart's disappearance. About midnight the *Midway* had begun pumping its cargo into the *Lurline*'s tanks, and at some point, as the tanker rose in the water, its guardrail had broken the surface.

The porthole theory was consistent with any of several scenarios. Brooke's abductors could have drugged him and taken him aboard the liner as a drunken reveler, or they could have left him elsewhere and boarded the liner themselves for a clean getaway. And the possibility of a hoax, perhaps orchestrated by Brooke himself, still had not been ruled out.

A boarding party of FBI men and police was waiting at 9:30, when the *Lurline* docked at San Pedro, the port for Los Angeles. Agent Philbrick and two police inspectors had flown from San Francisco at 3:00 that morning to overtake the ship. With them was Arthur Gossling, the general manager of Hart's store, to identify Brooke if need be. A platoon of twenty uniformed Los Angeles policemen had met them on arrival. The whole aggregation marched up the single gangplank that was lowered as the liner tied up to the pier.

The search was conducted with dispatch. All crew members and passengers, including Babe Ruth, were identified and interviewed before being allowed to disembark, but the screening was over before noon, and no one missed the ball game. The officers inspected every cabin, deck, lifeboat, and cargo hold, the engine room, and the bridge. But no stowaway, suspicious passenger or crewman, or person resembling Brooke Hart was found.

Philbrick, Gossling, and the San Francisco officers flew home dispirited. During their absence, their colleagues had been probing other ways Brooke's wallet might have gotten onto the *Midway*. A San Franciscan named Martin Smith had read about it in the papers and called the police.

"You know that Hart boy? I saw him, I'm sure," he said. "It was early Friday morning, about a half-hour after midnight. I was parked down by the waterfront, and this young fellow came up and asked me if I knew where Pier 32 was." The description Smith gave matched Hart's accurately.

Another tip came from a man who remembered that a storm sewer gushed into the bay between Piers 32 and 34. Could the wallet have come through it, he wondered? A detective called city hall and posed the question to J. C. Lineham, the city superintendent of sewers.

"That pipe drains a lot of territory," Lineham said, "everything bounded by Market, Tenth, Brannan, and the Embarcadero." The boundaries took in about eighty city blocks.

To Captain Dullea, the storm sewer theory was outlandish. All the catch basins had gratings that would have caught an object as large as Brooke's billfold. Moreover, had it come through the storm drain, its contents would have been wetter. When the *Examiner* had turned it over to the police, it was damp but not soaked through. The ink on some of the I.D. cards was smeared, but they were not pulpy, and the officers concluded that the wallet had not been under water for any great length of time.

At midday Saturday, Dullea and Vetterli made a walking reconnaissance of the waterfront. They found access to Pier 32 unhampered; any pedestrian could have thrown the wallet into the water, or it could have been tossed from a car.

Finally seaman Redinger returned to the *Midway*, and Vetterli sent an agent to interrogate him. The session was fruitless. Redinger knew nothing more than what he had told the people at the *Examiner*.

The investigation had evolved into one of the largest manhunts in California history. Officers from three counties searched cabins in the hills where Brooke's car had been found, the Santa Cruz Mountains, and the rugged terrain of the San Francisco Peninsula. Dozens of San Francisco inspectors were assigned to run down tips, and the police departments of twenty other Bay Area cities went on the alert. The 500 state highway patrolmen were ordered to watch for suspicious vehicles. Brooke's former classmates at Santa Clara University combed the back country, using cars donated by San Jose auto dealers. Two more FBI agents, Edward E. Conroy from Kansas City and Harold E. Andersen from New York, were flown in. But the results were minimal. The few meager leads that had shown promise on Friday petered out on Saturday. Brooke's car came up clean of fingerprints.

Gertrude Van Arsdale, it turned out, had been wrong about seeing Brooke driving east on Santa Clara Street. Only two green Studebaker President roadsters had been sold in San Jose, and Mrs. Van Arsdale had seen the other one. It belonged to Tom Holland, the manager of the San Jose Penney's store, who bore a broad resemblance to Brooke.

Likewise, rancher John Sepulveda's observation of a man alongside Brooke's car turned out to be uncertain.

"It could have been a shadow," he said when reinterviewed.

The weekend brought no further word from the kidnappers. On Saturday the investigators comforted the Hart family and themselves by pointing out that the banks (although normally open on Saturdays in 1933) were closed for the Armistice Day holiday. The conjecture was that the abductors were holding off until Monday, the earliest time Alex Hart could withdraw the ransom money from his account.

As early leads fizzled, new ones cropped up. A Hart's employee told of seeing a dark 1931 Buick sedan carrying two well-dressed men, "apparently both Americans," parked in Lightston Alley about 5:45 each evening for the past ten days or so. Since Brooke's disappearance, the car had not returned.

Another tip concerned a San Francisco woman who had purchased some furniture from Hart's store and failed to pay. The store had obtained a judgment against her, and she reportedly had vowed she would "make Mr. Hart pay for it some day." Philbrick and a San Francisco police inspector searched her Howard Street apartment but found nothing suspicious.

A puzzling circumstance, which strengthened the officers' growing conviction that they were dealing with amateurs, was the brevity of the time—only three and a half hours—between Brooke's disappearance and the first ransom call. The usual practice of professionals was to spirit a victim to a safe, remote retreat before contacting his family.

Some officers still clung to the belief that Brooke had eloped. They alerted the authorities in Reno and Tijuana to watch for him. Agent Conroy made inquiries of Dr. Heuschele, the youth's physician: The doctor said Brooke was in good health, in good spirits, with no signs of drug addiction.

As the investigation lagged, the newspapers seized on every shred of fact and fancy to keep the story out of the doldrums. The *Examiner* said Alphonse Bisceglia, a San Jose cannery owner, had been warned to "watch out or your boys and girls will be kidnapped." The *Chronicle* reported there had been a kidnap threat to San Francisco's wealthy Spreckels family, but Captain Dullea said he had never heard of it.

Behind the Ionic facade of the Hart home, life went on. The family was preoccupied with the telephone, whose every ring set off a surge of mingled hope and fear. The ailing Nettie Hart remained secluded in her room, refusing to countenance the possibility that her boy was truly in trouble. She clung to the conviction that this torment would pass, and that Brooke—like a son away at war—would soon rejoin the family circle. Remembering a melodramatic movie scene she had once seen, she envisioned her boy imprisoned in some dingy room, playing cards with his captors to pass the time until they were ready to set him free.

Friends gathered round. G. Logan Payne, the publisher of the *News*, dropped by to offer sympathy. From Stockton came Euphemia "Billie" Cohn, one of Nettie's closest friends. An elegant, bejeweled woman of dark Spanish-German beauty, Mrs. Cohn was more or less Nettie's counterpart in Stockton, where the Cohns had a store comparable to Hart's. She took on the duty of answering the doorbell and the telephone, dealing with the press, and fending off crackpots and uninvited visitors.

Another friend who came to help was Jay McCabe, an Irishman of good humor and great discretion, who had formerly run a San Jose hat store and was a political insider. He had moved to Los Angeles, but he returned at the first word of trouble. A bachelor, McCabe moved in with the Harts—with their gratitude—and took over the day-to-day management of their household. He became a semipermanent member of the family circle.

San Jose's churches were full on Sunday morning, and in many, there were special prayers for Brooke's safe return. Not among the churchgoers was Paddy Donovan. At age nineteen, Paddy was already a four-year veteran of the ragged 1930s army of homeless drifters, trudging the highways and riding the rails. At midday he climbed aboard a freight in the farm town of Gilroy for an hour's ride to San Jose, thirty miles north. Wracked by hunger, he left the train as it pulled into the San Jose yards and headed for The Alameda's row of mansions where tramps were seldom turned away.

Donovan had neither read a newspaper nor heard a radio in days. He was unaware that a young man named Brooke Hart was missing or that San Jose was aflame with fear and anger. Least of all did he know that the large white residence he unluckily selected as a likely place to get a meal was the Hart home. He made his way to the back door, where he knocked and asked for something to eat.

"Freeze, mister!"

Suddenly Donovan was looking into the muzzles of pistols held by cops closing on him from all sides. He was collared, dragged inside the house, and handcuffed. Within minutes he was in a sheriff's car, en route to the county jail where he was booked for investigation. Grilling began.

"I've been in and out of San Jose for four years," the dazed youth told his inquisitors. "I don't know anything about any kidnapping."

Finally, after some hours, his interrogators chose to believe him, and Paddy Donovan, the first suspect arrested in the Hart case, was freed to resume the itinerant trail.

Alviso, California, population 381, was a wretched conglomeration of shanties, shacks, pigsties, chicken coops, and decaying Victorian houses at the southern extremity of San Francisco Bay. In 1933 some people still nurtured an eighty-year-old dream that it would become a deep-water port for San Jose, nine miles to the southeast, but actually the little village stood on the bank of a slough that meandered inland through tidal marshes, far from the open water. The place stunk in summer because San Jose's sewer outfall gushed raw excrement and cannery waste nearby, and it flooded in winter when storm waters collided with the bay's inrushing tide. Alviso had independent municipal status, having been incorporated as a town in 1852, and as such it was a tolerant enclave for gambling joints, speakeasies, and whorehouses. It was also the site of the South Bay Yacht Club, whose name was more impressive than its squarish wooden clubhouse—a berthing place used by the few San Joseans who could afford pleasure craft.

One of the few was Marshall Hall, the twenty-five-year-old son of a prominent physician, who spent Sunday, November 12, cruising on the bay aboard his thirty-three-foot yacht, the *Mermaid*. The Halls were of the gentry; the family home was on The Alameda across the street from the Hart residence, to which its elegance was comparable if not equal. Marshall had graduated from Stanford Law School in February and taken the state bar examination in July. While awaiting the results he had become an unpaid clerk in Louis Oneal's law office. Now, having been notified that he had passed the exam, he was about to become a full-fledged member of the firm.

When Hall returned to the harbor late on this Sunday afternoon, he was told that Sheriff Emig, whom he knew well, had been there inquiring for him. As Oneal's protégé, Emig was in and out of the law office all the time. It took Hall a few minutes to reach him by phone.

"I hear you're looking for me, sheriff."

"Oh, hello, Marshall. I wanted you to take a little cruise down the bay for me, but I think it's too late now."

"What's up?"

"It's about the Hart case. There was a rumor that I wanted to check out on the Q.T."

Emig's "rumor" was a little-noted report on file since Thursday night with the police department in Hayward, a little Alameda County town between San Jose and Oakland, at the east end of the San Mateo Bridge. Vinton Ridley and Al Coley, who were partners in an Oakland wood business, had been scrounging for driftwood that evening on the mud flats beneath the bridge's eastern approach. At about 7:25 they had watched an automobile drive onto the darkened span, stop somewhere out over the water, and after a time, turn back. As the car stopped, a man's voice had cried "Help, help!" and "Leave me alone!" Finally they had heard, "I can't hang on much longer."

Ridley and Coley had made their way in the dark along the shore-line, toward the sound of the voice, but had found nothing. After the distress calls ceased, they had given up the search, driven to Hayward, and told the police of the episode. Friday morning, officers had gone out to the mud flats and looked around, but no further action had been taken.

"I wanted you to sail down and look around under that bridge," Emig told Hall, "but you'd never make it before dark now."

"Sorry I missed you."

"Don't worry about it, Marshall. It's only one lead out of a hundred we're trying to check out. I don't think it amounts to anything."

* * *

By this time the community's fear and anger were breeding suspicion and finger pointing. Concern grew for other potential kidnap victims, particularly the wealthy young men in whose circles Brooke Hart had moved. On Sunday night, two men described by the *Chronicle* as "obviously of the mobster type" had visited O'Brien's candy store and taken seats at the soda fountain, perusing the latest newspaper reports on the Hart case.

"From time to time," the *Chronicle* reported, "they studied young [Charlie] O'Brien, who assists his father in managing the place. Their appearance in the well-equipped store, with its atmosphere of refinement, struck a discordant note. They obviously did not fit their surroundings. But they sipped soda through a straw and talked in low tones."

Finally a suspicious employee had called the police but by the time they arrived the suspects had left. In a remarkable burst of surmise (which would raise eyebrows later), the *Chronicle* told its readers, "Officials were of the opinion that the two had visited the place with the intention of laying preliminary plans for using young O'Brien as an intermediary in the first effort to contact the Hart family."

The Silveria farm, four acres of apricots with a small house and a barn, had no running water and no plumbing. It was on Piedmont Road in the foothills northeast of San Jose, about two and a half miles south of the spot where Brooke Hart's car was found. Because of its isolation—no telephone, no radio, no newspaper—the distance could have been a hundred miles. So Delphine Silveria, wife and mother, did not learn of the Hart kidnapping until late Friday when she went to her sister's house to do the washing. On Monday morning, after talking earnestly throughout the weekend with her husband, the frightened woman appeared at the sheriff's office to tell what she had witnessed about 6:30 Thursday evening. At that hour, on her way back from the privy with her fourteen-year-old daughter, Isabelle, she had stopped at the barn for an armload of wood.

"We were standing in front of our barn about fifty feet from the road," she told Emig. "We heard a horn first, and then we saw the lights of a car coming from the south." The vehicle was traveling so fast that for a moment Mrs. Silveria had expected it to pile up on a turn not far from her house.

"As we were watching," she related, "the car stopped on the wide part of the road, right in front of the driveway to our barn, and the driver turned out the lights. It was a big, dark sedan about the size of a Buick or a Dodge, with a long hood, and there were three men in it. They talked and smoked for a minute or two, until a smaller car, a roadster with a canvas top, came up from the same direction. One man was driving, and there was a man on each running board. The roadster stopped right near the larger car, and the driver was told to get out. One of the men on the running boards went over to the men in the big car and said, 'Well, we got him all right.' "

Mrs. Silveria said the driver of the roadster was marched over to the sedan, and one of his guards told him, "Come on, big boy, get in here." He complied. Delphine was convinced she was watching a hijacking. She and her daughter, hidden by the barn door, remained silent.

"Are you sure we're on the right road?" she heard one of the men ask.

"Yes," replied another, "keep straight ahead and then turn down into Milpitas and onto the Oakland Road. Head for Stockton and then shoot to Sacramento. We'll take him to the cabin on the hill."

"What about the license plates?" Mrs. Silveria heard another of the men ask, and someone replied, "Leave them like they are."

"Have you got enough gas?"

"Sure, plenty."

One of the running-board men climbed into the roadster; all the others got into the sedan with their captive, and both cars sped away without lights. There was a rattling, like tin, in the back of the big automobile.

If Mrs. Silveria was right, at least five men now seemed to be involved in the abduction of Brooke Hart.

"Why did you wait so long to come and tell me about this?" Emig asked her.

"I was scared, Mr. Emig."

"Can you describe the men you saw?"

"Not very well; it was already dark." Mrs. Silveria said the captive had light-colored clothes—coat, hat, and trousers, and she thought "he probably had light hair."

"Did these men have any sort of foreign accent?" Emig wanted to know.

"No, they spoke good English. They were just regular Americans."

Despite the ingenuous sincerity of the woman confronting him, the sheriff was skeptical. She had no reason to fabricate, but could she really have seen, almost two hours after sunset, all that she related?

And how much of the conversation could she have heard from her hiding place near the barn fifty feet away?

"Thank you, Mrs. Silveria," Emig said, dismissing her. "Please stay home this evening. I may be out to see you."

As soon as the woman was out of earshot, the sheriff called in one of Vetterli's agents, who happened to be in his outer office.

"Come on," he said. "We've got to talk to a little girl."

The sheriff and the FBI man sped to Berryessa School, where Isabelle Silveria was enrolled, to interview her before she could talk to her mother again. The girl, called out of class by the principal, turned out to be a bright child, terrified by what she had seen and by the "real mean tone" of the men's voices. Her story, while not so detailed as her mother's, matched it. Like her mother, Isabelle said she saw five men plus their captive. She remembered their conversation about "plates," but she had not understood that. She put the time she saw the two cars at about 6:30.

"How do you remember what time it was?" Emig asked.

"It was right after dinner, and we always eat at six o'clock."

At dusk Monday Vetterli set up a mild ruse to test Delphine Silveria's story further. He and Emig, with some other detectives wearing suits of different shades and colors, drove out to Piedmont Road in Vetterli's car, a dark coupe. Agent Ramsey followed in Brooke Hart's Studebaker, newly released from the police lab. They pulled into the Silveria yard.

"We need your help, Mrs. Silveria," Emig said. "We want to reenact what you saw. Please show us exactly where the two cars were parked."

Mrs. Silveria was staring fixedly at the roadster.

"That's the same car!" she cried. "—the same car the prisoner was driving, with the men on the running boards."

"It can't be," Ramsey lied, laughing. "That's my buggy."

"Well, if it isn't the same car, it's one just like it."

With Mrs. Silveria's help, the officers positioned their automobiles, and a pertinent fact became apparent at once: The distance from the cars to her hiding place behind the barn door was little more than half the fifty feet she had estimated. Conversation in normal tones carried easily over the shorter span. Mrs. Silveria could easily distinguish between the light and dark suits the detectives wore.

Emig admonished the woman to "keep this to yourself," and Ramsey confessed the deception that had been perpetrated with the roadster.

"You didn't think you were fooling me, did you?" Delphine replied.

The sheriff, who was unconvinced by Mrs. Silveria's account, would keep it under wraps for eight more days.

About the same time Mrs. Silveria had arrived at Emig's office, Louis Rossi was going through the Monday morning mail at Hart's store. He sorted out the bulky trade papers, advertisements, and promotional pieces, and began to riffle through the letters, installment payments, and bills from eastern wholesalers. Suddenly he spotted it: a small envelope postmarked at Sacramento, the state capital 120 miles to the northeast, at midnight Friday. The address, to "A. J. Hart," was penciled in childish, uphill capital letters.

Following Vetterli's instructions, Rossi used tweezers to fish the envelope out of its stack and placed it between cellophane sheets. He carried it gingerly to his car, drove to the Hart home, and handed it to Ramsey. Inside was a postcard bearing a crudely lettered message:

YOUR SON IS O.K. AND TREATED WELL. ONE MORE PEEP TO POLICE WILL BE HIS FINISH. YOU HAVE MADE -1- SQUAWK ANOTHER WILL BE TOO BAD. WE WILL HAVE $40,000 YOU GET 500-$20'S (UN-MARKED) 2000-10'S—2000-5'S PUT IT IN A SATCHEL (BLACK) BE READY TO TAKE A WEEKS TRIP ON A HOUR NOTICE GET THE STUDE RDSTR HAVE RA-DIO INSTALLED. WHEN TOLD TO GO YOU WILL TAKE ORDERS FROM K.P.O. YOU BETTER DO AS TOLD.

6

"Await Further Contact"

Reed Vetterli studied the postcard from Sacramento and decided it was the work of a crank. Its crudity offended him.

Certainly, if real, it reinforced the growing conviction that the kidnappers were bumbling novices. It betrayed lack of preparation and sloppy execution, and it was devoid of criminal craftiness. Instructing Alex Hart to "take orders from K.P.O." was absurd. KPO was an NBC station in San Francisco; could the kidnappers have a confederate there? Not likely. But if they did, using him in the ransom process could only lead the cops to their doorstep. The discovery of Brooke's wallet also signaled the abductors' amateurism. By letting it get away from them, they had surrendered what could have been their best credential of authenticity in ransom negotiations.

Genuine or not, the note from Sacramento had to be dealt with. All agreed that for the present, its existence must be kept from the press; the less the kidnappers could learn from the newspapers, the better. By now the reporters were pouncing on every development, no matter how nebulous, and blowing it up into a big story. The *Chronicle* was on a conjectural spree merely because Victor Chargin, a lawyer friend of Alex Hart, had left for Los Angeles with William Pabst, the president of the San Jose National Bank. The trip was on bank business and both men said so, but the newspaper was insisting they must be headed south to arrange the ransom.

White Oaks Road was hardly worthy of its name. It was a narrow, unpaved gravel path through an orchard in the Campbell district, six miles southwest of downtown San Jose. On this crisp Monday morn-

56

ing Tom Shaves, his son Merle, and their friend Everett Mason were out in the newly pruned orchard, chopping up the prunings for firewood. Because the trees were leafless skeletons at this season, the men could see the road clearly, although they were some distance into the orchard's interior.

About eleven o'clock they saw a black Chevrolet sedan come down the road and stop not far away. A moment later a Pontiac pulled up behind it. Mason and the Shaveses thought this odd, for hardly any-body traveled White Oaks Road, let alone stopped there. Still, the woodchoppers would have paid the cars no further heed, had not Merle Shaves broken his ax handle just then. As he and Mason drove out of the orchard in their truck to get the ax fixed, they passed within a few feet of the two strange vehicles. Both drivers, who appeared to be in their late twenties, were sitting in the Pontiac, and the man behind the wheel was writing something on a paper propped against the vertical windshield. As Shaves and Mason passed, he stopped and buried his face in a newspaper. Shaves got a good look at him but could not see the other man well.

When Mason and Shaves returned from their errand a little later, the two automobiles were still there. Both bore 1933 California plates, and Mason made a note of the numbers. Soon the man who had been writing got out of the Pontiac, walked to the Chevrolet, and drove away. The other man moved into the driver's seat and sped off in the opposite direction.

All afternoon Mason and Merle Shaves debated whether to report the incident. They did not want to look foolish, and ordinarily there would have been nothing sinister in what they had observed: a couple of men sitting in a car with pencil and paper. Still, the Hart boy was missing, and everyone in the county was on the lookout for anything suspicious.

"It was the way the man covered his face with the newspaper that made the boys curious," remembered Mason's widow, Marjorie, in 1987.

Mason's father told the two young men it was their duty to report what they had seen. Finally, at six o'clock Monday evening, they went to see Deputy Sheriff Harry Evans, their neighbor in Campbell. After hearing their story he reached for the phone. It took him only a minute to reach Emig.

"Sheriff, I've got a couple of license numbers for you," he said.

Marjorie Mason recalled later that Emig "was not too enthusiastic about the report." He kept the information supplied by Shaves and Mason to himself; his only follow-up was to run the license numbers through the Department of Motor Vehicles in Sacramento. Word came back that the Pontiac belonged to Thomas J. Thurmond of 262 Leigh Avenue, Campbell, and the Chevrolet to John M. Holmes of 1070 Bird Avenue, San Jose. Nothing on record suggests that Emig checked out these names any further, and perhaps he felt he didn't need to, for he knew Holmes already. Jack was an old friend, a brother Mason; he and Emig had entered Golden Rule Lodge 479, F&AM, about the same time in the mid-1920s.

When the public finally learned of the orchard rendezvous five days later, Emig told a reporter there was "nothing to it." His casual dismissal of the episode, which would give rise to one of the great puzzles of the Hart case, may have reflected only that he was swamped with leads, good and bad, from all over California.

In San Francisco, a man named Ernest Lunes pointed a finger of suspicion at Robert Cicero,* an Italian-American from Louisiana who now lived in San Jose. Lunes told the *Examiner* that Cicero had become involved with a nineteen-year-old girl from a prominent San Jose family and asked her to join him in a string of holdups—to become his moll, no less. Off and on in 1931 and 1932, Cicero had worked at Hart's store. Vetterli made a note to check him out if he ever got a free minute.

From Sacramento came a telegram that set off a short-lived burst of hope within the Hart family. The sender, one James Nealis, proposed a ransom counteroffer of $20,000—half the amount demanded. At first Nealis was taken to be the kidnappers' negotiator. The excitement faded when he turned out to be a friend of Ray Renwick, just trying to help.

By this time, the "Klutas gang" theory of the abduction had been discounted. In Peoria, Illinois, however, a pistol duel erupted when police sought out a member of the gang, Russell Hughes, to question about the Hart case. When the shooting was over, Hughes was dead. Handsome Jack Klutas himself, meanwhile, was successfully eluding a coast-to-coast dragnet.

In Oakland the police received a strange tip by telephone: A male voice told them to watch for a certain license plate on East Twelfth Street, because "the man in that car knows all about the Hart case." The police spotted the vehicle, crowded it to the curb, and arrested Burton Moore,* a printer, who turned out to be the man who had made the call. In his possession was a note reading, "Contact Hart

*Fictitious name.

family. Phone Jack Klutas. Do not destroy." A call to Moore's wife established that he had been discharged from the psychopathic ward at Oakland's Highland Hospital. He was sent home after a night in jail.

In another home in Oakland, Evelyn Ridley was troubled. Not a word had appeared in the papers about the "Help!" cries that her husband, Vinton, and his partner had heard Thursday evening while gathering driftwood near the San Mateo Bridge. Mrs. Ridley would have been even more upset had she known of Emig's conclusion that the calls did not "amount to anything." In her heart she was sure the man in trouble was Brooke Hart, and she thought his father should be told. At her kitchen table she composed a letter to Alex Hart, with a covering note to Chief Black:

> The . . . calls for help were in earnest, and they were terrible to hear and sent chills up my husband's spine. . . . If you are interested you can get in touch with us at any time here in Oakland. There is quite a bit more we could tell that I don't know how to write about.

When she finished the letter, Evelyn Ridley lacked the heart to mail it. She set it aside for three days.

Alex Hart, thus unaware of what the Ridleys knew, wanted more than ever now to send a good-faith signal to his son's captors, and Monday afternoon the word was put out that he would have a statement that evening. A platoon of reporters gathered on the porch of the mansion.

Precisely at eight o'clock the front door was opened by Ramsey and Hicks, who invited the newsmen into the entrance hall. Only one representative of each paper or press association was admitted, twelve to fifteen in all. The door was closed and locked behind them. Soon Alex's stocky figure, drooping but impeccably groomed in a dark business suit, appeared at the top of a staircase. Fatigue and anguish etched his gray countenance as he descended slowly, carrying in his hand a sheaf of typewritten slips. At the foot of the stairs he distributed them to the reporters, greeting each with a quiet word or two and shaking hands. The half sheets of watermarked bond paper bore a statement drafted earlier in the day by Vetterli and his agents:

TO THE KIDNAPPERS OF BROOKE L. HART

We are anxious for the return of our son Brooke. We desire to negotiate for his return personally or through any intermediary who might be selected. When contact is made we will of course want evidence to prove that Brooke is held by you. All negotiations will be considered confidential by us and we will allow no interference from any outside source.

The newsmen tried to ask questions, but the weary father curtly cut them off.

"I have nothing more to say," he told them. "All I can say is in that statement. Good evening, gentlemen."

Hicks and Ramsey solemnly counted off the reporters as they filed out, and the door closed behind them. The Harts' message was on every front page up and down the West Coast on Tuesday morning.

The second ransom note arrived at Hart's store in Tuesday's mail. Rossi intercepted it and delivered it immediately to the residence before noon.

If this was what had been written Monday morning on the orchard road in Campbell, it had taken a 100-mile round trip in the day that had since elapsed. It had been postmarked in San Francisco at 6:30 Monday evening. The envelope was identical to the one in which the postcard had arrived from Sacramento, but this time the message filled two pages of cheap stationery, in the same crude pencil lettering. It combined reassurance with bullying arrogance:

WE PRESUME YOU HAVE GOTTEN OUR LETTER FROM SACRAMENTO. YOU HAVE MONEY AS DE-MANDED. INDICATE SAME WITH A NUMERAL AT THE MARKET STREET WINDOW OF YOUR STORE LIKE THIS: (1). YOU WILL BE ADVISED WHEN TO START YOUR TRIP AS NOTED IN FORMER NOTE. AS LONG AS CONTENTS OF THESE NOTES ARE KNOWN TO YOU ALONE BROOKE IS SAFE. BY NOW YOU KNOW FEDERALS OR ANYONE ELSE IS POW-ERLESS TO BRING BROOKE TO YOU EXCEPT THROUGH US.

WHEN A.J. HART, WHO WILL CARRY THE MONEY, STARTS HIS TRIP HE WILL CARRY THE

MONEY IN A BLACK SATCHEL (SMALL) BESIDE HIM IN SEAT OF STUDE ROADSTER. IF ANYONE FOLLOWS THIS CAR OR KNOWS ITS ERRAND BROOKE WILL NOT BE RETURNED ALIVE. OUR NEXT CONTACT WILL TELL YOU WHERE TO GO AND BE PREPARED TO START ON THE MINUTE. YOUR EVERY MOVE IS BEING OBSERVED—AWAIT FURTHER CONTACT.

Together, Alex and the FBI men scanned the two long paragraphs. Unquestionably this message originated with the same novice criminal as the previous one; it carried the same amateur flavor. The window-sign idea was grotesque. Moreover, professionals would have ascertained beforehand that Alex Hart could not drive a car and could not possibly comply with their ransom instructions. Vetterli, reversing his opinion, now decided the notes were from the real kidnappers, not hoaxers or swindlers—but simpletons nonetheless.

"I must give them an answer," Alex insisted. "I can't give them an excuse to hurt my boy."

The agents agreed that it was essential to open a dialogue. Writing on a large sheet of gray cardboard with a heavy marking crayon, Ramsey prepared the numerical recognition sign that was demanded:

He handed the completed placard to Rossi.

"Here, Louis, take this back to the store and put it in the window as soon as you can."

Then Vetterli picked up the phone and called Andersen at the Sainte Claire Hotel to brief him on what was happening.

"The numeral will be going up in the store window in just a few minutes, Harold. Get over to Market and Santa Clara streets right away and stake it out."

With the arrival of the second note, the tension in the Hart home mounted. Obviously Brooke's captors were becoming impatient—looking for a fast way to take their money and run. In their greed, they were sure to grow careless. The fear was that their mistakes could prove as perilous to Brooke as to themselves. As Rossi headed back to the store with the "-1-" placard, nothing remained for the family but to wait and hope and pray.

Across California the corrosion of fear, the dry rot of suspicion, and the flames of outrage grew. Hart-case paranoia afflicted well-meaning citizens whose judgments were at other times sound. Suspects were pointed out for the flimsiest of reasons. One man reported an acquaintance to the FBI on the sole ground that he always seemed to have money to spend and had once remarked, "There's no need for working as long as you can make money the easy way." In Sacramento a man named Anderson was subjected to an FBI investigation because he was reputed to be a "hard-boiled fellow" and had once been married to a woman named Jane Hammond.

At midafternoon Tuesday one of Alex Hart's brothers-in-law, a man he neither liked nor trusted, burst into Arthur Gossling's office at the department store.

"It's about the boy," he announced. "I've gotta talk to Alex right away."

"He's not here," said Gossling, unwilling to let anyone, least of all this ragtag relative, disturb the boss in this time of anguish. When the man grew defiant and refused to leave, claiming cryptically to have a message from the kidnappers, Gossling picked up the phone and called the FBI outpost in the Sainte Claire Hotel. A couple of Vetterli's men arrived within minutes and gave the brother-in-law a ride to the mansion on The Alameda. Alex Hart greeted him coolly, took him into another room, and shut the door.

"What is it this time?"

"First, Alex, you gotta promise me you won't tell the feds anything I'm gonna tell you."

Hart answered with an impassive stare.

"Alex, this guy called me today. He's a fellow I know here in San Jose, and he's got connections with the underground, I guess. Well, yesterday he was stopped on the street by some Italian with dark skin and a beard. This Italian asked him, 'How would you like to be an errand boy in the Hart thing? There's $7,500 in it for you.' My friend said he wouldn't get into it for any price, but then this wop started threatening him, and he came to me. Alex, I'm scared to death."

"What do you want from me?" Hart asked.

"My friend wants us to come to his house tonight, you and me, Alex, between 7:00 and 7:30, to go over the whole thing."

Alex was seething inside. For longer than he cared to remember he had been getting this brother-in-law out of jams, financial and otherwise; he had once hired a lawyer to clear the man of bigamy. The message he was getting now was out of step with everything else that was happening and had all the signs of a shakedown.

"I won't go," he said.

The brother-in-law looked crestfallen. "Well, then, I'll phone my guy and tell him." Nothing more was heard about it.

Late Tuesday Charlie O'Brien finished his shift at the candy store, left by the back door, and cut across a drab alley to the Plaza Garage where he rented a parking space. He got his car from its regular spot and left by a wide door opening onto Market Street, across from the city hall. As he inched across the sidewalk about 6:20, a thin-faced stranger approached from the passenger side and reached for his door handle as if to climb in. Then, apparently reconsidering, the man turned and sped away on foot. O'Brien got only a fleeting look at the blank, humorless face with deep-set blue eyes under heavy brows. The fellow had jug-handle ears.

It took O'Brien only a few minutes to drive to the family home on Thirteenth Street. Just after seven o'clock the phone rang. The caller, a man, was so casual that O'Brien at first took him to be some friend.

"Hello, is this Charlie?"

"Yes."

"I have a message for Mr. Hart. *Get this*: Tell him to place the money beside him on the seat of Brooke's car, right away, and head for L.A. Before he gets there he'll be relieved of the money by a man in a white mask."

"Who is this?"

"Never mind. Just tell him to take a satchel with the $40,000 and put it on the seat beside him. A man in a white mask will appear. D'ya get that?"

O'Brien sped across town to the Hart home. He was taken into a closed room, where he relayed the caller's message to Alex. Emerging, Alex repeated the gist of it to Ramsey, whose first reaction was frustration because O'Brien had let the call get away. He admonished O'Brien to stay on the line next time and jiggle the hook to signal the operator.

To Alex, the idea of heading for an unknown point of rendezvous with a masked man was silly melodrama.

"I don't think I should go," he said, after mulling the caller's instructions. "We don't know that this is a bona fide call or that the caller has my boy. Anyway, I can't drive a car."

Ramsey concurred. The agony of waiting resumed.

The phone rang next at 8:45. It was answered in the downstairs hall by Mrs. Cohn, who signaled Alex that the call was for him. He went to the upstairs extension as Deputy Sheriff Hicks picked up the instrument that Mrs. Cohn had left off the hook.

"Is this Mr. Hart?" a man's voice asked.

"Yes, this is Alex Hart."

"You didn't follow orders, Mr. Hart." The voice was smooth, calm, softly accusatory—the voice a schoolteacher might use with a recalcitrant pupil. "You did not drive south. You did not follow the instructions we gave Charlie O'Brien. Why not, Mr. Hart?"

"Look, I have no idea who you are. I'll do anything to get my boy back, but I need some proof that you really have him."

"You're going to have to trust us, Mr. Hart. Look, I can tell you exactly what your son was wearing when we took him. That ought to prove something, Mr. Hart. He had on an overcoat and a light felt hat, and he was carrying his glasses. That hasn't been in the newspapers."

This was true. The papers were running Brooke's description every day, but while they mentioned his gray suit, they said nothing about his topcoat, hat, or glasses. The *Chronicle*, in fact, had erroneously reported that he was hatless.

"Can you give me a sample of his handwriting, or one of his shoes, or something else he was carrying?"

"It would take two weeks to get anything like that, Mr. Hart. Brooke is a long way from San Jose. Besides, I'd have to get permission from my superiors." There was an awkward pause; then the caller revised the instructions: "This is your last chance, Mr. Hart. You still have time to catch the 9:30 train to Los Angeles. Catch it and the man in the mask will meet you. You won't have to wait. When the money is turned over, your boy will be released in the morning. Take that train . . . or it will be too bad."

There was a click as the caller replaced the receiver on its hook.

Alex Hart had been coached to stall, in any conversation with the kidnappers, while the call was traced. Almost as soon as Alex had come on the line, Ramsey in his upstairs hideaway had begun working with the telephone company operator downtown. Within seconds she had told him the call was from a pay station at 376 South Second Street. The address belonged to Perry's Parking Lot. Ramsey relayed the information instantly to Vetterli at the Sainte Claire and to Emig at his office.

The sheriff, with a carload of deputies, and Vetterli, with a carload of agents, converged on the parking lot within minutes. The cars braked to a halt alongside the office, where the officers confronted the attendant, Eugene Williams. There was a pay phone on the wall.

"Anybody use that phone lately?" the sheriff asked.

"Yeah, just a few minutes ago." Williams said a man looking to be twenty-five or thirty had appeared about 8:45 and inquired for a woman driving a Chevrolet. Then he had walked into the office and used the telephone while the attendants were at the other end of the lot.

"What did he look like?"

"Ruddy-faced, about five-feet-eleven, I'd say, 160 pounds. Pretty well dressed—light brown suit and overcoat and a light gray hat, I think."

"Did he wear glasses."

"No."

Was he smoking?

"No."

"Had you ever seen him before?"

"No, he was a stranger to me."

"How long has he been gone?"

"Not very long. Four or five minutes maybe."

Emig and Vetterli exchanged dejected glances. Using the phone on the desk, Vetterli called Ramsey on the private line at the Hart home.

"We missed the guy by four minutes," he said.

From his end, Ramsey gave Vetterli a full briefing on the kidnapper's call, including the ultimatum to Alex: "Take that 9:30 train or it will be too bad." Suddenly Vetterli broke off the conversation and turned back to the parking lot attendant.

"Mr. Williams, would you recognize the man who was here if you saw him again?"

"I think so."

"We need you to come with us, then. That man may be Brooke Hart's kidnapper, and he may be down at the depot right now, waiting for the train to Los Angeles." It was almost 9:15. Williams piled into the sheriff's automobile with Emig, to head for the Southern Pacific station about nine blocks away. The sheriff's car was behind the automobile of the FBI men.

Then, before the two cars could pull away from the parking lot, came an episode of farce. It was the misfortune of Melville Trengrove, a young bank teller who lived nearby, to be out for an evening stroll. The FBI men saw him first—a shadowy figure moving along in the dark. Surmising him to be the fleeing telephone caller, they sprung from their car and jumped him with drawn guns. Trengrove started to run, and one of the FBI men brought him down with a flying tackle. By the time Emig, who knew Trengrove, reached the scene and extricated him, a crowd had begun to gather.

The five-minute incident was an unmitigated calamity. The secrecy of the manhunt—especially its downtown focus and its instant response to the ransom phone call—had been compromised, an upright citizen had been roughed up, and critical minutes had been lost.

Emig, Vetterli, and Williams resumed the trip to the depot at high speed, while the other FBI men returned sheepishly to the hotel. At the station Williams took an inconspicuous vantage point and studied from afar the cluster of persons waiting for the train. He saw no one resembling the man who had used his phone, and there was nothing suspicious about any of the boarding passengers.

Nor was Alex Hart among them. In the house on The Alameda, he had stuck with his decision to ignore the kidnapper's ultimatum. As distraught as he was, he had instantly caught a slip that the otherwise smooth caller had made: In one breath the man had said Brooke was far from San Jose, and it would take two weeks to produce a handwriting sample. In the next breath the man had promised, "If you do as you're told, you won't have to wait. . . . Your boy will be released in the morning."

The inconsistency was glaring; the caller might or might not be the kidnapper, but for certain he was a liar. Beyond a doubt now, Alex knew he was dealing not with swaggering thugs but with an infinitely more dangerous sort—erratic, seat-of-the-pants operators who couldn't even keep their story straight. Having decided the train rendezvous was folly, he retired to his bedroom to try for sleep he knew would not come.

7

"Killing Him Is the Easy Way"

Marshall Hall, the lowliest man in Louis Oneal's law office, rose early on Wednesday morning, facing what was destined to be a memorable day.

By nine o'clock he had to be in San Francisco, to raise his hand before the state supreme court and be sworn in as a lawyer entitled to practice in California. He would have little time to linger and savor the moment, however, for at noon he had to be at a certain pier on the San Francisco waterfront to meet his mother and sister, returning from a Panama Canal cruise. Then he would have to race back to San Jose for his first appearance as an attorney, at an Industrial Accident Commission hearing. It was set for two o'clock in the old brick city hall in the City Plaza.

As he gulped his breakfast, Hall scanned the *Mercury Herald* and concluded that the investigation of the Hart kidnapping had bogged down. The newspaper—in the dark about the ransom notes and phone calls—had a dull story, mainly a roundup of nebulous leads that the detectives were pursuing to dead ends. Hall was intrigued, however, by a paragraph near the end of the piece, where it jumped to an inside page:

> Other tips, believed to be of minor value, were investigated yesterday. Officers went to the San Mateo Bridge to investigate reports that a man answering Hart's description had been seen with two husky men in a sedan crossing the span Thursday night.

Hall recognized this as a skewed version of the report Sheriff Emig had wanted him to check out on Sunday—the driftwood gatherers' tale of a man in distress on or under the bridge. It had taken three days for the report to surface in the San Jose press, which seemed to put no more stock in it than Emig had.

Also closely perusing the *Mercury Herald* that morning was Emig himself. He was relieved to see that the Melville Trengrove incident had not made the paper. Not only was it an embarrassment and a possible tip-off to the kidnappers that their calls were being intercepted, it was also certain to exacerbate the jealousies rising between him and Chief Black, his former boss. By default and bad luck, Black was coming off second best in the Hart case news stories, which were lionizing the sheriff. It was therefore uncomfortable to Emig to be caught up in a false arrest incident on Black's turf in the center of the city. (Later, when reporters finally learned about Trengrove's misfortune and asked Black what Emig was up to, the chief grunted, "I have no idea. I guess the sheriff's office is not going to cooperate with me on the Hart case.")

Sitting there in his office in the courthouse, Emig was at the center, if not in full command, of a law enforcement army equalling any that California had ever mustered. But for all that anyone could tell from the news accounts, it was an impotent army just marking time. That suited Emig fine; if the public was fooled, so Brooke's abductors might be. In their notes and telephone calls, they were revealing themselves to be more impatient and desperate—and more careless—with each hour that passed.

Reporters, meanwhile, were subsisting on scraps. The *Mercury Herald* reported that "vigilance at Hart's home on The Alameda was considerably relaxed yesterday." Once again the newspapers had been fed the subterfuge that all officers had been withdrawn from the residence, and either in ignorance or in complicity with the investigation they had accepted it. The *Chronicle* fleshed out its thin article with a report that pawn shops everywhere were on the alert for Brooke Hart's signet ring, inscribed *Universitas Santae Clarae '33*.

Politics was invading the story. Ex-sheriff George Lyle, still sulking over the way Emig had turned him out of office in 1930, told the *News* with feigned reluctance that a group of Alex Hart's friends had retained him to "advise" Emig in the lagging investigation. The newspaper identified Lyle as a "veteran manhunter and sleuth."

Also pouncing on the publicity opportunity was Los Angeles District Attorney Buron Fitts, 400 miles distant. He had gotten a good ride on his earlier declaration that Brooke had been "positively identified" in a Los Angeles cafe. Now he told reporters he did not think Brooke had been kidnapped at all, because there had been "no definite ransom demands." Emig allowed himself a thin-lipped smile when he read that statement, carried by the Associated Press.

Meanwhile there were two more "sightings" of young Hart in Los Angeles. A confused youth believed to be Brooke had visited an Army recruiting office there. And in Hollywood a "bashful" young man with "pale and sunken cheeks" entered a dress shop alone, asking money for food. A saleswoman, who said the fellow appeared dazed, identified him as Brooke from a photograph.

It was now six days since Brooke's disappearance, and the story was on the front pages all over the United States. Editors had grasped its impact. Kidnapping for ransom inspired terror in the thirties in the same way that political assassination would in the sixties, airplane hijacking in the seventies, and hostage-taking in the eighties. The fear spreading out of San Jose was reinforced from Miami, where County Solicitor Fred Pina reported a plot to kidnap three-year-old Mary Alice Kenlay. The little girl was the granddaughter of Chicago's late Mayor Anton Cermak, who had been slain in March by an assassin intending to shoot President-elect Franklin D. Roosevelt.

A third ransom letter reached Hart's store in the Wednesday afternoon mail, scarcely an hour after it had been postmarked at the main San Jose Post Office. Its envelope and its pencil printing matched those of the earlier notes. It filled four pages of note paper from a cheap writing tablet.

Rossi intercepted the letter and took it at once to the Hart residence, where Vetterli and Conroy were already in conference with Ramsey. The agents huddled with Alex, reading the message together as Vetterli turned the pages with tweezers. After six short paragraphs reviewing all previous communications, the note took on a cold, callous tone edged with sadism:

YOU WANT MORE PROOF. MR. HART, THIS IS NOT A BUSINESS TRANSACTION. THIS IS A KIDNAP-PING WITH EVERY AVAILABLE RESOURCE OF AID AT YOUR SERVICE. ANY THIRD PARTY CONTACT

WITH US IS OUR PERSONAL SUICIDE. IN SHORT, YOU DON'T TRUST US WE DON'T TRUST YOU, SO FURTHER DISCUSSION IS USELESS.

WE HOLD THE CARDS IN THIS CASE. BROOKE IS NOT WITH THE WRITER BUT IS HELD AT A REMOTE POINT. WHEN PAYMENT IS MADE A TELEGRAM BY CONTACTING PARTIES WILL RELEASE BROOKE. BROOKE IS BEING TREATED AS WELL AS POSSIBLE BUT THE CASE IS GETTING TOO MUCH PUBLICITY FOR US TO HOLD HIM ANY LONGER. WE ARE SORRY TO DO THIS BECAUSE BROOKE IS A MANLY LAD BUT HE HAS SEEN US AND IS TOO LIABLE TO IDENTIFY US.

KILLING HIM IS THE EASY WAY WITH LITTLE RISK FOR US. RETURNING HIM IS WHAT WE DE-MANDED THE RANSOM FOR. SORRY I CAN'T GET SOME FURTHER PROOF FOR YOU BUT I SAID THE WRITER IS A CONTACT MAN ONLY. WE DO NOT HOLD BROOKE HART HERE. MR. HART, UNLESS OUR PRINCIPALS HEAR FAVORABLY FROM US BY 7:30, 11-15-33 YOU WILL NOT BE CONTACTED AGAIN. IT WILL BE USELESS. IF YOU COMPLY TO OUR DEMANDS PUT A NUMERAL TWO WHERE THE 1 NOW IS AS SOON AS IT IS RECEIVED. STARTING 7:30 P.M. 11-15-33 DRIVE SOUTH ON MONTEREY ROAD TO LOS ANGELES, TAKE MALIBU HIWAY INTO L.A.

IF YOU ARE NOT STOPPED BEFORE L.A. STOP AT THE MAYFAIR HOTEL OVER NIGHT. W. SEVENTH STREET, L.A. RETURN 7:30 P.M. SAME ROUTE AS BEFORE. FOLLOWING NIGHT HAVE RUMBLE SEAT OPEN AT ALL TIMES. BAG WITH CURRENCY BESIDE YOU. DO AS TOLD AND YOU AND YOUR FAMILY WILL NOT BE MOLESTED FURTHER BY US OR ANY OTHER ORGANIZATION. FAIL US—YOU LOSE A SON AS WELL AS $40,000 BECAUSE YOU ARE SLATED TO MAKE THIS PAYMENT IRREGARDLESS.

SEE TO IT THAT YOU ARE NOT FOLLOWED AND THIS TIME START AT 7:30 P.M. IN THE STUDE ROAD-STER. THIS IS THE LAST CONTACT UNTIL YOU

MEET THE MAN WITH THE WHITE MASK. DO NOT
TRAVEL OVER 10 M.P.H. BE SURE YOU ARE ALONE.

Alex blanched at the cruelty of the ultimatum. Still, after a few
minutes' reflection he decided the letter gave new reason for hope.
Surely the kidnappers chose their cruel phrasing for purposes of shock.
And the complexity of the message, with its bizarre instructions,
betrayed their avidity for a quick end to the ransom impasse.

"I have to respond," Alex said. "But I still have the problem of
never having learned to drive an automobile."

"Let me drive, Mr. Hart," offered Rossi, whose solicitude for his
boss was without stint. "I'll go in your place and deliver the ransom."

"Oh, Louis, I can't ask you to do that."

"I *will* do that."

The FBI men thought Rossi's stand-in idea, while risky, had merit.
Despite the kidnappers' admonition that the Studebaker must be alone
on the road, the agents proposed to follow Rossi at some distance in
another car, armed with machine guns for a speedy rescue.

"The first thing we have to do," Vetterli said, "is put that new sign
in the window. Anybody got a piece of cardboard?" This time it was
he, not Ramsey, who demonstrated his artistic talent by preparing the
placard. With crayon he drew a large numeral "2" to signify accep-
tance of the kidnappers' demands, then added a postscript in thick
black lettering:

-2-
I CANNOT
DRIVE

The square of gray cardboard was given to Rossi, who left at once
for the store.

As the afternoon wore on, Alex Hart's anxiety about his inability to
drive, and his fear that the deficiency might cost his son's life, grew to
obsessive proportions. He had no confidence that Vetterli's terse message on the placard would satisfy Brooke's captors. At length Ramsey
and Vetterli suggested another appeal to them through the press. A
new call went out, inviting reporters to be on hand at seven o'clock.
The FBI men drafted a statement for Alex and Nettie to release:

TO THE KIDNAPPERS OF BROOKE L. HART

We have received numerous communications from various persons demanding ransom for the return of our son Brooke. Obviously not all these persons are acting in good faith. None have produced any proof that they have our boy in custody. We are anxious to negotiate, but must have evidence that Brooke is being held before we can deal with anyone.

We wish to reiterate that all negotiations will be considered confidential and that no interference will be allowed from any outside source.

As the newsmen were admitted to the residence, the scene was in contrast to that of the press reception two nights earlier. This time no law officers were in sight. The newsmen were greeted not by Hicks and Ramsey, but by Mrs. Cohn. They were shocked at the deterioration of Brooke's father in the forty-seven hours since they had seen him last. The *Chronicle* found him "worn and haggard"; the *Mercury Herald*, "white and drawn."

Yet there was a soft quality to the occasion. On Monday night Alex had abruptly, even brusquely, cut off all questions. Now he lingered, chatting with the reporters as friends sharing his ordeal. The journalists, scribbling with smudgy pencils on pads of copy paper, responded with self-conscious sympathy as Alex disclosed in general terms the kidnappers' demand that he drive alone to a rendezvous.

"Gentlemen," he said, "I bought my first automobile in 1913, and I've owned cars ever since, but I've never learned to drive one. Now it's too late to teach an old dog new tricks. I want you to make that very plain, please."

Alex took the opportunity to discredit ex-Sheriff Lyle's boast that he had been retained to bail out Emig in the bogged-down investigation.

"I have not discussed such a proposition with Mr. Lyle," the father said. "I have not engaged him, nor have I authorized anyone else to engage him. I have confidence in the men now in charge: the Department of Justice [FBI] agents, Sheriff Emig, and Chief Black."

A reporter inquired what form the communications with the supposed kidnappers had taken.

"Various forms—by letters, by telegrams, other ways." Alex did not mention the phone specifically, but the implication was clear.

Some of the newsmen tried to draw additional facts from Mrs. Cohn. Had the messages given any hint of Brooke's whereabouts?

"No."

Were negotiations in progress?

"There has been nothing you could call a negotiation."

As the session drew to a close, Alex reiterated his good-faith pledge. "I desire to play absolutely fair," he said. "If Brooke comes back, there will be no questions asked."

For the first time the curtain of privacy had parted and the torment within the Hart home was coming into public view. But for reasons of Brooke's safety the view was closely circumscribed. The journalists got no inkling of the vigil Ramsey and Hicks still kept in the rear room upstairs, nor could they hear the telephone ringing there at the very moment they were filing out the front door.

Rossi had posted the second numeral placard in the department store's window at midafternoon. But outside, hundreds of persons were passing afoot or in cars, and agent Andersen, staked out across the street, could not even guess at the would-be recipient of its message. After keeping watch for several hours, he abandoned the surveillance.

In adding the "I CANNOT DRIVE" postscript to the sign, Vetterli had baited a trap. The kidnappers, frustrated in their outlandish plan for a rolling rendezvous on the road, would need to communicate with Alex Hart again if they were to grasp the $40,000 prize he dangled before them. Would greed and anxiety move them to use the telephone once more—once too often? Ramsey was so sure they would take the bait that at 6:30 he had called the chief operator at the telephone company, who was tracing every incoming call, and exhorted her to special vigilance in the hours ahead. Now, at 7:20 his private line was ringing; she was already calling him back.

"Mr. Ramsey," she said, "two calls have been placed to the Hart home, Ballard 2013, in the past eight minutes. Each time, the calling party hung up before we could ring the number."

"Where were the calls made from?"

"The first was at 7:12 exactly, from a pay station, Ballard 5493, at the southwest corner of First and San Antonio streets."

Ramsey flipped through a city directory on his desk. The phone booth in question, he determined, was in the Montgomery Hotel.

"And the second call?"

"It came in just a few seconds ago, at 7:19. It was from Ballard 7591, which is a public phone in Tuggle's Drug Store at Tenth and Santa Clara streets."

"Thank you, operator. Get back to me at once if there is another call."

"I will, Mr. Ramsey."

As he returned the receiver to its hook and sat back to wait, Ramsey framed a picture of the kidnapper in his mind's eye: a man of average height and build, Caucasian, in his late twenties, panicky and torn between greed and fear. At this instant he was darting about downtown, using up nickels at one pay phone after another, each time—so far—aborting his call at the last moment. Obviously the man had a car; it was eleven blocks from the Montgomery Hotel to Tuggle's Drug Store, and he could scarcely have covered the distance in seven minutes on foot.

San Jose did not have dial phones; to place a call, one had to lift the receiver, wait until the operator answered "Number please?" and then tell her the number desired. Did the kidnapper realize that each time he asked for Ballard 2013, the operator was reporting his location to the cops on his tail?

Deputy Hicks arrived in the upstairs room, and Ramsey briefed him on the latest events. Hicks shifted his cigar from one side of his mouth to the other and flopped into a chair alongside the desk.

"Y'know, Bill, the guy who's out there knows San Jose like the palm of his hand. He knows where all the phone booths are."

The minutes ticked by. Half an hour passed. Then, thirty seconds before eight o'clock, the residence phone jangled again.

The Harts, Ramsey, and Hicks had rehearsed a precision drill for answering. The family had three telephones, all on the same line—in the little corridor between the side door and the entrance hall, in the kitchen, and in the front bedroom upstairs. When each call came, Mrs. Cohn would go to the corridor instrument and wait until Ramsey had reached the upstairs bedroom extension. Then, to avoid a click on the line when the officer cut in, Mrs. Cohn would begin counting in a loud voice, audible upstairs. On her count of three, she and Ramsey would lift their receivers simultaneously.

This time their drill went off without flaw. They picked up their phones at the same instant, six seconds before eight o'clock, and she said, "Hello."

"Is Mr. Hart there?" It was the smooth, soft male voice that both Alex and Miriam had described.

"I'll see. Please hold on." Mrs. Cohn passed the downstairs phone to Brooke's father.

There were a few seconds of silence, during which those in the house could hear a distant ringing on the private line in the communications center upstairs. With a surge of exultation and relief Ramsey heard Hicks answer it, and he knew the chief operator downtown was telling Hicks where the kidnapper was calling from. Then, as Alex came on the line, Ramsey's attention returned to the conversation with the kidnapper.

"Is this Mr. Hart?"*

"Yes."

"Mr. Hart, you had our serial number in your window this afternoon."

"Yes, it was there. I can't drive."

"Mr. Hart, you get Charles O'Brien, or some member of your family, and leave P.D.Q." The caller's voice took on a hard edge.

"I can't drive," Hart repeated, "and I'm in no physical condition to make a trip."

Ramsey smiled at Alex's repetition. Brooke's father was performing well in his assignment of stretching out the call.

"Mr. Hart," the caller said, "I want your answer. Yes or no, will you go?"

"I am willing to deal with you, to do anything in my power to get my boy back, but I am unable to leave now."

"You get Charlie O'Brien or some member of your family with you right away and start P.D.Q., and have the rumble seat of the car open and up!"

"I don't know whether I can get Charlie O'Brien to go or not."

"Well, I don't care. You get Charlie O'Brien or some member of your family and go P.D.Q.!"

It struck Ramsey as poetically just that the victimized father was cool and in command, while the kidnapper's agitation grew by the minute.

By now Hicks had learned from the operator that the kidnapper was calling from 222 South Market Street. He instantly recognized the address as that of the Plaza Garage—the place of the abortive attempt to intercept Charlie O'Brien's car on Tuesday evening! He asked the operator to connect him to the sheriff's office and then to stay on the line. Emig answered in seconds.

"Bill, our guy is calling again, from the Plaza Garage. He's on the line right now."

"Good work, Ray, thanks." Emig hung up and turned to Undersheriff Earle Hamilton and Deputy Felix Cordray, who were standing by in his office: "Come on, boys. Let's go!"

The three officers, wearing civilian clothes, jumped into the sher-

---

*Alex Hart's conversation with the kidnapper, as quoted here, follows Ramsey's verbatim notes, transcribed upon the completion of the call.

iff's car outside and headed through darkened streets toward the garage, four blocks south. Meanwhile the chief operator had returned to Hicks's line and put him through to the FBI room at the Sainte Claire. He couldn't tell whether it was Vetterli or Conroy who answered, but it made no difference.

"The bastard is talking to Alex Hart right now," Hicks said, "from the Plaza Garage at 222 South Market. He's a block away from you. Get going!"

While Hicks alerted the sheriff and the FBI, Alex Hart was further prolonging his conversation with the abductor by haggling over the Los Angeles trip. They were now three minutes into the call.

"I want to deal with you, to be fair, but I can't go," Hart repeated. "I'm ill. Can't we get somebody that will be satisfactory to you as a go-between?"

"Well, who would we get?"

"I don't know, somebody you name, or I can name somebody."

The kidnapper, his bluff called, fell back on his transparent pretense of being the lackey of someone higher up.

"Mr. Hart," he said, "I've got orders from headquarters, and this is the last time; this is your last chance. That's all I can say. Will you get Charlie O'Brien and go or not? If you won't *now*, it will be just *too bad*."

"No, I won't go. I haven't any assurance that you have the boy. Can't you give me any assurance?"

"We have your boy," the caller insisted. "Mr. Hart, I am one of the boys that wrote the letters you received. You remember the long one this afternoon?"

"Yes, I received it."

"Well, you get Charlie O'Brien and leave P.D.Q." The kidnapper seemed addicted to the slangy initials.

"Well, where shall I go? When?"

"Follow the instructions of that letter this afternoon. Leave for Los Angeles in the car. Your boy will be returned."

"How do I know I'll get my boy, or where?"

"The driver of your car will be told where he can pick up your boy at once," the caller promised.

"I know, but can't I have some assurance that I'll get my boy back?" Hart dragged the caller over the same ground again and again . . . stalling . . . stalling . . . stalling.

"Mr. Hart, you get Charlie O'Brien and go at once."

Downtown, the sheriff's car glided swiftly south on Market Street, past Hart's store, past the parking lot from which Brooke had vanished. It took only two or three minutes to reach the Plaza Garage, across the street from the old city hall—hardly 150 feet from San Jose police headquarters. As Emig parked on the street, he spotted Vetterli and Conroy approaching from the opposite direction on foot. They had all but sprinted the block from the Sainte Claire. In the garage office, in the front near the street, Emig found twenty-two-year-old Robert Cline, the night attendant.

"Who has used your telephone in the last few minutes?" he demanded.

No one had used the office phone. But Cline pointed to a wall phone in the rear of the cavernous, dimly lit garage. In the shadows Emig could make out the figure of a man still talking into it.

Emig, Hamilton, and Cordray started for the rear phone, with Cline trailing along. The way it was mounted, the user's back was toward them as he spoke into the fixed mouthpiece. Preoccupied with his conversation, he was oblivious to their silent approach. He hung up just as they got there and was startled as he turned and confronted them.

He was a thin-faced, ruddy young man with large ears and brown, wavy hair receding at the temples. A two-day stubble of dark beard covered his chin. He wore corduroy trousers with high-top boots and an old dark-blue sweater.

"What's your name, mister," Emig demanded.

The man stared dully from haunted steel-blue eyes, deep set under heavy, dark brows.

"Harold Thurmond," he said. "What's this all about, sheriff?"

It was not surprising that the suspect recognized Emig, whose picture was in the papers every day or two. The man offered no resistance. A quick frisk determined that he carried no weapon.

"Who were you just talking to?" Emig asked.

"My mother."

"Didn't you call Alex Hart?"

Thurmond's face whitened and he fell silent.

"Harold, you're under arrest," Emig said, locking the handcuffs.

II

THE
ATROCITY

8

The Collaborators

At San Jose High School in the early 1920s, everybody liked Jack Holmes except perhaps Doc Smith, the biology teacher, who thought him to be a showoff and a cheat.

The trouble between them came to a head in an incident in which Holmes may have been innocent, at least at the outset. A humorless disciplinarian, Smith was interrupted repeatedly during a lecture by the whispered wisecracks of some anonymous jester in the back of the room and by outbursts of giggling. Finally his patience snapped.

"All right," he told the class, "put your books on the floor, and no talking. You're going to take the final exam right now."

Everyone was caught unprepared. Clarisse DuBois, who sat near Jack and admired him, didn't even have a pen, and she asked if he had one she could borrow. Smith turned from the blackboard just in time to catch him answering.

"Holmes, I said no talking!" he exploded. "You don't need to take the final. I'm flunking you right now."

While the rest of the class struggled with the test, Holmes doodled in his notebook, producing a devastating cartoon of Smith's face on the body of a jackass. Smith saw it and, unamused, dispatched Holmes to the principal's office.

For a long time Jack had not been taking school seriously. He was bright when he chose to be, but the previous year he had squeaked by with mostly Ds. The principal, a stern ex-Army officer and character builder, expelled him on the spot, although probably not without regret. A muscular six-footer, Holmes played well on the football team and also drilled with the Cadet Corps, an ROTC-type outfit of which the old soldier was inordinately proud.

Clarisse was not the only girl attracted to Holmes. Evelyn Fleming, who was a year behind him in school, watched him at the football games and admired him from afar. While he could have enjoyed a variety of feminine companionship, the best recollections are that he did not. In high school he went steady with one girl, Gertrude Marsh, whose father ran a paint store.

Holmes was not without social graces. A self-taught pianist, he could play anything by ear. Most of the time he was quietly courteous and personable. Most people thought him handsome, although not classically so, with his ample pompadour of brown hair rising above magnetic blue eyes. A cleft chin and a hint of cruelty in his down-turned mouth line only heightened his magnetism. A man who knew him then said much later he was "a mean-looking bastard, but still good-looking. He'd remind you of Burt Reynolds—that type of guy."

Jack was the only child in a solid family. His father, Maurice Holmes, fifty-six years old at this time, was a tailor who had come to America from Denmark and married Hulda Peterson, an Iowa girl of Swedish birth. They had settled first in Los Angeles where Jack was born on March 20, 1904. The family moved to San Jose about 1915, and Maurice opened his own tailor shop downtown. They lived in a comfortable bungalow on Eleventh Street on the edge of Naglee Park, an older residential district much favored by San Jose's gentry. Maurice was accepted into the town's business establishment and fraternal life. He joined the Masons in 1920, and Hulda became a member of the San Jose Women's Club, a genteel, upper-crust group dedicated to culture and good works.

What pained Jack Holmes most about getting kicked out of school was losing his place on the football squad. He loved the game and dreamed of becoming a coach. His impetuous reaction to his expulsion was to enlist in the Marine Corps, but his hitch was short, for he pulled a ligament and was discharged before most people knew he was gone.

In the 1920s amateur radio was a great frontier, and Holmes was fascinated by it. While still in high school he got his ham's license and was elected vice-president of the San Jose Radio Club. With an old spark-gap rig he began transmitting from the Eleventh Street house. Needing gainful employment, he took a job in a radio shop.

*   *   *

Somewhere along the way, Jack's adolescent romance with Gertrude Marsh tapered off. So not long after his discharge from the Marines, when he was introduced to Evelyn Fleming at a dance, he turned on all his charm.

"He had all the personality in the world," she remembered long afterward. "He was very outgoing, easy to talk to. I was crazy about him. He was everything I ever dreamed of having."

On March 8, 1924, Jack and Evelyn were wed. He was twelve days short of his twentieth birthday, and she was six months younger. The wedding commenced a nine-year period of domesticity when, to all appearances, Holmes was close to a model husband and, later on, a good father.

Of material goods the newlyweds had few; of wealth little. They settled in with Evelyn's mother, Alice Fleming, in her yellow Victorian house on Bird Avenue, a charming place with a cupola and nineteenth-century gingerbread. It was a good arrangement, because when Evelyn's father had died in 1919, he had left nothing but a mortgage on the house. For five years Mrs. Fleming had worked as a dressmaker to support herself, Evelyn, and another daughter, but it was a precarious existence, and Jack's salary was a welcome augmentation to the household coffers. Jack went through a series of jobs but was never without one for long. A year after he and Evelyn married, he became a salesman for the Standard Oil Company.

As a salesman, Holmes demonstrated a public relations flair. Theron Fox, then sports editor of the *Mercury Herald*, was impressed when Jack appeared in the newsroom to hand-deliver his first credit card. Fox later recalled, "He was the type of guy that if your sister or daughter brought him home, you'd say, 'He's a great catch, the all-American boy.' " Not only was Holmes industrious, he sought community respect. In 1926, following in his father's footsteps, he became a Mason, joining Golden Rule Lodge 479.

There were a few, among Holmes's acquaintances, who knew that his engaging personality camouflaged a mean temper and a streak of ruthless rebellion. One who was exposed to this dark side was Al Jones, an auto salesman from whom Jack purchased a used Dodge touring car. When he missed the payments for three or four months, Jones was sent out to repossess the machine.

Holmes had acquired a partnership in a repair garage—a converted barn actually—and Jones spotted the touring car in front of it. He climbed in, found the key, and had started the engine before Holmes emerged from inside and lunged at him, lethally swinging a three-foot length of axle.

"You get the hell out of here or I'll brain you!" he yelled.

Jones, fearing for his life, ducked and retreated strategically but returned later with a deputy sheriff and reclaimed the automobile. Under threat of arrest, Holmes's defiance crumbled, but Jones concluded that he was "just a natural criminal."

In April 1927 the Holmeses became the parents of a son, David, and twenty months later a daughter, Joyce, came along. By all accounts, Jack adored the youngsters. He bought David a pair of roller skates, and father and son "raced" in front of the house. Jack took the boy fishing and to the movies and made kites that they flew together. But he was away much of the time. David would remember his father as a man who laughed a lot, but he said in 1989, "I didn't know him too well; we were hardly buddy-buddy. I don't know if he was a happy man or I was a happy boy."

Two weeks after David Holmes was born, Standard Oil transferred Jack to Half Moon Bay, then a bleak village on a sparsely populated San Mateo County coast. The family lived there two or three years. Some would come to believe this interlude had much to do with what happened later.

Half Moon Bay was mainly a farm center, but the little town's isolation, coupled with its proximity to San Francisco, had given it a new character in the 1920s as a port of entry for contraband booze. The gas station out of which Holmes worked became a hangout for Prohibition rumrunners and for bootleggers and hijackers ashore. Holmes soaked up their scofflaw braggadocio. Their contempt for the laws they broke and the cops they bribed touched his resonant chord of greed.

By 1932 the Great Depression had settled on the land like a stifling blanket, drying up the job market. The Holmeses were back in San Jose, and Jack still dreamed of becoming a coach. Having left school under a cloud, he decided to resume his education and registered for an industrial arts course at San Jose State. He took a battery of entrance examinations, including an intelligence test in which he scored well, and an "A and S" (ascendancy and submissiveness) test to discern leadership potential. In the latter his reactions were almost all on the "ascendancy" side of the scale. He scored "plus-13," placing in the upper fifth of the test group. He completed two terms at the college before dropping out. It was during this time that his fellow students noticed his "perfect crime" fixation. He would pore over the newspapers, analyzing the crimes reported and the errors that led to the perpetrators' detection. One friend considered him "almost devilishly clever" about it.

Along with this crime obsession went an affinity for policemen. On his way to and from the campus, Holmes often stopped to talk shop with the cops downtown.

"I was on the beat at the time and often met him at First and San Antonio," recalled one of them, Andy Anderson, fifty years later. "He used to come by almost every day. He was a nice-looking guy and a good-sized man; he had a very nice personality. He asked me several times what the chances were of getting on the police department." Another officer Holmes got to know was rookie Ray Blackmore, who would later serve as San Jose's chief of police. Blackmore thought of him as "a good man."

Jack's dreams of becoming a cop or a coach were passing fancies; he remained an oil salesman, working for both Standard and Shell at different times, eventually moving over to the Union Oil Company. Salesmanship came naturally for him, and making the rounds of service stations and garages suited his long-time interest in cars. He fitted in and enjoyed the banter around the grease pits. He felt at home amid the mingled aromas of gasoline, drained motor oil, rubber, and tube-patch cement.

It was late in 1932 or early in 1933 that Jack stopped at a service station at San Carlos Street and Delmas Avenue, a few blocks west of San Jose's downtown district, and introduced himself to a new attendant on duty, a stolid, thin-faced fellow close to his own age, with faintly troubled eyes.

The man offered his hand. "I'm Harold Thurmond," he said.

Jack Holmes's plus-13 score on the ascendancy and submissiveness test suggested his need for a foil at the opposite end of the scale—someone he could dominate. No one could have better filled the role than Thomas Harold Thurmond, for whom submissiveness was a way of life.

Thurmond had grown up as a plodding younger son in a devoutly Baptist home dominated by his mother and five sisters. Early in the century the family had lived in Lodi, a solid farm town in California's great Central Valley, where Harold was born on June 20, 1906. The Thurmonds moved to San Jose sometime during Harold's school years; he was a lackluster scholar in both towns. A girl who went to school with him in Lodi thought him "a kind of a queer duck"— queer in the sense of odd, not homosexual.

The service station where Harold Thurmond and Jack Holmes first met belonged to a man named Francis Wyatt. The exceptional circumstance by which Thurmond happened to be working there— how he had been thrown cynically into the deal when Wyatt purchased the station from Harold's father—is told in the preface. That transaction is one of the few clear views we have of the father, Thomas J. Thurmond, a Kentuckian by birth who remains in the shadows of history.

In what may have been a perennial quest for cheap rentals, the Thurmonds moved from house to house within San Jose and in the Campbell area to the southwest. The family took in student boarders from the teachers college to make ends meet.

Lillie Thurmond, the Missouri-born mother, was a handsome woman with sandy-gray hair, remembered by an acquaintance as "a very sweet person." She was a matriarchal personage, a pillar of the church. Under her roof no meal was begun until grace was said. To her, liquor was Satan's brew, and she militantly guarded her daughters and her boarders against its corruption. For this we have the testimony of Al Jones—the same who repossessed Jack Holmes's touring car. By a not-too-remarkable small-town coincidence, Jones knew both the Holmes and Thurmond families, and about 1924 he came a-courting one of the Thurmonds' boarders, a girl named Natalie from Modesto. For decades thereafter he would recall Lillie's sharp query: "Do you imbibe, young man?" (As a man-about-town, promoter, and political dilettante, Jones will pop up repeatedly, in widely diverse contexts, as this narrative continues.)

Thurmond's siblings were, by and large, intelligent and successful. One sister was a primary-grades teacher, married to the principal of the much-favored Willow Glen Elementary School that Louis Rossi's little girl attended. Another sister was a church organist, much in demand, and two others were respectively accountant and stenographer for a tax lawyer. The fifth sister had married a highway patrolman. Thurmond's only brother, Roy, was ordained in the Assemblies of God church and was its pastor at Chico, in the Sacramento Valley.

* * *

Lillie Thurmond regarded her son Harold as a "delicate" lad, especially after he suffered a severe head injury in early childhood. She also thought him "spiritually inclined." In 1923 he joined the San Jose First Baptist Church at age seventeen and was soon caught up in the youth program.

As he grew to manhood it became increasingly evident to most that Harold was a dullard in this family of high achievers. Policeman Andy Anderson, who had a nodding acquaintance with him, considered him "a funny little guy." Al Jones, while courting Natalie, knew him as a friendly youth obsessed with fast cars, dreaming of the time when he would have his own racer. He was good natured and "didn't have an ounce of meanness," as far as Jones could see, but was "a bit on the hesitant side" mentally.

Wyatt, who would know Harold almost ten years after Jones did, got the same impression: "I wouldn't classify him as retarded exactly, but he was just not very smart. I guess maybe he had about an 8-year-old mentality. He was very easily led."

Thurmond dropped out of San Jose High School before graduation. For four years in the mid-1920s he labored as a yard man at the McElroy-Cheim Lumber Company and then put in a stint with a paint store in Oakland. About 1931, back in San Jose, he returned to the lumber yard, working a day or two at a time until his father arranged the service station job for him.

None of these jobs paid much, and Thurmond's chronic penury brought on the first crisis of his adult life. Sometime in the late 1920s he had proposed to a San Jose girl and they became engaged. By his own account later, he loved her deeply. But for two years she made his life miserable, nagging him about his poor prospects, and finally broke the engagement. An invitation to her wedding to a rival suitor, which Harold found in his mail near the end of 1931, demolished his last remnant of self-esteem. Plunging into depression, he began to drink, frequenting San Jose's speakeasies and taking up with a lawless crowd he found in them. To his puritanical family, this behavior was an irrational and incomprehensible response to adversity.

Throughout this painful time, Lillie Thurmond consoled herself in the conviction that Harold, who sat at her side in church each Sunday, was after all "God-fearing," with a "kindly, gentle, and religious heart." What she never understood was the thinness of his commitment. Harold attended church out of habit, no more, no less. If his mother wanted him in the pew, he was there—

because he always acquiesced in the wishes of a stronger personality. The Christian concepts of good and evil held little meaning for him.

At the time Jack Holmes and Harold Thurmond first encountered each other, Holmes was to all appearances a happy man with a promising future—well liked, recognized, and respected around town. He and Evelyn still lived with her mother, and their Bird Avenue address enabled their son David to attend Willow Glen Elementary School, which, under the principalship of Thurmond's brother-in-law, was considered superior. Above all, Holmes was gainfully employed, which in itself was no mean status symbol in the spring of 1933. In May, riding high, he traded in his battered old Chevrolet on a handsome new model, a black 1933 Chevy "coach," as two-door automobiles were then called. It was a dressed-up vehicle with wire wheels.

Beneath the smooth surface of his life, however, restlessness and rebellion simmered within Jack Holmes. His work was humdrum, and his marriage to Evelyn had lost its excitement. So he was primed to react recklessly when Gertrude Marsh, the soft brunette who had been his high school sweetheart, unexpectedly reentered his life in the late spring of 1933. She was now a teacher at the rural Franklin School south of San Jose. Her name was now Gertrude Estensen; she had married Leonard Estensen, a service station operator, two years earlier.

Jack's renewed interest in Gertrude began innocently when he stopped one day at her father's paint store. He asked how she was and learned she was seriously ill in the hospital, following surgery. After that, he inquired about her every day or so. At home he told Evelyn that if she did not object, he would like to pay Gertrude a visit. Feeling secure in her marriage, Evelyn offered no opposition, so as soon as Gertrude came home from the hospital, Jack showed up at her door on Pierce Street.

The reunion of the old sweethearts was joyous and good-hearted, and Gertrude urged Jack to bring Evelyn over. Soon the Holmeses and Estensens were a foursome, spending many evenings together.*

---

*An understanding of the association between the Holmeses and Estensens, before and on the night Brooke Hart was kidnapped, is critical to any valid conclusion about the events of that night. The generally accepted account of how the couples got together, as given here, was disputed by the late Leonard Estensen in a 1989 interview with the author. See Chapter 22, "Lingering Doubts."

Almost from the start, however, behind Evelyn's back, Jack began visiting Gertrude by day also. Within a month he was pleading with her to leave Leonard and run away with him. Her response was cool but not wholly discouraging. By fall, he had gotten her away for a Saturday trip to San Francisco and had taken her to a football game. The fantasy of making love to her besieged Jack's troubled mind. He came to realize that possessing Gertrude, whether as wife, mistress, or playmate, would require far more money than he would ever make selling gasoline and oil.

Thurmond, whose own poverty had cost him a woman's love, was a sympathetic listener to Holmes's woes. The two had hit it off from their first meeting, and more and more, in his off hours, Jack hung out with Harold at Wyatt's service station.

During this time, Wyatt began experiencing strange little misfortunes. While closing one night, he told Harold he had hidden the day's receipts under a certain thirty-gallon oil tank, so that the cash would be ready the next day. No one else knew the hiding place, but by dawn's light the money was gone. Next Wyatt had a problem collecting from his bootlegger customers, who accounted for a major part of his credit business. When he dunned them for the money, they produced charge slips signed by Harold, proving they had already paid. And before he could confront Thurmond on that, one of his gas tanks came up 100 gallons short, in what had to be an inside job.

Wyatt summoned both Harold and his father for a showdown. Harold squirmed and alibied, but the evidence of his embezzlement was too strong to be denied. Without confessing openly, he gave Wyatt a promissory note to cover the losses, which ran to $250 or $300, and his father countersigned it. But although fired, Harold still hung around.

"He had these bootlegger friends," Wyatt recalled later, "and occasionally he'd come into the station half-looped and give me a case of fine bootleg hooch, just as a friendly gesture."

Wyatt also discovered that his dim-witted, larcenous ex-employee could fix speeding tickets. One week Wyatt accumulated about five of them, and Harold said, "Give them to me." He took them to his ex-brother-in-law, the highway patrolman, and they were never heard of again.

For a while Harold made regular payments on the note, giving Wyatt a $25 postal money order each week. Then he began to skip. Wyatt drove to Harold's home to demand payment and ran into a buzz saw in the person of Lillie Thurmond. In an emotional show of offended dignity, she accused him of persecuting her fine Christian son. He left empty-handed. His next stop was at the district attorney's office, where an assistant district attorney listened sympathetically. Finally the assistant, who had a private law practice on the side, spoke for the first time.

"Well," he said, "I had more or less expected you, but I can't help you. You see, I represent the Thurmond family."

Wyatt gave up.

To Jack Holmes, a flawless felony was something to be admired, like a perfect diamond. A botched crime was an affront. Throughout 1933, the news provided a rich vein of violence and terror to satisfy his dilettantish obsession with crime and its execution. Poring over the newspapers, he must have been impressed with the way kidnapping was paying off. It was the felony of fashion. Ransoms paid by families of wealthy victims were enormous in the currency of the time: $60,000 for Charles Boettcher, Jr., in Denver; $50,000 for Jerome Factor, son of John "Jake the Barber" Factor in Chicago; $70,000 for a child, Margaret McGrath, in Harwick, Massachusetts; $30,000 for Mary McElroy in Kansas City; $100,000 for William Hamm of the beer family in St. Paul. There had been three big payoffs in July alone: $100,000 for John Factor himself, $40,000 for John J. O'Connell in Albany, and $200,000 for oil millionaire Charles Urschel in Oklahoma City.

At some point, it appears, Holmes began to ponder seriously whether he could execute a kidnapping for that kind of money. As a self-deemed crime expert, he should have dropped the idea in an instant, for police and prosecutors across the land had launched an all-out antikidnapping campaign and were getting verdicts ranging from fifteen years to death. As an egotist, however, Holmes convinced himself that he was smarter than those who had been caught. In that frame of mind he must have noticed, in the September 19 *Mercury Herald*, the overwritten account of the gala Hart's Department Store dinner at the De Anza the night before. The headline read:

BROOKE L. HART
MADE EXECUTIVE
IN FATHER'S FIRM

Slowly a plan for self-enrichment began to germinate in Holmes's fertile, criminally attuned, sexually haunted mind. He would have to work it in easy stages, and he would need a partner who would follow orders blindly—someone with a ruthless streak, not overly sensitive to the difference between right and wrong, but nonetheless reliable.

Who?

Holmes laughed. The question answered itself. Who but poor, dim-witted, eager-to-please Harold, who would happily stick his head in a hot oven for anyone who told him to? Holmes sought out his friend and, talking partly cold turkey and partly in riddles, outlined the first phase of his idea.

"Are you with me?" he asked.

Thurmond flashed his weak grin.

"Sure Jack, I'll do it."

Late Monday, September 25, Thurmond waited in Holmes's Chevrolet on Stockton Avenue, watching a certain car Holmes had described to him, parked outside the Union Oil Company plant. When a man emerged and drove away in it, Thurmond followed. The driver was M. J. Michel, a clerk Holmes said would be en route to the bank with the day's receipts.

As Michel slowed for a turn three blocks away, Thurmond ran him to the curb and entered his car at gunpoint. Thurmond was steady on the trigger, his face blank, his manner devoid of emotion. Only the bulging of a neck muscle betrayed whatever concern Lillie's "spiritual" son might be feeling as, for the first time, he crossed the line between upright citizen and outlaw.

In a voice soft but cold, Thurmond gave a bewildering series of left and right turn commands, to which Michel responded in terrified obedience. The circuitous route led into the countryside, and presently, with no one in sight, Thurmond told his captive to stop by a pear orchard north of town.

"Take your shoes off and get out," he ordered, as he confiscated Michel's money bag. Thurmond tied the barefoot clerk to a tree and drove off to a rendezvous point where Holmes waited.

"How did it go, Harold?"

"Just the way you said." Thurmond handed Holmes the money bag.

"Oho, look here!" Holmes whooped as he thrust in his hand and withdrew thick packets of greenbacks. The collaborators clapped each other on the back and roared with laughter. It took but a few minutes to count the money, which came to $716. Holmes doled out Thurmond's share and gave it to him, putting the rest in his pocket. There were also checks and coupons totaling $471.34, and Holmes said, "We'll hide these for now."

It had been so easy, so *incredibly* easy. Now the partners had more money in their pockets than honest work would pay them over the next three months. Holmes danced a little jig; the holdup formula, as he had devised it, was foolproof. Both men knew it was only a matter of time until they employed it again.

Thurmond had proved his mettle. Holmes decided, however, to give him a few days off before broaching his next idea, one that might take a little getting used to for even so dumb an ox as Harold.

Soon after the Michel hijacking, Francis Wyatt was surprised to receive another $25 payment on Thurmond's long-defaulted promissory note. He wondered where Harold had got the money.

When Holmes finally broached his next idea, for a big score that would make the Michel loot look like small change, Thurmond registered no dismay. Not a flicker crossed his stolid face. The collaborators, cruising around downtown in Holmes's car, passed Brooke Hart on the street one day not long thereafter. Holmes spotted him first.

"Look at that curly-haired rich bastard," he said.

"If we could pick him up we could get a piece of change out of him," Thurmond mused.

"What would we do with him?"

"I don't know. We'd have to figure that out."

"We might put him on a boat or something."

If the kidnapping of Brooke Hart had begun as Jack Holmes's idea, he had now maneuvered his partner into the role of its chief advocate and defender. Once motivated, the sluggish mind of Harold Thurmond ran wild. Ideas came and went. Gradually the plan grew firmer, and its appeal to the greedy minds of the partners increased.

At length Thurmond observed, offhand, "You know, Jack, the smart thing would be to dump that guy overboard someplace."

About October 15 Holmes called on one of his oil route customers, a man named Meyer who ran a garage on Willow Street. He steered the conversation around to guns, remembering that another of Meyer's friends had left town, leaving behind a .41 caliber pistol he hoped the garageman could sell for him.

"How much does your buddy want for that gun?" Holmes asked.

"He told me to try to get six bucks."

"I know a guy who's looking for a gun like this. I'll send him around."

Thurmond showed up later. From the awkward way he handled the weapon, Meyer concluded he had little experience with firearms.

"I'll take it," Thurmond said without a quibble, tossing down a $10 bill. Meyer gave him $4 in change and entered the sale in his cash book.

A week later the collaborators put the Hart kidnap on the back burner, deciding to replenish their dwindling cash reserves first with a reprise of the earlier holdup. This time Holmes chose J. W. Scott, who did the banking for his former firm, the Shell Oil Company, as the victim. The job was set up for October 23, again a Monday when Scott's money bag would be swollen with the weekend receipts. Once more Thurmond turned in a letter-perfect performance.

"Hot damn!" Holmes cried, laughing as he counted out $675 in cash and checks. Once more, from his share, Thurmond conscientiously sent Wyatt a postal money order for $25.

As the partners refocused their attention on Brooke Hart, they reached a firm understanding that their criminal career would be a passing thing, not a permanent vocation. Neither man had a police record (though by now each richly deserved one), so they would quit while they were ahead. Once they had made their big score with Brooke, they would resume their lives as upstanding citizens—affluent ones.

Frank McKee, a boating hobbyist, had known Jack Holmes for ten years. On Tuesday, October 31, he was surprised to see his old friend approaching him at the South Bay Yacht Club's rundown marina on Alviso Slough.

"Hello, Frank," Holmes called. "Any boats for sale around here?"

McKee pointed to his own craft, a sailboat he had been trying to sell.

"You can have this one for fifteen hundred bucks," he said.

Holmes said he had been to every yacht club in San Francisco, and McKee's boat was closer to what he wanted than anything else he had seen. If he decided to buy it, he would return to let his partner, a friend named Harold, look it over. Neither Holmes nor Harold ever came back, however.

*   *   *

About the same time Holmes was dickering for the boat, a customer at the California Concrete Products Company, on the south side of San Jose, was making a vivid impression on Tony Carvalho, the yard man. The fellow drove into the yard and parked his dark-colored coupe in front of the office. He was in his late twenties, attired in dark suit and hat, of medium height and build, with receding brown hair, prominent ears, and deep-set blue eyes in which fear seemed to mingle with confusion.

"Do you have any brick tile?" he wanted to know.

Carvalho, not quite understanding what the man meant, took him to a brick pile in back of the office and picked up a 12½-pound concrete building block.

"How about this?"

Without even lifting it, the stranger said, "No, that's too light."

Next Carvalho found a block that weighed 19½ pounds. The customer took it in his hands, balanced it, and hefted it up and down.

"No, that's not heavy enough either."

"Well, then, try one of these." Carvalho offered a sample from a stack of twenty-two-pound blocks measuring five by eight by twelve inches. Two holes for reinforcing steel traversed the five-inch dimension, and the blocks had notched and corrugated ends that would fit together snugly in construction.

The customer grasped the sample, hefted it, and said, "I'll take two of these." Then, after picking up another one and weighing it in both hands, he changed his mind: "Make it three."

Concrete block sales in less than bulk lots were so rare that Carvalho didn't know how much to charge, so he went to the office to find out.

"Charge him a dime apiece," said the manager, John Demicheli. Carvalho returned to find his customer, who was stowing the blocks in his car, still strangely obsessed with their weight.

"Yes, these are heavy enough. They're cheap at the price," the man said matter-of-factly. He followed Carvalho into the office and paid for them with a fifty-cent piece. Demicheli gave him twenty cents change. Because the transaction was so trivial, Demicheli made no sales slip, but weeks later he would remember this odd customer as clearly as Carvalho, who would unhesitatingly identify the man as Harold Thurmond.

The next time Thurmond reported to Holmes, he was still concerned about the weight of his blocks.

"I bought three twenty-two pounders, Jack," he said. "Do you think that's enough?"

"Don't worry," Holmes laughed. "Forty pounds would hold a horse on the bottom of the bay."

As a man pursuing another's wife, launching a criminal career, and negotiating to buy a boat, Jack Holmes did not need further complication in his life. But on November 1, he showed up at Kay's Service Station on South Third Street with the dismal news that he had lost his Union Oil job.

"Personal reasons," he told Seaman Kay, the proprietor. "The manager had a prejudice against me. Officially I resigned, but actually I was canned."

The probable reason was that he was now giving his customers short shrift, as he spent more and more of his time wooing Gertrude and plotting the abduction of Brooke Hart. The boss who fired him was of course unaware that with the Michel hijacking, Holmes had already helped himself to his salary for the next several months.

"Come to work for me, Jack," suggested Kay, whose firm was more than a filling station. It delivered oil to farmers throughout the countryside, and by working up a route, Holmes could make $100 to $200 a week on commission, Kay told him.

"You'll need a truck," he added, "and I know where you can pick up an old one cheap. There's one for sale for $350 at the Western Oil Company on River Street."

Holmes returned nearly every day that first week of November to talk with Kay about his job offer, giving every sign of considering it seriously. But all the while he was giving out other stories all over town. On Saturday, November 4, the partners were cruising on First Street near Pierce, when Holmes spotted Gertrude Estensen on the other side of the street. He wheeled around and pulled up alongside her, introducing her to "my friend Harold."

"Where are you boys headed," she asked.

"Just fooling around."

Gertrude later remembered the brief encounter clearly as the only time in her life she ever met Harold Thurmond. And she distinctly recalled Holmes telling her that he was going back to work for his old outfit, the Shell Oil Company.

* * *

Among the 2,800 residents of the orchard village of Campbell, none was more respected or better loved than Lillie Shaw. A widow for the last half of her seventy-six years, she had devoted her life to the community, serving as president of the Country Women's Club and leading the campaign for a public library. When she died on Sunday, November 5, the merchants unanimously resolved to close for her funeral Tuesday afternoon in the Congregational Church, of which she had been secretary.

Lillie was the aunt of Evelyn Holmes—the sister of her late father—and Jack Holmes accompanied his wife to the services. After the burial, he picked up a family-style Italian dinner downtown and took it home for the funeral guests. So as it turned out, Mrs. Shaw's demise upset the original timetable for Brooke Hart's abduction, which Holmes and Thurmond had first planned for that Tuesday, November 7.

At three o'clock Wednesday afternoon, as Brooke parked his car in the lot at Market and Post streets and walked the few feet north to the department store, Thurmond was watching from afar. A little later, when Thurmond and Holmes met by prearrangement, Harold excitedly reported the sighting.

"Shall we stick around and see when he comes out again?" he asked.

Now it was Holmes, the architect of the kidnapping, who was chickening out.

"Harold," he said, "the more I think about this harebrained idea, the less I like it."

"It could be done mighty easy," said Thurmond, the follower, who in his role reversal had bought the plan hook, line, and sinker and was now its protagonist.

The collaborators found a parking place with a view of both Brooke's car and the side door of the department store, which Brooke habitually used. For almost three hours they waited, as dusk descended. Then, just at six o'clock, Thurmond nudged his partner. The side door opened, and in the glow of a streetlamp he recognized Brooke's golden mop of hair. Holmes tentatively placed his hand on the car door handle, ready to go into action. Then:

"Damn!"

Alongside Brooke's trim figure had appeared the stocky frame of Alex Hart. It would be madness to snatch the son in the company of the father. Agreeing to meet the next afternoon, the partners parted and went home.

The next day, Thursday, Thurmond acted to remedy two oversights in the kidnapping preparations. First, he obtained a large pillowcase from his nephew's bed. Then he drove his father's car to Santa Clara and bought a seventy-five-foot coil of clothesline wire.

While Harold was thus occupied, Holmes was busy with machinations of his own. About four o'clock he telephoned Gertrude Estensen.

"What are you doing tonight, honey?" he asked.

"I don't know, Jack."

"Let's do something."

"We just went to the show last night," Gertrude said. "Why don't you bring Evelyn over and play bridge?"

"All right. If I can't come I'll call you."

After he hung up, Holmes headed for the home of Harvey and Ruth Gum in the Cottage Grove neighborhood on the south edge of town. The Holmeses and Gums were social friends. Ruth answered the doorbell when Jack rang it about five o'clock, taking her by surprise. She invited him in, and he stayed a short time, conversing aimlessly. From the Gums', he drove downtown to meet Thurmond, as they had agreed. As Thurmond got into Holmes's car, he asked, "Do you want to pipe that guy off again?"

"Yeah, sure, let's go," Holmes replied.

They took up their surveillance anew, from a parking place a little south of Hart's store.

"Do you know Brooke Hart?" Holmes asked his partner as they waited.

"I've seen him a few times and I can identify him," Thurmond said. "He'd recognize me, so you'll have to grab him."

The sky was darkening rapidly. Both plotters grew jumpy as the store's quitting time approached. Then at 5:55, Brooke again emerged from the store, a fashion plate in gray. There he was, alone, striding briskly down the sidewalk."

"Get going, Jack," Harold said. "We'll do it just the way we planned."

Holmes had ample time to position himself. Brooke's walk to his car was only about sixty yards, but he took several minutes to cover the distance, exchanging greetings with Louise Hartz and chatting with the parking lot attendant Henry Kuehn.

As Brooke at last got into his automobile and began creeping along the lot's lone driveway toward Market Street, he must have seen the man standing at the curb in the gathering dusk. But he had no reason to sense anything sinister about the lone figure, who might have been waiting for a ride, or killing time before an appointment, or just enjoying a cigarette.

As the front bumper of the Studebaker crossed the curbline, Brooke braked gently to a full stop, just for an instant, waiting for the street traffic to clear. In that instant, with sure and silent movements, Jack Holmes placed his foot on the roadster's right running board, opened the door, slipped into the car, and pressed the muzzle of Thurmond's pistol into Brooke's ribs.

The boarding was so swift and natural that later, no one nearby remembered seeing it happen.

9

After the Fact

Seventy-one new miles had been clocked on the odometer of Jack Holmes's black Chevy as he braked it to a stop at Fourth and Santa Clara streets, four blocks east of the point where he had taken Brooke Hart captive. The elapsed time, which would become a matter of critical concern, was just under two hours by the best later reckoning. It was now a few minutes before eight o'clock.

"Jeez, Harold," Holmes said, as he cut off the ignition, "I never thought I could participate in a thing like that."

"I don't know how I did it either," Thurmond replied.

Their agonizing was brief.

"Well," said Holmes after a pause, "as long as it's done we might as well go through with the rest of it. How much shall we ask?"

"Fifty grand?"

"Don't be greedy, Harold. Let's let the old man off easy. Forty thousand, OK?"

"OK with me, Jack."

Holmes withdrew a postcard and a pencil from his pocket and, by the car's dim dome light, laboriously printed in capitals a message to Alex Hart, Sr., composing it as he went along. It was the one which began "YOUR SON IS O.K. AND TREATED WELL. . . ." When finished, Holmes handed the card to Thurmond, who put it in his pocket, along with Brooke Hart's wallet.

"We better not see each other again till Monday," Holmes said. "You sure you know what to do, Harold?" As in the Michel and Scott holdups, which had been dress rehearsals, Holmes had conceived a plan for this job that stuck his compliant partner with most of the work and risk.

"Don't worry, Jack, I'll do it right," Thurmond replied as he got out of the car.

Holmes sped away into the night. No more than ten minutes later he arrived at his house on Bird Avenue to pick up Evelyn for their date with the Estensens. His father, Maurice Holmes, and his mother, Hulda, were already there to baby-sit. While waiting for Jack, Evelyn had been helping Hulda fit a dress.

"Come on, honey, we're running late," Holmes called to his wife as he entered. He greeted his parents cheerfully if perfunctorily. Within two or three minutes Evelyn and Jack left for the short ride to the Estensen home. It was nearing 8:15. *

At the Estensens', Gertrude and Leonard had finished the dishes and were playing bridge when the Holmeses arrived, probably about 8:20. Gertrude's idea of continuing the bridge game was quickly abandoned in favor of another night at the movies. The two couples killed an unhurried fifteen minutes before leaving for the Hester Theater, a neighborhood movie house then showing Walt Disney's cartoon sensation, "The Three Little Pigs." Later Gertrude was certain they arrived before the first show ended about nine, because the house was full and they had to wait for seating. During the picture, she recalled, Holmes was "just as natural as could be," laughing heartily at the huffing and puffing of the Big Bad Wolf.

When the second show ended sometime after eleven o'clock, the couples drove downtown for a snack at Maggi's Restaurant on South First Street. They returned to the Estensen house about midnight, and while parked in front they laid plans for the weekend. Saturday afternoon the San Jose State football team would be hosting the Cal Aggies, and they tentatively decided to see the game; Gertrude said her mother would probably want to go, too. †

While his partner socialized at the cinema, Thurmond undertook the lonely mission Holmes had assigned him for the remainder of the

---

* This and certain other time estimates in this chapter are based on the kidnappers' confessions, FBI documents, and press reports. Later, Holmes's survivors and the Estensens would offer differing time frames for the evening's events, raising substantive questions about the validity of Holmes's confession. See Chapter 13, "The Woman and the Alibi," and Chapter 22, "Lingering Doubts."
† The California Agricultural College was the predecessor of today's Davis campus of the University of California.

night. In his father's car he set out on a desolate ride to San Francisco. Mile after mile he sped through the dark along El Camino Real, the thin ribbon of gray asphalt that was the only direct highway up the San Francisco Peninsula in 1933. The route was rural for much of the way; Harold maintained a steady fifty miles an hour except through the towns. Traffic was light and he could have driven faster, but he took care to stay close to the speed limit. He did not want this trip documented by a traffic ticket.

Before 9:30 Thurmond arrived in the 1000 block of San Francisco's Market Street and headed for Dan Dwyer's speakeasy, where he had several stiff drinks to steady his nerves and dispel the chill of his ride. Then he picked up the phone on the bar and asked for long distance.

"Operator, I want to place a call to Ballard 2013 in San Jose." He had jotted down the Hart residence number before leaving home. There was clicking on the line, and then Thurmond could hear the ringing at the other end and then a woman's voice: "Hello." He could not identify the voice (which belonged to Aleese Hart). The call lasted little more than a minute. He imparted the information that Brooke was kidnapped but little else before losing his nerve and hanging up. * As he did so, he realized he had botched the call and would have to make it again. But he dared not use the same phone twice.

Leaving the speakeasy, he walked up Market Street to the Whitcomb Hotel, where he found a pay phone in the lobby. From there he placed his second call at 10:30, giving assurance that Brooke was safe and specifying the $40,000 ransom figure. He hung up with Miriam's anguished plea, "Oh, please don't hurt him!" resounding in his ears.

Thurmond's instructions from Holmes now called for him to take a ferry to Oakland and, somewhere in midbay when unwatched, toss Brooke Hart's wallet over the rail. It had been a long day, however, and Harold was reeling from fatigue and the delayed jolt of Dan Dwyer's whiskey. Emerging from the hotel into the cool night air, he walked toward the foot of Market Street, where the Ferry Building beckoned at the waterfront. Instead of catching a boat, however, he turned south along the Embarcadero to Pier 32. There loomed the silhouette of the liner *Lurline*, fueling for its next cruise to Hawaii. The pier was deserted and unguarded at this hour, and Thurmond proceeded to its edge without challenge. With a quick glance about, to confirm that no one was watching, he withdrew Brooke's wallet

---

* In his confession, Thurmond said the Harts' line was busy at 9:30. However, Aleese clearly remembered receiving the call.

from his pocket and with a casual gesture dropped it. He heard a small splash in the water far below.

Friday was a day of rest for Thurmond, in preparation for a second grueling night on the road. Holmes had decided that the ransom notes should bear widely scattered postmarks; it was Harold's job to mail them. In the evening he again borrowed his father's car and set out alone for Sacramento, 120 miles to the northeast. Under the best conditions it was a three-hour trip, some of it over a steep, tortuous road hugging the sides of mountains.

By 8:30 he had the mountainous part of the ride—the treacherous Altamont Pass east of Livermore—behind him. Emerging onto the flat floor of the Central Valley at Tracy, he retrieved from his pocket the postcard note that Holmes had given him and inserted it into an envelope he had brought from home. After sealing and addressing it in juvenile pencil printing, he continued on his way, turning north through Stockton and his birthplace, Lodi. Arriving in Sacramento about ten o'clock, he mailed the note in a box within sight of the state capitol's illuminated dome. After a bite to eat, he drove back home, reaching San Jose about 1:30 Saturday morning.

For Holmes, business, pleasure, and the social whirl went on.

On Friday morning, refreshed after several hours' sleep, he made the rounds of his usual haunts, dropping in at Seaman Kay's service station for the first time since Tuesday. He had been on the verge of accepting Kay's offer of a truck-route job then. Now he told Kay he probably wouldn't need it; he said he had a new offer from the Shell Oil Company.

Saturday afternoon Jack and Evelyn kept their football date with the Estensens and Gertrude's mother. As they entered the stadium, they ran into Theron Fox, former *Mercury Herald* sports editor. The conversation was mainly about football; the Hart case was not mentioned. To Fox, Holmes appeared genial, relaxed, and natural, cheering himself hoarse as San Jose State routed the Aggies 20–0.

In the evening, after the game, the two couples went to another picture show. To Evelyn, it became painfully clear that the game and movie were chiefly enjoyable for Jack as opportunities for romancing Gertrude. There were limits to Evelyn's tolerance and patience, and this was the night they were reached. She had been naive, but she was not blind.

102

As the marathon of double-dating with the Estensens had progressed since summer, Jack had grown more and more demonstrative of affection for his old sweetheart. Now he had abandoned all pretense of hiding his infatuation. The syrupy compliments, the casual caresses, the hugs—all of which Gertrude seemed to enjoy—could no longer be ignored. By the time the Holmeses got home from the theater, around midnight, Evelyn was seething. She met the issue head on.

"Are you in love with that woman?" Her eyes flashed.

"And if I am?"

"Do you think she'd have you, Jack? Do you think she'd leave Leonard? She's playing you for a fool."

"She'll leave him anytime I'm ready. Ask her."

"Then she's a fool!" Evelyn threw down the gauntlet. "Either you leave her alone, Jack, or get out of this house!"

Evelyn was jealous of her husband and did not want to lose him, but in delivering her ultimatum she felt little jeopardy. As a serious bridge player, she knew she held trump cards. More than half a century later she remembered, "Oh, yes, he thought he was definitely in love with Gertrude. But we also had two children; he wasn't about to leave them. Especially he wasn't going to leave his son."

Tossing and turning the rest of the night, Evelyn resolved to have a showdown with her rival as soon as the new day dawned. Early Sunday morning she rang the Estensens' bell. Gertrude, still in bed, sleepily donned a robe and came to the front door.

Evelyn struck like a coiled snake: "Why are you trying to steal my husband?"

"My God!"

"I'm no fool, Gertrude. I saw everything that happened yesterday. He couldn't keep his hands off you. He says you're going to leave Leonard and run away with him."

Gertrude was flabbergasted. "He's dreaming, Evelyn. It's an illusion. It's his idea, not mine. I have no intention of leaving Leonard or running away with Jack. I don't want to, and I've never tried to. Even if I wanted to I wouldn't, on account of you and the children."

"I've seen this coming all these months," Evelyn said, calmer now. "I thought by going out with you and Leonard, throwing him into your company, he'd get over his infatuation, but I guess it was the wrong thing."

"Jack will get over this silliness sooner or later," Gertrude predicted. "It's just something left over from high school. He has always been erratic—I guess you know."

The two women parted on an amiable if not wholly satisfying basis. They little imagined that within five days they would be partners in a desperate effort to save Jack's name and his life.

Back home, Evelyn found her husband unrepentant. They endured Sunday under a surly pall of hostility. Early Monday Jack packed a suitcase and left 1070 Bird Avenue for the last time, not telling Evelyn his destination. Downtown he checked into the California Hotel, a cheap, slightly seedy but respectable place on South First Street, two doors south of O'Brien's candy store. He told the clerk he would be staying a couple of weeks and was given a room on the third floor.

As it would turn out, Holmes's timing for leaving his wife could not have been worse. Three days earlier (the day after the kidnapping) Lillie Shaw's will had been filed for probate. To her niece Evelyn, she left a half-interest in two lots on Monte Verde Street in Carmel, purchased some years earlier for $50 apiece. On one of them was a cabin. Had Jack stayed with his family, he could have enjoyed a comfortable old age, for in 1990 the property was estimated to be worth no less than $800,000.

Harold's weekend was much less stressful than that of his partner. On Sunday morning, at the First Baptist Church, he sat with Lillie Thurmond in her accustomed pew. Mother and son rose and stood with heads bowed as the Reverend Andrew L. Fraser offered a special supplication:

"Our Heavenly Father, we pray for the safe return of Brooke Hart to his family, and for the righting of this cruel wrong."

The minister went on to deliver a sermon condemning the rising tide of crime.

After checking into the hotel and breakfasting at a cafe, Holmes drove southwest at midmorning Monday, into the farm country south of Campbell. By prearrangement he stopped on remote White Oaks Road, the thin, gravelly lane that meandered between the orchards on the bank of Los Gatos Creek. Upon Harold's arrival in his father's Pontiac, scarcely a minute later, Holmes left his car and walked back to rejoin his accomplice for the first time since their deed. He carried a newspaper with the headline, "Liner Searched on Wallet Clue to Missing Heir."

"You idiot!" he muttered, as he climbed into the driver's seat of the Thurmond car, Harold sliding over to accommodate him. "I told you to throw the wallet in the middle of the bay. How did it end up on that ship?"

"By that time I was too tired to ride a ferryboat all the way to Oakland and back. I threw the wallet off the pier. I heard it splash in the water, Jack, honest I did."

"You lazy son of a bitch. You want to get us hung?"

"Hell, all it did was confuse 'em," Thurmond grinned. "Hey, did you read how they rousted old Babe Ruth out of bed? We're in the big leagues now!"

Holmes's anger speedily dissipated. Thurmond was right; the latest news accounts showed the cops to be thrashing around in disarray.

"Did you mail the note?" Holmes asked.

"Sure, Jack, about ten o'clock Friday night in Sacramento."

"That means old man Hart is reading it just about now. I'd like to see the bastard's face. Now we've got to give him some more orders. Did you bring the paper and envelopes?" Holmes had given his confederate the responsibility for supplying the stationery, which might be traced.

Thurmond produced a small writing tablet and a pencil and handed them to his partner, who made a great show of handling the paper so as not to leave fingerprints. He propped the tablet against the windshield of the old Pontiac and began to compose note number two.

Holmes had meanwhile conceived the window-placard idea, which he thought to be a brilliant strategem for risk-free coded communication with the Harts. After writing instructions for the "-1-" sign, he once more told Alex to prepare for a trip and repeated the assurance, "BROOKE IS SAFE."

For the first ten or fifteen minutes of the kidnappers' rendezvous, no other vehicle passed them on the lonely road. Then suddenly, as Holmes labored over the note, they were startled when a truck with two men in the cab chugged out of the orchard nearby. Until then neither Holmes nor Thurmond had noticed the workers among the trees some distance away. As the truck turned toward the kidnappers, Holmes dropped the note and, in a jerky movement, picked up the newspaper on the seat beside him as if to read. Leaving the scene, the truck passed within inches of them, the road being barely wide enough for two vehicles side by side.

Presently the truck returned with its two occupants and reentered the orchard. Soon thereafter Holmes completed the new message, scanned it with satisfaction, and sealed it in an envelope provided by Thurmond. He affixed a three-cent stamp for first-class postage. Handing it to Thurmond for mailing, he opened the car door and stepped out.

"Oh, one other thing, Harold," he said as they parted. "I split up with my old lady this morning. I'm in the California Hotel now, Room 91 on the third floor."

Thurmond made a U-turn, with difficulty on the narrow road, and departed for San Francisco, where Holmes had told him to mail this second letter. Holmes returned to his Chevrolet and drove away in the opposite direction, confident that all was well. When he got out of Thurmond's car, however, he failed to notice that a scrap of paper had fallen from the floorboard and landed in a roadside furrow. Nor did he have any inkling that his hasty movement, dropping the note and picking up the newspaper, had aroused the suspicion of the orchard workers, one of whom had taken the license numbers of both strange vehicles.

It took Thurmond more than an hour to drive to San Francisco. He mailed the new note there sometime around one o'clock and was back in San Jose by midafternoon.

Once again, Holmes had arranged things so that while Thurmond worked, he would be free to pursue the affections of Gertrude Estensen. He showed up at her door at two o'clock that Monday. We do not know whether, at this point, he was aware of the previous morning's confrontation between Evelyn and Gertrude, or of Gertrude's disavowal of romantic interest in him. In any event, he made little headway with Gertrude during his visit, for her mother was present, and he decided against breaking the news that he and Evelyn had parted. The conversation turned instead to the day's news and the Hart kidnapping.

"Who could do a thing like that?" the mother mused.

"Only the lowest kind of person," said Gertrude.

"Yes, that's right," Holmes agreed. He said he knew little about the crime because he had not read the papers much lately, only scanned the headlines.

Late Tuesday afternoon, a full day after Thurmond had mailed the second note in San Francisco, the kidnappers sauntered past Hart's store and stole furtive glances at the window. They quickly spied the numeral posted there by Rossi. It meant that Alex Hart was ready to deal. The ball was now in the kidnappers' court.

As a registered guest at the California Hotel, Holmes had parking privileges at the Plaza Garage, which backed up to the hotel across the rear alley. Fronting on Market Street just south of the police station, the garage was used by several of the neighborhood businessmen, including the Paynes, who published the *News*, and the O'Briens of the candy store. During Holmes's first twenty-four hours of using the garage, he identified the automobile of young Charlie O'Brien, who, the *Mercury Herald* had reported, was Brooke Hart's "lifetime chum." Suddenly inspiration struck: He would use O'Brien as a ransom go-between.

His vaunted criminal expertise should have sent up red flares and rockets; bringing a third party into the negotiations could only multiply the risk. But impatience coupled with greed overpowered judgment. He had doubtless read about the role of Dr. John F. "Jafsie" Condon as middleman for the Lindbergh ransom. That payoff, made at night in a Bronx graveyard, had come off without a hitch, though the Lindbergh baby was already dead. The kidnapper had collected $50,000 and was still at liberty.

If an intermediary was to be employed in dealing with Alex Hart, Charlie O'Brien was the ideal candidate. He had the trust of the Hart family, and the set-up was perfect. As a tenant of the California Hotel, Holmes could hang around O'Brien's restaurant and keep Charlie under surveillance without creating suspicion. Of course that left only Thurmond with the advantage of unrecognizability to handle face-to-face contacts in collecting the ransom. But that was Holmes's game plan anyway: Let poor, dumb, faithful Harold take the risks.

At six o'clock Tuesday evening, when Charlie's shift at the candy store was ending, Thurmond lurked in the dusk of South Market Street near the Plaza Garage driveway. Holmes had told him what to do. As Charlie's car emerged, moving slowly, Harold approached it from the right, placed his hand on the door handle, pulled his coat upward to display a gun, and started to step onto the running board. It was the same maneuver with which he had intercepted the two oil company clerks, and identical to the approach Holmes had used in entering Brooke Hart's roadster. But as Thurmond was on the verge of opening O'Brien's car door, he changed his mind, let go of the handle, turned, and fled down Market Street.

We can only speculate upon the precise purpose of Harold's aborted effort. Was O'Brien to be dragooned into the ransom negotiations? Was he to be bribed into complicity? Was he to have become a second hostage? Whatever the intent, Holmes speedily scrubbed the interception from his seat-of-the pants scenario. For the next half hour the kidnappers drove around pondering their next step. Then, reckoning that O'Brien must have reached home by now, Jack decided to contact him by telephone. He went to a pay booth and gave the operator the number of the O'Brien residence.

"Charlie?" he asked when young O'Brien answered.

"Yes, this is Charlie."

"I have a message for Mr. Hart. *Get this*: Tell him to put the cash beside him on the seat of Brooke's car, right away, and head for Los Angeles. Somewhere along the way a man in a white mask will take the money."

The kidnappers resumed their cruising, allowing an hour for O'Brien to relay their message to Alex Hart, and for Hart to go into action. Then they drove south on Monterey Road, the highway to Los Angeles, scrutinizing every southbound car they overtook. They rode for twenty miles, as far as Morgan Hill, before turning around and heading back, continuing to study the cars passing them in the other direction. It was dark on the road, but the silhouette of Brooke's roadster would have been unmistakable. They did not see it. Alex Hart was not rising to their bait.

"He needs the shit scared out of him," Holmes said, as they arrived back in San Jose about 8:30.

This business was not going as Jack Holmes had contemplated. Alex Hart's canny pluckiness and refusal to capitulate to Jack's every erratic whim gave rise within him to a consuming frustration and fury. He could not help but reflect on the way his circumstances had deteriorated. Little more than two weeks ago he had been a profitably employed householder and family man of good repute. Now he was a jobless criminal, estranged from his family, sleeping alone in a dismal room of a cheap hotel, the anonymous object of community revulsion and the greatest manhunt of recent times. The mistress he craved eluded him, and the ransom fortune with which he might win her was nowhere in sight. With every hour that passed, Holmes was unraveling more.

He had to get that money.

So now he let his guard down, abandoning whatever caution his imagined criminal craftiness had dictated. The time was past for such ruses as had sent Thurmond traveling all over Central California to ensure remote postmarks on the ransom letters.

The indirect approach to Alex Hart through Charlie O'Brien had failed, so now Holmes decided they must hit the old man head-on. At 8:45, back from their fruitless ride to Morgan Hill, they parked on South Second Street near San Salvador, and Jack dispatched Harold to a phone at Perry's Parking Lot. From there Thurmond called the Hart home, and Alex answered.

As we have seen, Thurmond found himself on the defensive before the call was a minute old. Respectfully but insistently, Alex renewed the demand for evidence that Harold was in truth one of Brooke's abductors. Harold did his dismal best to establish his credentials and offered his fanciful instructions for a "last chance" payoff on the train to Los Angeles.

"Take that nine-thirty train—or it will be too bad," was his final warning before he hung up and fled.

Alex Hart's failure to comply, because he had no confidence in the outcome, compounded the consternation of the kidnappers, who—like Emig and Vetterli—watched glumly from afar as the train left the depot.

At noon the next day, Wednesday, Holmes and Thurmond sat in a car in front of the San Jose YMCA, three blocks east of Hart's store, pondering their next move.

"That old man is no dummy," Holmes said. "Hell, I wouldn't hand over the dough, either. For all he knows we could have nothing to do with Brooke, just be a couple of bloodsucking sons of bitches."

"Instead of the nice guys we are," Thurmond giggled.

"Let's write another letter to convince him."

Thurmond again produced a writing tablet. "What do you want to say?"

"Harold, you can't spell your own name. Give me the tablet."

For most of the next hour Holmes laboriously composed the third ransom letter—the rambling, sadistic epistle that warned Alex Hart, "FAIL US—YOU LOSE A SON AS WELL AS $40,000."

Holmes gave new instructions, compounded in their absurdity, for Alex Hart's trip to Los Angeles and the ransom delivery. The father must leave with the money bag in Brooke's roadster, alone and unfollowed, at 7:30 that night and must travel no faster than ten miles per hour. The rumble seat must be open at all times. If agreeable, Alex was to replace the "-1-" numeral in his store window with a "-2-."

The kidnappers had refined their plans for taking the ransom. The masked man would be Holmes himself, abandoning his preference for operating in the shadows, far from the action and peril. He would be poised on the running board of his own black Chevy, with Thurmond at the wheel. When they spotted Brooke's car headed out of town, they would overtake it, and Holmes would grab the black satchel from Alex as they passed.

"There, that ought to bring the old man around," Holmes said as he folded the four-page letter and sealed it in an envelope. The kidnappers parted, and a few minutes later, at about one o'clock, Holmes mailed the new message at the main post office a block south of Hart's store. With any luck it would reach the store in the afternoon delivery, and Alex Hart would be reading it in an hour or two. From the post office, Holmes drove on to the Normandin-Campen Garage on West Santa Clara Street, where he had an appointment to have the radio in his car repaired. Thurmond spent the afternoon prowling the downtown district afoot.

At a quarter to six, when the partners rejoined each other downtown, Holmes greeted Thurmond with the news that the "-1-" placard in Hart's window had already been replaced. The new "-2-" sign told them that the note they had composed at noon, outside the YMCA, had hardly slowed down going through the post office. It also signified that Alex Hart was ready to deal. But there was the new problem of the unexpected words "I CANNOT DRIVE" below the numeral.

"Damn!" Holmes grunted. His criminal mind had never contemplated the chance that in this thirty-third year of the twentieth century, San Jose's leading store owner would not know how to operate an automobile. With their peril growing by the hour, the kidnappers could only regard this unforeseen snag as a catastrophe. Their need now was to grab their money and run. Their white-mask plan to take Alex Hart's $40,000 from his moving vehicle was idiotic, but it was the only plan they had, and this could destroy it. They drove around for more than an hour debating the risk of another telephone call; in the end they decided to chance it.

A few minutes after seven o'clock Holmes parked near First and San Antonio streets and went to a pay phone in the Montgomery Hotel. At exactly 7:12 he deposited his nickel and gave the operator the number of the Hart home. Then, even before the ringing started, he panicked and hung up.

At 7:19, having raced a mile to the east, Holmes tried again. This time he called from a booth in Tuggle's Drug Store at Tenth and Santa Clara. Once more he terminated the call before it began.

"Chickened out again, huh?" Thurmond chided, as Holmes returned to his automobile. "Hell, let me try."

That was precisely what Holmes intended; making the call himself was too risky. He drove back downtown and parked on South Market Street outside the Plaza Garage.

"There's a wall phone out in the back," he told Thurmond. "Everybody uses it." Harold entered the garage just before eight o'clock.

From his vantage point, with a clear view of the garage entrance, Jack should have seen Sheriff Emig enter the building seven minutes later. He should have noticed the business-suited and felt-hatted FBI agents racing down the sidewalk from the Sainte Claire Hotel. Perhaps he nodded off. Maybe he was scanning the latest news about the kidnapping. Whatever the reason, all the danger signals escaped him.

Time ticked by. When Harold had been gone for more time than a phone call ought to take, Jack circled the block a couple of times and then drove aimlessly around the city.

Now was the moment for him to fall back on whatever escape plan his scenario called for. But brash Jack Holmes had never considered the eventuality of failure; there was no plan. His cunning and caution had failed under the overload of a lost job, a lost family, frustrated sexual fantasies, and his secret career as a desperado.

He should have fled. He could have been out of the county in fifteen minutes, out of the state by morning, and out of the country within a day. But now, at his instant of peak peril, he resignedly drove back to the Plaza Garage and parked his car.

Robert Cline, the night man, remembered when Holmes returned, about nine o'clock—a jaunty figure in a light-blue suit and a Panama hat. They exchanged cheerful banter for a few minutes. Leaving the garage, Holmes walked to the nearby White Front Tavern for a late supper, returned to his lonely hotel room, and went to bed.

10

Confession and Incrimination

Within a minute after his capture in the Plaza Garage, Harold Thurmond found himself in the rear of Sheriff Emig's car, sandwiched between two of the cops who had arrested him. As they sped away, passing the spot where Holmes had been parked, Harold must have seen that his partner had fled.

A hasty consultation between the officers produced a decision to take the prisoner first to the FBI's outpost in the Sainte Claire Hotel, less than a block away. From there, Emig could phone ahead to his jail and make arrangements for incarcerating Thurmond unobserved by newsmen. For sufficient reasons, the sheriff did not want the word out, just yet, that a suspect was in custody.

At the hotel, the officers managed to hustle their captive through the lobby to the elevators without attracting attention. As Vetterli and Emig began to question him upstairs in the FBI suite, agent Conroy slipped away, out of earshot, and called Ramsey at the Hart home.

"We caught the guy, Bill, just as he hung up," he announced. "Name's Thurmond. We've got him here at the hotel."

"Hot diggity-dog! Congratulations."

"Bill, ring us right back. We'll put him on the line cold. Talk to him a little and see if you recognize his voice."

A minute later the phone rang as Ramsey complied. Conroy answered it and handed it to Thurmond: "It's for you." Perplexed, the prisoner took the receiver.

"Hello. This is Harold Thurmond. Who is this?"

From the first syllable, Ramsey was positive that this smooth, soft voice was the one he had been listening to not more than half an hour earlier, bullying Alex Hart. The tone, pronunciation, cadence, inflection, and modulation were identical.

Presently Thurmond was loaded into Emig's car again for the ride to the jail. To avoid reporters on arrival, Emig steered clear of the jail proper and whisked his prisoner instead into the massive, neoclassic courthouse which stood in front of it. Inside the building, Thurmond was led through dark corridors to Emig's office in the rear, its window facing the jail across an alley perhaps twenty-five feet wide.

"You know why we brought you in, don't you, Harold?" Emig asked him.

"No, sheriff, I've never been in trouble in my life. This is horrible for me."

"Harold, where have you got Brooke Hart hidden?"

Thurmond squirmed. Fine beads of sweat appeared on his forehead.

"My God, Mr. Emig, I'm a good boy. I go to church every Sunday."

"Then why did you snatch Brooke?"

"I didn't, I tell you. We're all religious people. My brother Roy, he's a preacher. And my sister's a church organist."

At some point Emig left the questioning to his deputies and the FBI and went to the phone in his inner office to make two calls. The first was to Chief of Police Black at home. This was a matter of professional courtesy; Emig had nabbed Thurmond in the center of the city, the heart of Black's jurisdiction—in embarrassing proximity to his office, in fact. The chief accepted Emig's offer to drive over and pick him up, to take part in the interrogation.

Emig's second call was to his mentor and protector, Louis Oneal. It is not known why the sheriff invited the old political boss to witness the grilling, but he probably acted from an instinct for self-preservation in San Jose's treacherous political arena. From the moment that Emig had discovered Brooke Hart's green roadster, he had sensed that this case could hold his future in the balance. The dynamics were clearly present: Brooke's high visibility and popularity, the prestige and wealth of the Harts, and their influence within the mercantile and civic establishments, the Jewish community, and the Jesuit community at Santa Clara University.

The sheriff felt the need for counsel. The hardness of the times, with thousands jobless and homeless, had bred frustration and desperation among San Joseans and people everywhere. Fear was abroad, borne on a nationwide wave of killing, kidnapping, and extortion. The prevailing mood, Emig knew, could revive the vigilante vengeance that had ruled California in Gold Rush times. Edgy and fearful of making a false step, he dared not depend solely on District Attorney Fred Thomas, who was a good man but reluctant to tread on the toes of the gentry. Oneal's instincts would be surer. Nowadays Oneal's clients were mainly from the upper crust, but he had once had a gamy clientele of hoodlums, and in criminal law his savvy was unsurpassed.

Another likely reason for Emig's call to Oneal opens up a rich vein of conjecture: Had the boss asked—even ordered—that he be kept abreast of this sensitive situation? Had he asked leave to grill the suspects himself? As will be seen, from the moment he entered the interrogation room, Oneal was never far from the Hart case. Some would later guess him to be the éminence grise of all that transpired thereafter.

While Emig used the telephone, the FBI men seated Thurmond at a table in the outer office and placed a pencil and paper before him.

"Harold, I want you to hand-print what I tell you," Vetterli said. He began to dictate from the first ransom note—the postcard mailed from Sacramento: "YOUR SON IS O.K. AND TREATED WELL. . . ." When Thurmond had reproduced the full message, Vetterli pocketed the paper for comparison with the original at the FBI laboratory.

The federal agents then placed another call to the Hart residence and had Thurmond talk successively with Alex Hart, Miriam, Aleese, and Hicks, all of whom had heard the kidnapper's telephone voice during the ransom calls. Unanimously they declared Thurmond's voice to be the same.

Emig's short ride across town to pick up Chief Black took but a few minutes; the chief was waiting for him at the curb. Substantive interrogation resumed upon their return, with a formidable phalanx of inquisitors confronting the suspect: Emig with his undersheriff, Earle Hamilton; Vetterli, Conroy, and Andersen of the FBI; the dour Black; and off to one side, the white-maned Oneal.*

Vetterli's haymaker lead-off question, "Why did you kill Brooke Hart?" assumed a fact not in evidence; at this point there was still reason to hope that Brooke was alive.

---

* Records of the interrogation are sketchy. In this narrative, specific questions are attributed where possible to the officers who actually asked them, otherwise to the most likely interrogators.

"Look, this is terrible," Thurmond protested, affecting high indignation. "It's outrageous to treat an innocent person, a good Christian, this way."

"Why were you talking to Mr. Hart on the phone, Harold?"

"I don't know anything about what you're asking me. I told you, I was calling my mother."

"The people at Mr. Hart's house have all identified your voice."

"They're wrong," Thurmond whitened and his perspiration became profuse, but he stuck to his denial as the questioning seesawed back and forth, over and over the same ground. Minutes grew to hours.

At length one of the agents said quietly, "Harold, we were listening in on you."

The prisoner shuddered convulsively. His face, now a gray mask of anguish, betrayed desperate cerebral exertion as he strove for a plausible explanation of the actions in which he had been caught red-handed.

"All right, all right!" he cried out finally. "I made the phone call. But I didn't have anything to do with the kidnapping."

"Tell us about it, Harold."

A remarkable mixture of fact and fiction gushed out. Thurmond said he had once been in love, but the girl had turned him down and married another. He had not seen her again until that very afternoon, when he had caught a glimpse of her on the street and gone to pieces. He had retreated into a movie house for solace, and there, in the dark, he had overheard two men talking about a numeral "-2-" in Hart's window. The notion to pose as Brooke's kidnapper and collect the ransom had come to him, and he had acted on it. Apart from that, he insisted, he had no connection with the case. The sweat was running off his brow in small rivulets now.

Toward midnight, Vetterli called a break. The interrogators left the room except for Conroy and Andersen, who lingered behind in "good cop" roles. They offered Thurmond a cigarette and addressed him in Dutch-uncle earnestness:

"You're in a lot of trouble, Harold. Don't make it worse than it is. Your best bet is to lay it on the line."

When the grilling resumed, Vetterli again posed the first question.

"There's something I don't understand, Harold. What did you mean when you told Mr. Hart you were 'one of the boys who wrote the letters'?"

"I pretended I had written the ransom notes."

"What ransom notes, Harold?"

Thurmond knew he had trapped himself. The papers had carried not a word about the messages he and Holmes had sent. Apart from the spurious story in Saturday's *Examiner*, which had been categorically denied, there had been no public report of ransom notes at all.

"Harold," said one of the agents, after a pause to let the prisoner contemplate his error, "you asked Mr. Hart if he remembered a long letter this afternoon. How did you know about that?"

"I was just bluffing."

"You knew about that letter because you wrote it, didn't you?"

"No, no! I didn't write it. I swear I didn't."

"Well, then, how did you know everything that was in it?"

"I don't know what you mean."

"How did you know that Mr. Hart had been told to drive to L.A.? How did you know he was supposed to keep the rumble seat open? You talked to him about all these things."

"I told you. I heard two men talking in the theater." It was the only pitiful ploy Thurmond could think of as the quicksand rose around him.

"What did these two men look like?"

"I don't know. It was dark in there."

"You brought up the name of Charlie O'Brien when you were talking to Mr. Hart," one of the officers commented, changing the subject.

"Charlie O'Brien is Brooke Hart's best friend. I read it in the newspapers."

"And it just came to you, out of the blue tonight, to have Mr. Hart use him for a driver?"

"Yes."

"Come on now, Harold."

"It's true."

"Then why were you talking about Charlie in your earlier call, too?"

"What earlier call?"

"The one you made Tuesday night from Perry's Parking Lot."

A spasm contorted Thurmond's face, as if a bullet had struck him.

"Deputy Hicks listened in on that one, Harold," Emig said. "He recognizes your voice, too."

Thurmond sat mute. His brain raced, still trying to fabricate a credible story short of a full confession.

"OK," he said at length, taking a deep breath, "I admit it. We wrote that letter, and I made that other phone call. But really, we're not the kidnappers. We were just trying to cash in."

"And this was before you saw your old girl friend this afternoon. She had nothing to do with it, did she, Harold?"

"Not really."

"And you didn't hear anyone talking about the case in the picture show. You made all that up, didn't you?"

"Yes, sir."

"Harold, was it you who called Charlie O'Brien too, Tuesday night?"

"I don't know what you're talking about."

"Sure you do, Harold. We'll get Charlie O'Brien on the phone later and let him listen to you also."

As the jousting went on, the officers mixed bluff, educated guess, and damning fact to keep the prisoner off balance. Thurmond, in turn self-righteous, defiant, and humble, retreated to one fallback position after another. Working backwards chronologically, the interrogators successively obtained his admissions of complicity in each step of the ransom process: the numeral instructions, the notes from San Francisco and Sacramento. At last, when he acknowledged his San Francisco trip on the night of the abduction and his phone call from the Whitcomb Hotel, Vetterli felt a surge of exultation. Until then Thurmond had adamantly denied involvement in the kidnapping, as opposed to a tawdry ransom swindle, and although the denial had no color of plausibility, it had remained a theoretical possibility. But with his admission of the Whitcomb call, the possibility evaporated. That call had been made less than five hours after the kidnapping, when Brooke's absence was known to few outside his family. No impostor could have placed it.

A little before 2:00 A.M. another recess was declared. This time it was Vetterli who stayed behind with the prisoner.

"Harold," he said, after some small talk, "you told us you're a good boy; you come from a good Christian family. I believe that."

"It's true, Mr. Vetterli." Thurmond's eyes lit up at the FBI man's unexpected recognition of the rectitude he had been professing all night.

"And your mother taught you to fear God, didn't she?"

"Yes."

"Well, Harold, how do you think God feels about making that poor Hart family suffer?"

Thurmond's mouth fell open. He began to tremble and whimper softly.

Vetterli allowed nearly a minute to pass before speaking again, gently.

"Those people have been suffering for a week, Harold, because their boy is gone. God wants you to show mercy now and put a stop to that. Tell me, can you swear before Almighty God that you did not kill Brooke Hart?"

There was a pause of a few seconds' duration. Then suddenly the prisoner broke into uncontrollable sobbing.

"Brooke Hart is dead," he blubbered.

"What did you do with him?"

"We threw him off the San Mateo Bridge."

Vetterli glanced at his watch. It was 2:30. When Thurmond had recovered his composure, the FBI man asked, "Who's in this with you, Harold?"

"The man who planned it is in Los Angeles. I only do what he tells me. It's crazy. I don't know what I'm doing since I lost my girl."

"What's the other man's name?"

Thurmond sat mute. From the time in September when he had hijacked the Union Oil receipts, he had been a slave to Jack Holmes, albeit a willing and complaisant one. Even now, having come to disaster, he still shrunk from the prospect of Holmes's displeasure. It was not repugnance at the informer's role that stayed him from identifying his partner; it was the hypnotic grip in which Holmes held him, even from afar.

"You're an idiot, Harold, to protect anybody who's in this thing with you," Vetterli said. "He wouldn't protect you. You can bet your last buck on that."

"His name is Jack Holmes."

"And he's in Los Angeles?"

"No, Mr. Vetterli, I just made that up. He lives here in San Jose."

"Whereabouts?"

"His home is on Bird Avenue, but he and his wife split up three days ago. If he hasn't skipped out on me, he's at the California Hotel."

Vetterli called the other officers back into the room, along with Oneal and Belle Gallagher, a court reporter summoned to record the confession. Around the courthouse, she was known as part of Oneal's coterie; she owed him her job in the district attorney's office. Some said she was his girlfriend.

"Harold's ready to tell us all about it now," Vetterli announced.

It was decided that reducing Thurmond's confession to writing took priority over arresting Holmes. As Vetterli explained later in a memo to J. Edgar Hoover, the officers wanted to get Thurmond's signature on the document "before he had an opportunity to secure legal counsel."

The same soft, dispassionate voice that had tormented Miriam and

Alex Hart now echoed through the empty chambers of the courthouse, as Thurmond began his eerie recitation.

Belle Gallagher's transcript, as it comes down to us, tells only the words of the suspect, not the interspersed interruptions of the interrogators. However, their prompting is obvious behind the turgid legalistic prose that is attributed to the simple Thurmond as he plods ahead with his story:

> I, Thomas Harold Thurmond, voluntarily make this statement . . . that I have known Jack Holmes approximately one year in San Jose, California; that approximately five or six weeks ago he approached me with a plan to kidnap Brooke Hart and hold him for ransom.
>
> We discussed this matter on one or two occasions, and on Thursday, November 9, 1933, shortly before six o'clock P.M., Jack Holmes and I saw Brooke Hart come towards the parking lot where he used to park his Studebaker roadster.

At this point Thurmond strayed off into the fantasizing and planning he and Holmes had done beforehand—clear evidence of premeditation. Then he resumed the chronological narrative, describing in detail Holmes's forcible interception of Brooke's car at the parking lot's edge. Harold, driving Holmes's Chevrolet, had followed the Studebaker to the remote rendezvous point on Evans Road where Brooke had been transferred to the Chevy and his car abandoned. From there his captors had driven him directly to his death scene.

> We stopped about half a mile out on the San Mateo Bridge, at which time Brooke Hart was ordered out of the car, and Jack Holmes walked back of the car . . . and hit him over the head with a brick which I had obtained at a cement company in San Jose before we started on this trip with Brooke Hart.
>
> When Jack Holmes first hit Brooke Hart over the head with this brick, he hollered "Help help," but Jack Holmes hit him over the head again with the brick and knocked Brooke Hart unconscious, and then I took some baling wire from the car which I had previously purchased on the afternoon of the 9th of November, 1933, at a hardware store in Santa Clara for 55 cents and bound the arms of Brooke Hart around his body close to his shoulders.

Jack Holmes then told me to get rid of him. Jack Holmes took the upper part of Brooke Hart's body and I took hold of him from his knees down, and together we lifted Brooke Hart onto the railing of the San Mateo Bridge and tossed him into the bay. I recall as we lifted him up onto the San Mateo Bridge he struggled slightly.

Thurmond next described the return trip to San Jose, during which he and Holmes divided $7.50 in currency and small change, which they found in Brooke's wallet. Finally he told of his trips to San Francisco and Sacramento, the ransom notes, and the follow-up phone calls.

The inquisitors sat rapt as Harold admitted his slovenly decision to toss Brooke's pocketbook from the pier, rather than into the middle of the bay from a ferry. They were appalled, not alone by the sheer brutality of the crime. Apart from that, it had to be the dumbest crime of the decade, consisting—as the *Chronicle* would later observe—of "one idiocy after another." The white-mask ransom scheme was incredibly childish; the store-window numerals were ludicrous melodrama. Committing the murder on a bridge with only two exits had been foolhardy. The kidnappers' greatest folly of all had been darting around downtown for two days, placing one call after another from at least five different booths within a half-mile radius, the last of which was 150 feet from the San Jose police station.

It was after 3:00 A.M. when Thurmond concluded his recitation. As Belle Gallagher went to a typewriter to transcribe her notes, Thurmond's captors piled him back into a car for a trip through silent, empty streets to the California Hotel. They detoured by way of the Plaza Garage, the scene of his arrest some seven hours earlier, where he now pointed out Holmes's black Chevrolet among the cars parked there. Vetterli and Black searched it without finding the .41 caliber Colt pistol that Harold said should be under the rear seat. A pair of Thurmond's gloves were found in a side pocket, however—palpable evidence linking the crime partners.

Vetterli took note of the car's newly repaired radio, an uncommon accessory in the autos of ordinary people at that time. Recalling the abductors' strange instruction to "take orders from K.P.O.," he could only guess what bizarre scheme their warped minds had concocted. But the radio in this car strengthened its link to the kidnapping. Before leaving the garage, Black summoned Cline, the attendant, and had him remove Holmes's distributor rotor to preclude his quick getaway if he were still lurking close by.

Now, about 3:30 Thursday morning, a mixed squad of federal and local officers led Thurmond across the alleyway behind the garage and into the California Hotel by the back door. From the sleepy desk clerk, it was learned that Holmes was in Room 91 on the third floor. Quietly the party made its way upstairs. The FBI trio of Vetterli, Conroy, and Andersen ranged themselves in the hall outside the room with guns drawn, as Emig and his deputies stood by. Thurmond was thrust forward and, following orders, knocked on the door.

"Jack?"

"Who is it?" The voice from within was thick from slumber.

"It's me—Harold."

"Just a minute."

Seconds later the door opened to reveal the rangy, six-foot frame of John Maurice Holmes in nightclothes.

"Police officers! You're under arrest," Emig shouted, as the six officers swarmed into the room to pin him.

"What the hell!" Holmes cried out. "What am I under arrest for?"

"Murder."

"This is all bullshit. I'm an honest family man, and I have to be out first thing in the morning looking for a job. You bastards come storming in here when I need my sleep." Holmes turned and addressed the sheriff directly: "Dammit, Bill Emig, tell these other sons of bitches who I am!"

The other officers glanced at Emig inquiringly.

"Yeah, I know him," the sheriff told his puzzled colleagues, quietly and without elaboration. Whatever elation Emig was feeling at the capture of his quarry must have been mixed with distress as he stared at Jack Holmes, his Masonic brother in Golden Rule Lodge 479 for the past seven years.

More than forty-eight hours earlier Emig had learned that Holmes was the registered owner of one of the cars in the orchard on White Oaks Road. For whatever reason—possibly because he could not believe a Mason capable of so nefarious a crime—he had not followed up. Did he realize now that with more diligence, he might have made this arrest two days sooner?

Thurmond now spoke to his partner. "Well, Jack, I've told them everything."

Holmes fixed him with a contemptuous stare. "The hell you did. What did you do that for?"

The officers made Holmes dress, and within minutes they were back at the courthouse with both suspects. Under questioning there, Holmes remained cool, affecting a defiant nonchalance.

"If you think you've got anything on me, shoot the works."

"Your partner has implicated you, Jack," one of the FBI men told him. "It will be better for you to tell us the truth."

"I don't understand any of this," Holmes responded. "It has nothing to do with me."

At two o'clock Wednesday afternoon Marshall Hall had arrived at San Jose's old city hall in the plaza. Having been sworn in as an attorney five hours earlier, he was set for his debut at an Industrial Accident Commission hearing in the courtroom above the police station. The proceeding dragged on into the evening and was still in progress when, unknown to the participants, Thurmond was arrested in the garage just across the street. By the time the hearing adjourned at nine o'clock, new lawyer Hall was reeling with fatigue and a headache. He drove home and went to bed early. Sometime before 4:00 A.M. he became aware of the telephone's jangling and answered sleepily. A voice he thought he recognized said, "Mr. Hall?"

"Yes."

"I want you to listen carefully and do exactly as I say. Do not ask any questions."

"Is this Mr. Oneal?" Hall inquired, certain that he was speaking with the head of his law firm.

"I told you, no questions. Come immediately to the First Street entrance of the courthouse. There will be someone waiting for you. Do not tell anyone your destination."

The caller hung up.

Half a century later Hall—by then a retired judge of the superior court—recalled his response to the peculiar summons, which could have been a trap.

"Being one who liked a little excitement," he said, "I didn't want to refuse. But I had in mind that young Brooke Hart had been kidnapped, and I thought, 'Well, I'll be prepared.' So I reached into a drawer and got my grandfather's .38 caliber Colt. But being only half awake, I could find only three shells for it."

Hall drove to the courthouse, which was dark except for a light in the sheriff's office window and another upstairs. He parked and reached for his half-loaded gun, on the dashboard. Then, suddenly unable to remember whether a Colt cylinder revolved to the right or left, he changed his mind about taking the weapon and left it on the seat. As he climbed the courthouse steps, he discerned Undersheriff Earle Hamilton inside the door, in the dark of the foyer. Greatly excited, Hamilton told him two Hart kidnapping suspects, named Thurmond and Holmes, had been caught.

"Marshall," the undersheriff said, "there's a special job we need you to do later, but in the meantime, go into the sheriff's office and guard the man you'll find there. We haven't got anybody else to watch him right now. Everybody's upstairs listening to the read-back of Thurmond's confession."

"So I went in there," Hall related in 1983, "and this fellow was sitting reading a newspaper, and he looked awfully rough and tough to me. And I sat there, with my hand in the empty pocket of my overcoat for what seemed like an hour before anybody came to relieve me of that responsibility—guarding Jack Holmes."

Actually, Hall's tour of guard duty may have lasted no more than a few minutes, but whatever the interval, neither he nor Holmes uttered a word during their time together.

"All he'd have had to do was break one of the windows and jump out, and he'd have been gone," Hall later acknowledged. "But he didn't know, I suppose, what was on the other end of my hand, or who I was. I guess he figured I was armed—and I wasn't. Had he moved, I think now that I probably would have let him move."

Emig could have called one of his own men to guard the prisoner, but as Hall surmised, "He didn't have all the confidence in the world in the judgement or size of the mouth of any of his deputies." It was Oneal, the sheriff's mentor, who had suggested using Hall. The summons was as high a compliment as the new lawyer could have received from his boss during his first twenty-four hours on the job.

Daybreak was not far off when Thomas Harold Thurmond at last affixed his name to his confession in what could have been a fifth grader's cramped penmanship. Vetterli, Emig, Black, Andersen, Conroy, and Hamilton signed as witnesses, and Miss Gallagher notarized the document. The grilling team then returned downstairs to retrieve Holmes from the reluctant custody of Marshall Hall.

Holmes was made to duplicate the task his partner had performed earlier, hand-lettering the text of the first ransom note for comparison purposes. Then Thurmond's confession was read to him, drawing a flippant retort: "If you've got that, there's no use talking." And then, after a pause, "I didn't know Harold would be a snitch."

As Earle Hamilton had told Marshall Hall at the courthouse door, he had not been summoned primarily to guard Jack Holmes, but for a rigorous job more in line with his talents. It was his seamanship Emig needed now. He wanted to reinstate without delay the reconnaissance of the San Mateo Bridge's eastern footings. On Sunday the driftwood gatherers' tale of distress cries from beneath the bridge had not impressed the sheriff. Now, hindsight illuminated his misjudgment.

"It was still thought that other suspects might be involved, besides Holmes and Thurmond," Hall later explained, "and so they tried to keep this all very secret. That was the reason for old man Oneal's mysterious call to me. They didn't want it known that anyone had been caught until they could prove the corpus delicti. What they wanted me to do—without telling anybody—was to go out there on the bay and try to find Brooke's body or anything else of an incriminating nature to support the story Thurmond had told."

Before sunup, Hall was on the phone rounding up a crew for his *Mermaid*.

"I got two close friends of mine," he recalled. "One was Sam Weston, a pear grower. I also got Clarence Rich, who was also a farmer. They were my regular crew. I made a big mystery out of it and told them, 'Hurry as fast as you can and get out to Alviso.' "

From the courthouse to the Alviso marina was a straight shot out North First Street for Hall. Keyed up, he floored his gas pedal and was soon flagged down by two officers in a police car. After some discussion, he persuaded them he was on an assignment for the sheriff and was allowed to proceed, but the secrecy of his mission had been compromised. By the time he reached his boat, the mystified Weston and Rich had it fueled up and ready to get under way. It was not yet light when the *Mermaid* glided down the slough and out onto the open water.

A fifteen-mile cruise took the vessel to the bridge, where it arrived just at sunrise. To Hall's amazement, the bridge deck was already teeming with reporters and cameramen who, having no one else to claim their attention, began to interview and photograph *him*. Word of the arrests had been leaked too late for the morning papers, but now in the light of day the press was all over the story. With the sheriff's hopes for covert action dashed, Hall little envisioned the grief ahead. Nor could he guess that nearly all of his first week as a lawyer would be spent in a grueling waterborne search for the body of his across-the-street neighbor, Brooke Leopold Hart.

III

OUTRAGE

11

The Brittle City

Never before had Bill Emig seen the temper of the town so brittle.

Since the day after Brooke Hart's disappearance, a surly, swollen tide of unrest had risen. It saturated the establishment circles in which the Hart family moved, the bully-boy rednecks of the street, the youthful thrill-seekers, and the desperate ranks of the idle jobless. The First Street businessmen were as much a part of it as Brooke's stalwart friends at Santa Clara University.

For the first time in fifty years, lynch talk was in the air. Before the capture of Thurmond and Holmes, the muttering had been desultory and unfocused, but Emig had heard enough of it to make him apprehensive now about his prisoners' safety.

California had nurtured a hardy strain of drumhead justice from Gold Rush times. San Francisco's vigilantes of 1851, who had hanged at least four scoundrels after a breakdown of the corrupt and impotent law enforcement system, were treated as heroes in the history books that schoolchildren studied. Another San Francisco vigilance committee in 1856 had grown to 3,000 armed members, who proudly displayed steel-engraved membership certificates.

Closer to San Jose, a fight in a Los Gatos saloon had triggered a less elegant outburst of vigilantism in 1883—exactly half a century before the Hart case. An ex-bandit named Encarnacion Garcia lost his gold to a companion, Rafael Maraval, in a card game, and the latter soon lay dead in the mud, stuck by Garcia's Spanish dagger. Garcia fled to the hills but was quickly captured. As evening approached a band of enraged citizens marched on the Los Gatos jail, took possession of the slayer, and hanged him from a new wooden bridge spanning Los Gatos Creek. A coroner's jury could find "no evidence to implicate anyone."

With the taming of the West, vigilantism had mainly passed from the California scene. Still, as recently as 1920 three members of San Francisco's Howard Street Gang, who had killed three peace officers, had been hanged from a tree in Santa Rosa.

Emig's concern for the security of his prisoners on this Thursday morning, therefore, was not farfetched. In the interest of keeping them alive to stand trial, not to mention surviving politically himself, he resolved to get them out of San Jose at once—certainly before the courthouse opened for the day. The San Francisco City Prison seemed their safest haven.

Although the morning papers carried no word of the arrests, the news that the sheriff had two men in custody was already circulating by word of mouth. Pulling aside the blind on his office window, Emig saw fifty to seventy-five persons milling in the alley outside. He could not risk taking the suspects from the courthouse into that assemblage. A ruse to divert the crowd began to take shape in his mind.

At about eight o'clock he placed a call to George Truman "Skimp" Letcher, who owned a garage across the street from the courthouse in the next block.

"Do me a favor, Skimp," he asked. "Come over here right away with a mechanic. Drive your car and park in front of the courthouse."

It may not have been wholly coincidental that Letcher was a crony of Louis Oneal. A few years earlier San Jose had been shocked and titillated when Letcher's father, Clarence, a pioneer auto dealer, had been done in by his second wife, Helen, after she caught him dallying with a paramour. She had pumped four bullets into him, then put her pistol to her own head and pulled the trigger. As a pillar of the community, Clarence had a big Elks funeral, which Helen shared. Leading a double file of his lodge brethren past their side-by-side, flower-banked coffins were Oneal and Sunny Jim Rolph, the latter then mayor of San Francisco.

Now, minutes after Emig's summons, Skimp Letcher and his mechanic arrived at the courthouse in coveralls, arousing no suspicion. In the sheriff's office they exchanged clothes with the kidnappers, and then the mechanic, wearing Thurmond's garb, was hustled roughly out of the courthouse back door and across the alley toward the jail. As the crowd surged in on him and photographers fired their flashguns, Emig and Vetterli took the genuine Thurmond, attired in coveralls, out the front door to Letcher's waiting car.

By the time the decoy in the rear reached the jail door, the onlookers realized they had been gulled. Then someone spotted the real Thurmond entering the car out front, and the crowd wheeled off in that direction. Within seconds the back alleyway was clear, enabling Undersheriff Hamilton to drive Emig's automobile, unimpeded, up to the courthouse back door. Agents Conroy and Andersen emerged therefrom with Holmes, who was shoved into the car's rear seat. Hamilton opened the siren, and as it dawned on the onlookers that they had been twice deceived, both vehicles roared off toward San Francisco with their separate prisoners.

Evelyn Holmes, with her marriage crumbling and two children to support, had gone back to school to refresh long-dormant office skills. On this Thursday morning she was in class at Heald's Business College, which occupied the second floor of a new commercial building near Hart's store. Fifty-six years later she would vividly remember being summoned from class to take a phone call from her mother.

"Something has happened, Evelyn. Come home right away." Her mother's voice was tense but gave no clue to what the problem was.

From the outside, nothing seemed amiss as Evelyn approached her home on Bird Avenue a short time thereafter. She had arrived ahead of a platoon of newsmen who would soon descend on the old Victorian. Inside, her mother broke the news: "Jack has been arrested."

The next hours and days would remain forever in Evelyn's mind as a nightmarish montage of scenes little understood. David Holmes, six years old at the time, would remember the surprise of his mother's midday appearance at his school to pull him out of class. He would retain a vivid image of photographers surrounding the Bird Avenue house, trying to shoot pictures through the windows. Their flashguns lit up the interior like lightning flashes until his mother pulled down the blinds.

Curiously, neither the police nor the sheriff's people nor the FBI put in any appearance at all. A man from the district attorney's office showed up for what turned out to be nothing more than informal chat; Evelyn told him it was "utterly impossible" that Jack could have had anything to do with the Hart case. During the crucial hours of Brooke's disappearance and ostensible murder, she insisted, he had been with her at home.

Finally Evelyn's sister, Beatrice Stice, arrived and drove her and the children to a refuge in the Stice home at Stockton, some eighty miles away. Joyce Holmes, not yet five years old, would remember being bundled under a blanket on the car floor during the trip.

Two thirds of the way up the San Francisco Peninsula, the automobiles bearing Holmes and Thurmond detoured east onto the San Mateo Bridge. By daylight it was a graceless low-level span nearly nine miles long, including its approaches and its six-mile water crossing. Except in its drawbridge section, its narrow deck was probably less than twenty feet above the cold, raw surface of the bay.

In Skimp Letcher's car, Thurmond agreed to cooperate by showing his captors where Brooke Hart's body had been thrown off the bridge. About half a mile from the Alameda shore, near where the *Mermaid* was getting set to start dragging, he signaled a halt. Let out of the car and released from his manacles, Harold walked to the railing and gazed into the water below, perhaps ten feet deep. Close to here, he thought, was where they had tossed Brooke over the side, but he could not really tell. The bridge's two-lane roadway, between the homely concrete guardrails, was straight for its whole distance, except for one dogleg near the San Mateo shore, and devoid of features to distinguish one spot from another.

In the sheriff's car, agents Conroy and Andersen bantered lightly with Jack Holmes during the ride to San Francisco. They stopped and bought him breakfast, which he wolfed down, and gave him a pack of cigarettes. He affected elaborate unconcern for his situation and whistled during most of the trip. Near the end, the agents sobered the mood a bit.

"You know, Jack, you ought to thank us for this ride."

"Why should I thank you for anything?"

"Hell, it's not just a murder rap you're facing. You saw that crowd back at the courthouse. Those people want to string you up right now."

For the first time Holmes seemed ill at ease. By the time they reached San Francisco, Conroy and Andersen knew he would break down and talk sooner or later.

All the way up the San Francisco Peninsula, Emig had kept an eye on his rear-view mirror. After his trickery in dodging the crowd at San Jose, he knew the newsmen would be in hot pursuit, and possibly would-be lynchers too. For a high-risk transfer like this, he should have put together a heavily armed convoy. Undertaking it with just side arms and two cars, one of them a civilian vehicle, had been a bold move dictated by urgency but foolhardy nonetheless.

On arrival in San Francisco, having determined with relief that no one was following, Emig headed not for police headquarters, which would be crawling with reporters, but for a rendezvous point outside the Palace Hotel. From there, under a San Francisco police escort, the prisoners were taken to the Potrero station, off the beaten track on the south edge of the city, and lodged in separate cells, remote from each other with no communication possible. Conroy and Andersen had sized Holmes up correctly; his bravado melted as soon as his cell key was turned, leaving him alone behind the bars.

A short time later Emig paid his Masonic friend a visit. "Sorry to see you like this, Jack."

"What'll I do, Bill?"

"Well, Jack, as a Mason and a lodge brother, I can tell you that it will be best if you sign a confession."

Holmes began his statement at one o'clock, with Emig and Hamilton facing him across the table, and Belle Gallagher taking notes. After a pro forma declaration that he was speaking "freely and voluntarily," he lapsed into a rambling, disjointed narrative. Just as Thurmond had characterized Holmes as the chief perpetrator of their crime, Holmes now depicted Thurmond as the instigator:

He [Thurmond] and I went to a show one afternoon a couple of days before the kidnapping, in fact it was the day before—no, I guess it was two days before—and after we came out of there, he grabbed me by the arm, grabbed me just like that [indicating] and says, "There goes Brooke Hart. If we could pick him up, we could get a piece of change out if him." I said, "Yes, where would you keep him?" and he said, "We would have to figure that out."

Frankly, I said that the idea did not appeal to me one iota, and I thought he was just talking through his hat. But he said that it could be done mighty easy. I said, "I guess it could," and he said, "What do you say we watch this guy?"

Holmes recounted in detail how he and Thurmond parked outside Hart's store and finally, after sweltering in the car for three hours (during which Jack left for beer at least once), observed Alex and Brooke leave work together at six o'clock. Harold wondered aloud where they might hide Brooke if they snatched him, and Holmes suggested putting him "on a boat or something." The recitation continued:

> We talked it over at some length, and the idea suddenly seemed to be a smart one, and as we were driving home that night Harold said, "You know the smart thing is to dump that guy overboard some place." . . . We really discussed it more as a joke then.

On Thursday evening the kidnappers renewed their surveillance of the department store about five o'clock. They agreed that Jack would carry out any physical interception they might undertake, because Harold had seen Brooke a few times and might be recognized.

> We really didn't expect to find him that night alone. We figured he would be with his father, and [we] just looked up, and lo and behold he walked down the line himself.
>
> I don't see very good at close range, I am farsighted; and Harold recognized him first and saw that he was alone and decided to get him. So I walked over to the edge of the sidewalk by his car . . . and waited for him until he came out [of the parking lot], and I climbed on his running board and had my hand in my pocket like that [indicating], and stuck my fingers against his ribs.
>
> By Sheriff Emig: You didn't have a gun, Jack?
>
> A. No. Let me correct myself, yes, I did have a gun against him and told him to "get going," which he agreed to do.

Holmes detailed the circuitous, zigzag route he had ordered Brooke to follow through the city streets, to reach the highway to Milpitas. They passed several other automobiles before reaching the rendezvous point on Evans Road. Thurmond, following in Holmes's car, arrived a minute later.

> I told Hart to get out and get in the other car, which he did. I then gave the gun to Harold and said, "Hold this on him while I go back and wipe off the doors and steering wheel."
>
> Q. That was to eliminate any fingerprints being on there?
>
> A. Yes, I wanted to eliminate any fingerprints. On the way out Brooke Hart asked for a cigarette, which I gave him out of his pocket. I didn't get the pack back in his pocket, but it

dropped on the seat. I had intended to continue on that [Evans] road and go to Oakland Highway, but in a short time I remembered the cigarettes on the seat, and I turned the car around and went back and picked up the cigarettes and gave them to Hart. We then proceeded back the way we come [sic] originally to Milpitas and then turned to the right and followed the highway to the San Mateo Bridge. . . .

First the idea was to take him [Brooke] into Oakland and get an apartment or a room in a rooming house. . . . Naturally he was quite excited, and we told him as long as he behaved himself he wouldn't be hurt.

Just a minute, I am getting ahead of my story—it is about that wire and a couple of concrete blocks.

Q. Harold got those?

A. Yes, stole the blocks, the two concrete blocks from Mc-Elroy-Cheim in San Jose.* Well, then we proceeded on from that point. . . . And on the way up Harold said, "If we dump this guy, it would be slick and write a note and get a quick turnover before they get too worried."

Brooke was blindfolded with a pillow slip before the kidnappers approached the bridge; as they drove onto it he had no idea of his whereabouts. Under Emig's prodding, Holmes told coldly how the youth was duped into a false sense of security.

When we got to the middle of the San Mateo Bridge and by the draw, there was no cars around. . . . We led him to believe he was going to be transferred from one machine to another and while we were doing that, getting ready to do that, Hart got fussing around, and a car came by and he started to shout, and I hauled off and hit him with my fist. I guess he hit his head on the concrete as he fell, as he laid quite still a few minutes. Then Harold reached in the car and got the wire and started wrapping his feet and hands, and at that time he passed me the gun. I don't think after that Hart ever snapped out of it. I think he hit the curb; I was watching him and he fell. I hit him with my fist. I hit him pretty hard; I wanted him to know that we meant business. After that we were

* Holmes was in error. As told earlier, Thurmond had purchased three blocks, not stolen two, from the California Concrete Products Company.

holding the gun on him so if he decided to get up again I intended to threaten him with it. Harold got the two concrete blocks and tied them around his feet and we tossed him overboard.

After that I don't know what it was, but maybe the water revived him and he made some sound and fanned around, and Harold said, "Give me that gun," and he climbed down on the stringers and fired the cartridges that were in the pistol where he imagined Hart would be. Afterwards he said he thought he hit him, but he wasn't sure.

While he was doing that, I drove up the bridge a ways and turned around and came back. I looked for Harold on the same side of the bridge he had gone down on but I finally saw him coming back and crawling over the railing on the other side of the bridge and looking down in the water. He climbed down on the stringers . . . and listened for some disturbance, but he was satisfied there wasn't none because when he got in the car I asked him what had happened and Harold said, "I am not sure. . . . I don't think he will ever come up again."

While Holmes's account was at odds with Thurmond's in certain matters of detail, it tallied closely with what the officers already knew. Holmes went on to relate how the kidnappers returned to San Jose and set the $40,000 ransom figure for their already-dead victim before parting at Fourth and Santa Clara streets.

"What finally became of the gun, Jack?" Emig asked.

"Harold had the gun."

As the session ended, after the best part of an hour, Holmes's iron control snapped.

"He put his head in his hand and cried like a baby," the sheriff reported later.

Holmes quickly regained his swagger. When the typewritten copy of his confession was given to him for signing, he read it carefully, borrowed Emig's fountain pen to correct several errors, and affixed his signature.

A swarm of cameramen awaited him as he emerged from the interrogation room. Chain-smoking cigarettes, he hammed up the scene for them, flashing a grin and turning first left, then right, then to face his captors at their command, the shutters clicking all the while.

* * *

134

While Holmes was confessing, there was a diversion for his obsequious partner. San Francisco Police Inspector Sydney Du Bose took Thurmond to lunch at an Italian restaurant near the Potrero station. While devouring a steak, Harold once more blamed his troubles on the woman who had jilted him.

"She kept complaining that I was too poor," he said. "She finally left me. Two years ago she married another guy, and I got an invitation to her wedding. That just broke me up. I've been nuts ever since."

The warm meal and the restaurant surroundings lifted Thurmond's gloom and loosened his tongue in a manic monologue of new confession. From the hungry suspect, the police got their first glimpse of Holmes's sexual frustrations and his obsession with Gertrude Estensen.

"She's got something on him," Thurmond told Du Bose. "Every so often she taps him for a bunch of jack and he has to come through."

As the inspector picked up the tab, Harold portrayed himself as a misunderstood man.

"You know," he whined, "everybody gives me a dirty look as though I was a tough guy. But I ain't. I'm just screwy."

From the Potrero station, the prisoners were taken late in the day to the city prison on the eighth floor of the San Francisco Hall of Justice. They presented contrasting images as they submitted to fingerprinting. Attired in his blue suit, gray felt hat, tan shirt, and shiny black shoes, Holmes kept up a stream of wisecracks. Thurmond, wearing his old blue sweater with corduroy trousers tucked into boots, was silent and swiftly obedient to instructions. He languidly chewed gum.

After the booking, the prisoners were ordered to sit on the same bench to discard their shoes. Thurmond's squinty gaze momentarily met Holmes's hard blue eyes, and glares of contempt passed between them. Then they were led away to widely separated cells.

Again alone behind bars, Holmes whistled, laughed, and sang at the top of his voice, finally falling into deep, untroubled slumber.

In the Hart home fifty miles to the south, toward evening, Ramsey and Hicks called Aleese and Miriam Hart to their station upstairs.

"Sit down," Ramsey said. "We have something to tell you."

In the pause before he continued, Aleese allowed herself a flicker of hope that the news would be good—that her brother had been found and would be coming home. But then the officers, as gently as they could, told the sisters that the kidnappers had confessed to killing him. Both girls collapsed. When they regained their composure, Ramsey said, "We don't know what to do about your folks. It would probably be best if you were the ones to tell them." The scene that followed, as the sisters carried the news to their parents, was remembered long afterward by Alex, Jr., their teenage brother, as "just tremendous upheaval, traumatic experiences all over the house." From Nettie's sickroom a terrible scream was heard as she learned her son was dead.

As the arrests and confessions became known, angry grief pervaded San Jose and the state. And terror. Rumors purportedly based on the kidnappers' off-the-record disclosures, about other victims supposedly on their hit list, circulated wildly. Charlie O'Brien was supposed to have been marked for abduction, along with James Rolph, III, the governor's son; Bob Payne, the son of the *Evening News* publisher; Dan and Lou Oneal, small grandchildren of the political boss; and a member of the Lion family, which owned a big San Jose furniture store. The fact that Holmes and Thurmond were in custody did not allay the fears of the families believed targeted, for there was no certainty that other accomplices were not still at large.

All day long messages of condolence and great baskets of flowers poured into the white mansion on the The Alameda. One telegram, from Washington, D.C., was signed Franklin D. Roosevelt.

Brooke's aunts, uncles, and cousins, arriving from throughout the area, talked to the newsmen hovering outside the house, passing on little insights into the family's agony. They said Nettie was refusing to accept the kidnappers' word that her boy was gone. One of Brooke's uncles, Harry Morris, spoke to reporters sadly of Jack Holmes's father Maurice, the tailor.

"For years he has made my clothes," Morris said.

Downtown, shaken almost to the point of incoherence, fifty-six-year-old Maurice Holmes went to the Santa Clara County Jail five times that day, seeking to see his son and disbelieving the jailers who told him Jack was not there. By the time of his last visit, in midafternoon, he and an unidentified friend had to push their way through a growing throng of 500 persons to reach the jail door.

"What is this crowd gathering for?" the father asked dazedly. "What do they intend to do?"

No one answered. Finally the old man turned away, shoulders sagging. To reporters who tried to follow and question him, he cried, "I will make no statement. No, not a word. Get away from me. Leave me alone." He retreated down the street and disappeared into a store.

Later an *Examiner* reporter called at the Holmeses' neat frame bungalow on Eleventh Street. Hulda Holmes, Jack's mother, sat in the comfortable living room with friends who sought to keep intruders at bay. Like Nettie Hart, she denied the reality of the nightmare engulfing her. She would not read the newspaper accounts of her son's arrest and confession.

"Why should I?" she demanded. "These things are only ugly rumors. Jack will tell me they aren't true." She told the *Examiner*'s man she could disprove her son's guilt, and she planted the seed of an alibi.

"I was over at my son's house that night," she declared, "and his wife helped fit a dress for me. He was just as sweet as he always was. He wasn't under any strain. I'm his mother, and I would know if there was anything wrong with him, which there wasn't."

Once Hulda began talking, her words became a compulsive nonstop monologue.

"Boys that are going to get into trouble are in trouble from the time they are little," she said. "Our boy never got into difficulties of any sort in his whole life. He had no bad companions. We guarded him carefully . . . I'm terribly sorry for the Harts, but I feel our position is even worse than theirs. No one has said their son was guilty of a hideous crime. But I don't and won't believe it about Jack."

Other newswriters, seeking Jack's wife, found the yellow Victorian on Bird Avenue locked and empty. They caught up with Evelyn Thursday night at the Stice home in Stockton and learned that she had seen an attorney there, Ira B. Langdon, about defending her newly-estranged husband. Evelyn rejected the reporters' demands for interviews.

"I know Jack never could have done this thing," she screamed at them. "He couldn't! Do they think that just because he was out of work he would become a kidnapper? Do they think he would murder? No, I can't believe it; I will not."

Len Kullmann of the *News* visited Thurmond's home among the orchards on Leigh Avenue in Campbell and found Harold's parents huddled together in a darkened living room. Lillie Thurmond, clad in a housedress with a sweater drawn over her shoulders, spoke for the family as usual, affirming their faith in Harold's innocence. Her words echoed his original protestations before his confession.

"We can't think that he did it," she said. "We raised him as a Christian boy. He always went to church. We're Christian people. It's unbelievable that my boy could do this. . . . Everybody I've talked to tells me Jack Holmes wound my son around his little finger."

As Kullmann turned to leave, Lillie followed him to the porch.

"You won't print anything against him, will you?" she pleaded, before fleeing back into the house, sobbing.

So far, by design or chance, Louis Oneal had kept his finger on all that had happened since the arrest of Thurmond and Holmes. Not only had he sat in on the grilling; he had summoned Marshall Hall to stand guard; his friend Belle Gallagher had transcribed the confessions; and his crony Skimp Letcher had provided the deception to hustle the suspects out of town.

When his role in eliciting Thurmond's confession leaked out, Oneal at first disavowed it, declaring with a straight face, "My interest in the case is no different than that of any other citizen concerned in the welfare of his home county." His actions soon stripped the disavowal of credibility, however.

Ordinarily the old boss preferred to operate behind the scenes, letting publicity's glare fall upon others. Nonetheless, he had a fondness for the bold gesture. Now his flair for the flamboyant surfaced, as he summoned reporters and released Thurmond's confession transcript from his own law office, rather than letting it come from the sheriff as might be expected. Holmes's confession followed.

In the cluttered office of the *News*, a storefront building just around the corner from the Plaza Garage, publisher G. Logan Payne read the confessions with mounting anger. A reserved, impressive man who dressed well and wore his iron-gray hair slicked back, Payne had been the publisher of a Hearst daily in Washington, D.C., before purchasing the San Jose paper in 1927. He retained his Hearstian capacity for outrage.

At midafternoon he went to his desk and began to compose an editorial. By the time he finished, all regular editions of the *News* were off the press, but he ordered that it run anyway. It ran on the front page of the Fourth Extra, the day's last edition, directly below a portrait of Brooke Hart. Payne's aroused prose had the clarity of a bugle sounding the charge:

HUMAN DEVILS

If mob violence could ever be justified it would be in a case like this and we believe the general public will agree with us. There never was a more fiendish crime committed anywhere in the United States, and we are of the belief that unless these two prisoners are kept safely away from San Jose there is likely to be a hanging without waiting for the courts of justice. To read the confession [of] both of these criminals . . . makes one feel like he wanted to go out and be a part of that mob. If you could have been with the writer who called at the Hart home to offer our sympathy and assistance in this time of their great trial—it would have made you feel like going out and committing a lynching yourself.

A few hours after Payne's editorial appeared, the San Jose City Council adjourned a brief business meeting in Brooke Hart's memory, resolving:

It is the hope that justice will be sure and swift and that the subterfuges and technicalities of law that frequently thwart or delay justice will not be taken in this instance.

12

"As Swift as Law Allows"

Under his own byline in Friday morning's *Chronicle*, Sheriff Emig looked ahead to the trial of Jack Holmes and Harold Thurmond:

> We intend to clear up every detail as far as possible so there will be no flaw in the prosecution of these men. I want to see justice done, and justice in this case should be simple. The men have confessed to a cold-blooded, wanton murder and the law has only one answer to that.

The sheriff (or more likely some ghostwriter) was not coming clean. He well knew that "justice in this case" would not be simple at all—certainly not so cut and dried as his article suggested. The kidnappers' confessions left many questions unanswered and raised some new ones.

It did not greatly concern Emig that Holmes's time sequence was out of step with Thurmond's; the discrepancies were understandable, probably reconcilable, and anyway, not critical to prosecution. Other uncertainties, however, were substantive and more troubling:

Where was the gun each suspect said was in the other's possession? What precisely had caused Brooke's death: the blow to his head, the gunfire, or drowning? Which kidnapper had taken the lethal action? Above all, were the suspects shielding other accomplices still uncaught? Delphine Silveria's story of watching five men—not just two—transfer a captive from one car to another on Piedmont Road carried too much conviction to be dismissed out of hand. Moreover, Emig had received garbled reports of a third man, elderly with white hair, joining Holmes and Thurmond at the orchard rendezvous on White Oaks Road.

Not least among the enigmas arose from the kidnappers' contradictory accounts of precisely where the murder had taken place. Thurmond placed the site about half a mile from the east end of the San Mateo Bridge; Holmes said it was "by the draw" in the middle of the span. Not only did the discrepancy complicate the search for Brooke's body; it also raised a thorny jurisdictional problem. A northwest-southeast map line marked the watery boundary between Alameda and San Mateo counties in San Francisco Bay, intersecting the San Mateo Bridge about two and a half miles west of the Alameda shore. If Holmes was correct about the killing site, it was in San Mateo County, and a murder prosecution would appropriately take place there. If Thurmond was right, the homicide jurisdiction would rest with Alameda County. In the latter, the district attorney's office was held by an ambitious forty-two-year-old prosecutor with the bespectacled look of a mathematics professor: Earl Warren, destined to become governor of California and chief justice of the United States. He was already telling reporters he was prepared to file murder charges.

In San Jose, however, District Attorney Fred Thomas was determined that Holmes and Thurmond be tried in Santa Clara County. Regardless of where the killing had occurred, Brooke Hart had been kidnapped in San Jose, and the Harts lived there. San Joseans lusted for hometown vengeance.

At fifty-nine, Thomas was a towering figure in the courthouse, an Oneal man of long standing, having begun his law studies in the Oneal office about the turn of the century. His horn-rimmed glasses and gray hair gave him a judicial look that he nurtured with care; his dearest wish was to become a judge. By inclination as well as registration he was a Republican, which was fortunate, because judges were appointed by governors, and no Democrat had occupied California's gubernatorial chair in this century. A gregarious man, Thomas was a Scottish Rite Mason and past exalted ruler of the San Jose Elks lodge, where the card games were his only recreation. He had been district attorney since 1926 and next year would be on the ballot for his third term. Convicting the kidnappers would make him unbeatable.

Thomas had a personal reason, as well as professional and political ones, for wanting to handle the Hart case; the crime against Brooke struck a tender nerve with him. As a prosecutor he had made his share of enemies, and some years earlier there had been the same kind of threats against his own little girl, Jeanne, now twelve. Even now she was never allowed away from the house alone—not even for school.

In prosecuting Holmes and Thurmond, Thomas would have the advantage of a new state law, which had been on the books for only three weeks. After Congress had enacted its 1932 Lindbergh Act, making interstate kidnap for ransom a federal felony, the California legislature had followed suit in 1933 with a "Little Lindbergh Act," which went to the matter of penalty. Under the old law, the penalty for ransom kidnapping had been ten years to life, with parole possible after seven years; the new law gave juries only two choices if bodily harm was involved: death or life imprisonment without possibility of parole. Holmes and Thurmond had committed their crime only fifteen days after the October 25 effective date of this harsh new statute. A second advantage of the Little Lindbergh Act for Thomas was that a kidnapping conviction did not require the corpus delicti needed for a murder conviction.

In San Francisco another prosecutor was also preparing charges against the suspects. H. H. McPike, the United States attorney for Northern California, announced he would seek four-count federal indictments, charging use of the mails to extort. The maximum penalties would be twenty years and a $5,000 fine for each count. McPike emphasized that he was not in competition with the local prosecutors; his indictments would be held in reserve, for use only if the state's case hit a snag. But that was not expected. "The state has an ironclad case," said the FBI's Vetterli.

In San Jose the tension grew. Hundreds of the curious swelled the throng around the jail, unaware or disbelieving that Holmes and Thurmond were not inside.

"They ought to get a fast trial in this crowd," one man shouted.

Other jail inmates, edgy about the hostility outside, were relieved when Emig announced that because of the inflamed atmosphere, no effort would be made to return the kidnappers to San Jose.

Ira Langdon, the attorney Evelyn Holmes had retained in Stockton, was not ready to concede that the state's case was a sure thing. Early Friday he drove Evelyn back to San Jose, where they obtained statements from the Estensens confirming Holmes's theater attendance on the night of the kidnapping. This testimony could rip a large, jagged hole in the "ironclad" case of which Vetterli boasted. Later on Friday Langdon took Evelyn and the dazed Maurice Holmes to San Francisco to visit Jack.

"Son, what does this mean?" the old man cried, as they embraced in the attorneys' conference room. There was no answer, but momentarily Jack's cockiness dissolved. He collapsed and cried like a child, hanging onto his father's shoulders.

Soon Maurice and the lawyer withdrew, leaving Evelyn and her estranged husband alone for the first time since he had stalked out of the house on Monday morning.

"Why on earth did you sign a confession, Jack?" she wanted to know. It was incredible to her that he had done so. Again and again during the past forty-eight hours she had tried to recall every detail of what they had done on the kidnapping night, and had convinced herself that they had been together the whole time.

"They sweated me twelve or thirteen hours," Jack told her. "They wouldn't let me sleep, and they dripped water down my back. Finally I'd have signed anything, just to get some rest."

Jack also related how Emig, "as a lodge brother," had counseled him to confess. Unless he did so, he said, the sheriff was going to turn him over to the San Jose mob. In the end he had decided to go along, believing he could easily prove his innocence once he got into court.

Evelyn accepted her husband's story at face value. For the past two days she had read no newspapers and knew nothing of the circumstances of his arrest—not even that he had been staying at a hotel. Otherwise she would have realized he was exaggerating, if not lying outright to her. Presumably he had enjoyed the best part of a night's sleep before his arrest in Thursday's predawn, and his confession had come by early afternoon with much of the intervening time taken up by his transfer to San Francisco. The time element alone ruled out the sort of marathon grilling he described.

Reporters pounced on Langdon as he escorted Evelyn and Maurice from the jail. He made it clear Jack's strategy would be to repudiate the confession he had signed in the absence of counsel.

"I have infallible proof that my client spent the night of November 9 in his home," he told the newsmen. "I'll do the rest of my talking in court."

After a night's rest, Emig was on the road back to San Francisco Friday to question the kidnappers again, taking with him Deputy District Attorney Herbert Bridges and, once more, Belle Gallagher. This time, to escape the commotion at the hall of justice, the suspects were taken to the FBI's San Francisco office in a Market Street business building. Vetterli, Conroy, Andersen, and four San Francisco police inspectors joined the San Joseans in the interrogation, which began after lunch.

The fawning Thurmond talked all afternoon, fleshing out his earlier confession with new, chilling precision. He related how, at the death scene, Brooke had been taken from the car and faced to the rear, back toward the shoreline. Then, while Thurmond circled the car to get the concrete blocks, Holmes had slipped up behind the victim and bashed in his head with the pistol. In so doing he had dropped the gun, accidentally discharging one round, which went astray. (This contradicted Thurmond's earlier confession, in which a concrete block was named as the bashing weapon. Holmes's version was that he had slugged Brooke with his fist, and that the youth's head had struck the pavement when he fell.)

The completion of the murder had been incredibly callous. When Brooke had screamed for help to a passing car, he had thrown his kidnappers into momentary panic. It was probably only because of the pillowcase over his head, muffling his screams, that the vehicle had failed to stop and Brooke's best chance for life had been lost. The kidnappers nonetheless had decided their greatest peril lay in the likelihood that the next car's occupants *would* stop at the sight of a hooded man. They therefore had removed the pillowcase, then knocked Brooke down again to finish their deed in a hurry.

Thurmond had been thorough and businesslike in attaching the weights intended to pull the victim to the bottom of the bay. Conveniently, the concrete blocks had holes to accommodate reinforcing rods. Thurmond had threaded the clothesline wire through them and, with Holmes holding Brooke immobile, bound one block to his ankles. A second was placed in the middle of his back, in line with the armpits, and trussed to his body with a loop of the wire, pinning his upper arms to his sides.

Although stunned, Brooke had continued crying and muttering as the kidnappers, grasping his shoulders and feet, hoisted him atop the bridge railing and pushed him off. In the water, he had struggled frantically, trying to paddle with his forearms, which remained free. Holmes, recovering the pistol from the bridge deck, had leaned over the rail and fired one shot at the flailing form. Then, as already related, Thurmond had climbed down to the understructure and fired three more shots into the water, aiming in the direction of a "gurgling sound." Heading back toward the Alameda shore, the slayers had driven a distance equal to about two city blocks before jettisoning their last block and the rest of the wire.

Thurmond also told his inquisitors how Lillie Shaw's funeral had caused a delay of the kidnapping, giving Brooke an additional forty-eight hours of life.

Holmes, questioned separately in another room, had fully regained his bravado after his morning breakdown in his father's arms. He evinced none of his partner's terror. While Harold groveled, Jack offered cynical bluster. In their session with him, the interrogators learned that the kidnappers, to save their own skins, had been ready to murder anyone who made the ransom payoff face to face.

"What would you have done if Mr. Rossi had delivered the ransom?" Holmes was asked.

"Well, you understand, he knew me," he replied. "His daughter and my son went to kindergarten together. I guess we would have had to do the same to him as we did to Brooke Hart."

On another crucial matter, the crime partners were in full accord. Asked repeatedly if they had other accomplices, both said no. The crime was their show, and no one else except Brooke Hart was in the cast.

Late in the day a newsreel crew, tipped off to the suspects' whereabouts, showed up at the building that housed the FBI office. Word quickly spread on the street that the kidnappers were there, and a small crowd gathered on the sidewalk outside. When the handcuffed Thurmond emerged for his ride back to jail, he was recognized, and a cry went up:

"Lynch him! Lynch him!"

The commotion did not pose a serious threat. No one moved toward the prisoner and the guards quickly bundled him into a car at the curb and drove him away. Nevertheless this first direct confrontation with a mob in anger reduced Thurmond to a cowering simpleton.

"Don't let 'em get me, Mr. Vetterli," he whimpered. "You like me a little bit, don't you? Don't let 'em get me."

Back at the prison Thurmond paced his cell, stared out through the steel grating, and rolled and tossed on his bunk, smoking one cigarette after another. While away during the afternoon, he had missed his first visitors. Two of his sisters had appeared, accompanied by Emmett Gottenberg and Philip Sheehy, the San Jose lawyers for whom both of them worked. The attorneys, whose specialty was tax law rather than criminal, nonetheless displayed a paper from Thurmond's father authorizing them to represent him. The visitors were informed that only the lawyers, not the sisters, would be permitted to see the prisoner when he returned. Finally they departed after leaving him a change of clothes. To reporters, the women dropped hints that an insanity plea would be entered.

Friday night Thurmond's nerves snapped and he broke into uncontrollable sobbing, as the *Examiner* reported, "with all the distress and terror of a child discovering he is lost." It continued for hours. Meanwhile, in a distant cell on the other side of the prison, Holmes whistled, laughed, and sang at the top of his voice.

"Why shouldn't I sing?" he demanded of jailer Antone DePaoli.

Later on he "slept like a baby," DePaoli reported. "He never moved a muscle and took care of a hearty breakfast."

Thurmond was not the only person upset by the "Lynch him!" cries outside the FBI office. Three thousand miles to the east, J. Edgar Hoover was furious when he read about the demonstration in the *New York Times*. Underlining the obscure paragraph that told of it, he jotted a memo, in his squatty round handwriting, to an assistant: "Please call Vetterli at once & tell him to stop taking these two criminals out of jail. If they should be lynched *while in our custody* it would be terrible." (Author's italics)

The sullen tide of outrage was now awash in San Francisco as well as San Jose; the *Chronicle* articulated it on page one of its Saturday editions:

EDITORIAL

AS SWIFT AS LAW ALLOWS

There is only one thing to do with the murderers of Brooke Hart.

That is to hang them, legally but promptly. The forms of the law must be followed, but in this case they are only forms.

The guilt of the culprits is unquestioned. They have confessed. There is no defense or mitigation. The crime was cold-blooded, premeditated, fiendish and sordid. It had not even the poor motive of anger or passion.

The first twelve persons called will be competent jurors; the plea should be guilty; the facts can be quickly presented, and there can be only one verdict and one sentence.

Then, without the law's needless delays, at the earliest legal date, the gallows should end two lives which have forfeited all rights except that to be executed by the law.

Something is owed to public feeling.

Less inflamed, but little different in import, was the rhetoric of the *Mercury Herald*'s "Editorial Analysis" column:

It is to be hoped that the proceeding will be swift; that the accused men will be given a fair and impartial trial before twelve good men and true. It is to be hoped that the trivialities and technicalities which are so often resorted to by attorneys for the one and only purpose of clogging the wheels of justice will not be permitted.

While the interrogators in San Francisco worked to extract incriminating detail from the suspects, other officers fanned out across the Santa Clara Valley to confirm their appalling stories. With Holmes's lawyer already giving signals that his client would repudiate his confession, and the possibility that Thurmond might do likewise, independent corroboration of the corpus delicti was crucial.

"We must have an airtight hanging case," District Attorney Thomas told reporters. "There must be no slip-up. These men deserve hanging, and that's what they're going to get."

Ramsey and Hicks, liberated from their stakeout in the Hart home, were sent to Campbell to reinterview Merle Shaves and Everett Mason, the woodchopper-witnesses to the suspects' strange meeting amid the orchards. After examining photographs of Holmes, both were certain he was the man they had observed writing on a paper propped against a windshield. As for the other man at the rendezvous, they had not had a clear view of him and could not say for certain whether he was Thurmond.

Further corroboration of the orchard meeting would come a week later from Mrs. James Turner, a Campbell woman. A scrap of paper she found near the site turned out to be a crude map, in pencil, showing routes from San Jose to Oakland by way of Milpitas. The turnoff to the San Mateo Bridge was clearly designated. Mrs. Turner took the map to Harry Evans, the deputy sheriff in Campbell, who turned it over to Emig.

*   *   *

At the California Concrete Products Company, where Thurmond said he had purchased the blocks, Ramsey and Deputy Sheriff John Moore found Tony Carvalho, the yard man who had sold them. They showed him newspaper pictures of the kidnappers with inadvertently transposed captions—Holmes's name under Thurmond's likeness and vice versa. Carvalho nevertheless pointed unerringly to the photo of Thurmond and exclaimed, "How could I ever forget that fellow?" The officers listened amazed as Carvalho told of Thurmond's curious concern with the weight of the blocks and his grotesque behavior of successively hefting and rejecting smaller ones before settling on the twenty-two-pounders.

In Santa Clara, Deputies Moore and Cordray went from store to store, trying to substantiate Thurmond's statement that the wire with which Brooke Hart had been trussed was bought in that city. At the Vargas Brothers Merchandise Store, the officers located Dominic Condensa, a clerk, who remembered the fifty-five-cent transaction. Thurmond had described his purchase as baling wire, but Condensa said it was a regular seventy-five-foot coil of clothesline. He remembered the purchaser as "rather tall," about thirty-five, wearing a light suit, and he thought the sale had taken place November 8, the day before the kidnapping, not the next day as Thurmond had said. The deputies had not brought pictures of the kidnappers with them, so Condensa could not make a positive identification.

Because the kidnappers had discussed hiding Brooke "on a boat or something," Chief Black took pains to check out Frank McKee, the man approached by Holmes at the Alviso marina about selling his yacht. McKee was able to pin down the date, Tuesday, October 31, because it was the day before duck season opened. His recollection not only provided further corroboration of Holmes's confession, it also strengthened the circumstantial case for premeditation. The only reason the boat deal had fallen through, McKee thought, was that Holmes and Thurmond could not come up with his $1,500 asking price.

The absence of the gun was a matter of major concern to District Attorney Thomas. If it turned out that Brooke had died of gunshot wounds, the weapon could be crucial to the proof. Each kidnapper, in his confession, had placed the pistol in the hands of the other; both said it had not been thrown away. But as things stood, if the confessions were withdrawn it would be hard to show that such a weapon even existed. It took Ramsey and Hicks only a short time to track down the man named Meyer, a customer on Holmes's oil route, from whom the gun supposedly had been purchased.

"Yes," he said. "I sold a .41 caliber pistol to Thurmond for six bucks. Holmes sent him around to see me."

"How well did you know Holmes?"

"He'd been coming around for about a year. Nice guy, lots of fun. We got along fine."

Meyer could not verify the exact date he sold the gun. His cash book showed separate $6 sales on three consecutive days—October 15, 16, and 17. One of them was the gun transaction, but he had no way of telling which.

In San Francisco, Thurmond was still insisting the gun should be under the rear seat of Holmes's car, and the investigators decided to have another look. A tip had come in that there was a secret chamber under the dashboard. Cordray and Ramsey went over the machine inside and out but found no trace of the weapon; the so-called secret compartment was empty. But the search was not in vain; Holmes's floor mat yielded concrete crumbs—evidence that the blocks had indeed been there. Also discovered were two safety pins, possibly used to fasten the pillow slip over Brooke Hart's head. A registration slip under the rear floor mat, in a leather courtesy-card case of the Union Oil Company, showed the car had first been sold on May 24, 1933, and registered to Holmes on July 25. The legal owner was a finance company in San Francisco. (In 1989, Evelyn Holmes would remember that "they tore the car all to pieces" and she never got it back.)

Holmes's automobile also yielded a Union Oil Company statement, from the firm's San Francisco district office, made out to Kay's Service Station in San Jose. On a hunch, Ramsey paid a visit to the station, on South Third Street.

"Sure, I know Holmes," said Seaman Kay. "I almost gave him a job."

It became clear that whatever had impelled Holmes to kidnapping, murder, and extortion, it was not abject poverty. Unlike many of the jobless in 1933, he was not "up against it." His unemployment was only in passing; within his grasp was a position that might pay $100 to $200 a week—several times what many families were living on in comfort.

* * *

From Thurmond's nonstop talking, the investigators first learned of Holmes's strange visit to Ruth Gum late on the afternoon of November 9, less than an hour before the kidnapping. The call had not been so purposeless as it must have seemed to her. Holmes had boasted to his partner that Ruth would provide his alibi. He had tarried at her home until not long before six o'clock; could he plausibly be accused of abducting Brooke—a major enterprise demanding preparation and careful timing—at five minutes past the hour?

Summoned by Ramsey, Mrs. Gum appeared at the sheriff's office with her husband to give a statement. Yes, Jack had come to see her on the ninth. She could not say why; he had rambled on and on, saying little that meant much. She was certain he had been there between five and six but could not recall exactly when he left. At least once since the kidnapping she had seen him again, but he had neither hinted at his complicity nor solicited an alibi. The Gums and the Holmeses were social friends, she said, emphatically denying any romantic involvement with Jack; he had never shown that kind of interest in her. Although Mrs. Gum was positive about the date of his visit, she could not come up with any event or circumstance to pin it down. Ramsey concluded it could just as well have been on Wednesday or Friday as on Thursday, and her testimony would be less than convincing before a jury.

All day Friday the malignant tide of outrage washed through the city, carrying the stink of vengeance. "The temper of San Jose citizens is still at white heat," the *Examiner* reported. *Chronicle* reporter Royce Brier was among the first to gauge the malignancy's virulence, writing bluntly that Brooke's friends were ready to take justice into their own hands.

Rabbi Karesh, Brooke's friend and his family's spiritual counselor, heard the mutterings within his own Temple Bickur Cholim. The twenty-six-year-old rabbi, who would later give up the rabbinate for the law and become an eminent California judge, mourned Brooke's death in a Friday night sermon, but added an admonition:

"Maybe you've heard talk of a lynching. Don't participate in any way. Once you unleash the forces of violence, there's no end to it. Spread the word to your neighbors. Let the law take its course. As Jews, we have to believe in the law."

150

13

The Woman and the Alibi

"What a dish!"

Deputy Sheriff Howard Buffington could only think the words, not utter them. But as he faced Gertrude Estensen for the first time, he understood how she might have tantalized Jack Holmes—led him to abandon home, family, job, and good name.

Had his craving for her also impelled him to murder?

She possessed a patrician beauty. At twenty-eight, this San Jose housewife and grade-school teacher was a serene-appearing woman with classic, inviting features—large eyes; a full, sensuous mouth; slender neck; and dark bobbed hair, softly waved. Buffington, a veteran cop, would never take her for a blackmailer, but this was the woman who, according to Thurmond, "had something" on Holmes and kept him broke.

The investigators had tracked Gertrude down within hours after she had given her "alibi" statement to Holmes's lawyer Friday morning. Now it was Friday night, and by request, she had come to the sheriff's office for questioning. Buffington and Undersheriff Earle G. Hamilton, her interrogators, led her to an inner room and introduced her to Lenore Ghetti, a special deputy and stenographer.

The interview got off to a rocky, confrontational start as the officers, gesturing toward Gertrude's escort, told her, "Your husband will have to stay outside. . . . We don't want to ask questions in front of him; we don't want to cause any hard feelings."

"There is nothing I would not want to answer in front of my husband, that is what I am trying to tell you," Gertrude protested. Her ire rose at the implication that the questioners anticipated salacious disclosures. She did not tell them that the man they had excluded from the room was not her husband but her father. Leonard Estensen had not come; he could ill afford the time away from his job in Redwood City.

The door closed and Buffington led off the questioning: "You went to school with Jack Holmes?"

"Yes, high school."

"You have known Jack Holmes for how many years?"

"About twelve or thirteen years."

"Did you and he keep company when you were kids?"

"Yes, for two years, that is while I was sixteen and seventeen."

"You were sort of sweethearts?"

"Yes, we were."

Abruptly the line of questioning shifted: "How well do you know Mrs. Holmes?"

"I have known Mrs. Holmes some length of time." Gertrude's answer was as incomplete as it was indefinite. The two women had attended San Jose High in the same era, but their acquaintance then had been casual at best. After that they had had no contact until Jack set up the family double-dating routine as camouflage for his amorous pursuit of Gertrude.

"Do you visit with Mrs. Holmes, and does she visit your home?" Buffington inquired.

"Yes, we always visit between houses."

"Do you know that Mrs. Holmes and Jack Holmes separated?"

"Yes, I do."

"Do you know the cause?"

"No, I do not. I understand it is a personal matter."

Hamilton, who had remained silent until now, asked his first question, direct and to the point: "Did you know they separated over you?"

"No, I did not." Gertrude was equivocating; it was only five days since Evelyn had appeared at her door, demanding, "Why are you trying to steal my husband?" Still, the answer was technically truthful.

"When were they separated?"

"Tuesday of this week." Here, Gertrude was in error by a day; the split-up had come on Monday.

"Did you have any idea why they separated?"

"No."

Suddenly Buffington took another new tack: "Did you see Jack Holmes that Thursday, the ninth of November, the night Hart was kidnapped?"

"Yes, that evening at my home."

"Who was present?"

"Mr. and Mrs. Holmes, my husband, and I."

Hamilton sensed at once that Buffington's new line of interrogation might produce an alibi for Holmes. Seeming to dread uncovering one, he cut in and resumed the clumsy probing for a sexual liaison.

"Did you ever see Holmes when anyone else was not around?"

"No."

"Did you ever meet Jack alone?"

"Yes, when I was sixteen."

"Do you ever meet him alone now?"

"I have been with him alone, but I never meet him alone."

"What do you mean by being alone?" Hamilton asked.

"Mr. Holmes comes to the house in the daytime without his wife, in the presence of my mother. Sometimes, however, my mother is not in the room."

"When was the last time you saw Jack Holmes?"

"Monday afternoon of this week, 2:00 P.M. exactly, at my home."

"Alone?"

"Yes."

"Was your mother there?"

"Yes."

"How long did he stay?"

"About half an hour."

"Did he talk to you about having money?"

"He never mentioned money. We were not that friendly that we discussed money matters."

"Did he at any time say he expected to get some money in a couple of weeks?"

"No. He always seemed to have plenty of money when we were out together, the four of us, but never any superfluous amount."

Clearly the officers were as titillated by the prospect of bedroom disclosures as they were curious about what light Gertrude might shed on Jack's guilt or innocence.

"Did he discuss with you leaving your husband and going away with him here lately?" Hamilton asked.

The question flustered Gertrude, and her reply was nonresponsive: "It was merely because we did not see each other for so long a time. I had been very ill, and after he found out about that, he called."

"Since you were ill he has been seeing you quite a bit?"

"No, I wouldn't say that."

"He had not discussed leaving your husband and making you go with him?"

Gertrude was still fuming at the officers' voyeuristic determination to paint her as an adulteress. Whatever her dalliance with Jack Holmes, it was no business of theirs. It had nothing to do with the Hart case.

"Do I have to answer that?"

"Not unless you want to."

"Yes, he did discuss it."

"Did he discuss money matters ever?" Hamilton asked, reverting to a subject Gertrude thought had been dropped. "When he wanted you to go away with him, didn't he discuss how he was going to get the money?"

"No. There was no intention on my part of running away with him, so I would not be interested in any money matters. If I were interested in his idea, naturally I would have such a discussion . . . I possibly could have found out if I inquired, but I did not."

"How long has he been talking about this to you?" Buffington inquired.

"Since about last June . . . I got out of the hospital toward the end of May, and that was the first time I had seen him for ten years."

"How did this meeting come about?"

Gertrude explained how Jack had learned of her surgery from her father during a chance visit to his paint store.

"When did he start bringing his wife to your home?"

"Right away."

"Did you insist on that?"

"Certainly."

"Did your mother know the proposal he made to you that you leave with him?" Buffington inquired.

"Yes, of course, and my husband knew also."

Just when this line of questioning seemed to be exhausted, Buffington struck unexpected pay dirt: "Really, then, you have never been out with him at all?"

"Yes," the demure woman sitting before him acknowledged, "I have been with him twice."

"Was it out for a ride or something?"

"I went to San Francisco one Saturday, and the following Saturday I went to a football game."

"Did Mrs. Holmes know that you did?"

"Not that I know of."

"Did your mother know it?"

"Mother knew it and my husband knew it."

"How did your husband feel about this thing?"

"I did not know," Gertrude answered, fumbling for words, "but I do not think he was too happy about the idea."

"When did you see Mrs. Holmes last?"

"This morning. She came to my home."

"Did she say anything this morning about your breaking up their home?"

"No."

"When she called last Sunday did she say something about it?"

"I told her I had no intention of going away with her husband or leaving my husband, and that I did not want to take her husband away from her, and I never tried to. I thought it was just an infatuation and an illusion on his part. Well, we just talked it over . . . and we parted very good friends."

"That was Sunday. . . . Then you did not see her again until this morning." said Buffington, recapitulating. "When she came this morning, what did she say to you?"

Evelyn's mission in the aftermath of Jack's arrest, Gertrude explained, had nothing at all to do with her marital woes. All she wanted now was to document her husband's whereabouts on the night Brooke Hart vanished. "She was at my house with her lawyer. He came to get a statement from me."

"And did he get it?" Buffington jumped at the chance to get a line on what Holmes's defense was up to.

"Yes."

"Did he get a statement from your husband?"

"Certainly."

Buffington tried another sudden change of direction: "Where did you go last Thursday evening, the night of the kidnapping?"

"We went to the Hester Theater to see 'The Three Little Pigs.' "

"How do you fix the time?"

"We were there before the end of the first show. They (Jack and Evelyn) called at my house shortly after dinner. We had done the dishes and we were playing bridge when they walked in."

"What time was that?" Buffington asked the question casually. The answer it produced would be the crucial nub of Gertrude's statement—the time factor that could either reinforce or shatter Holmes's confession.

"Between 7:30 and 8:00," she replied, "possibly a quarter to eight. I cannot say the definite time, but I do know it was about that time."

If Gertrude was truthful and her memory correct, she had seriously impaired the credibility of both suspects' confessions. Could Holmes have intercepted Brooke Hart, taken him thirty-eight miles to the bridge, helped kill him, tossed him in the bay, returned to San Jose, picked up his wife, and driven to the Estensen home, all in little more than ninety minutes? Possibly, perhaps, with precision timing—but this crime had been dogged by delay at every step. Holmes had forced Brooke Hart to drive out of the city by a roundabout route and then detour onto hill-country back roads, and the stopover to change cars had been time-consuming. Then, after a false start for the bridge, the kidnappers had doubled back to recover Brooke's cigarettes. At the killing site, it had taken more than a few minutes to bash in the victim's head, truss him up, and wire the concrete blocks to him. More time had elapsed while Thurmond descended to the bridge's underpinnings and fired the volley of bullets in Brooke's direction after he hit the water. There had been additional delays as the killers jettisoned their leftover block and wire, divided Brooke's pocket money, and composed the first ransom note.

All this before half past seven or eight o'clock? Hard to believe.

Moreover it defied reason that Brooke, doubtless hemorrhaging from his head wound, could have been thrown in the water much before 7:25 when the wood gatherers heard his distress calls. Now Gertrude was saying that at that time or not long afterward, Holmes was at her front door.

So the inquisitors were confronted with two main possibilities which a jury would have to weigh later: Either Gertrude was mistaken or lying, or much of Holmes's confession was fiction probably concocted under duress.

Again Buffington exercised his penchant for repetitive questioning: "How do you fix the time that you went to the show?"

"I know we had planned to go to the show one night that week, and we went Wednesday night. Then the Holmeses came over unexpectedly and we went to the show again on Thursday." Gertrude briefly summarized Holmes's phone call at four o'clock that Thursday afternoon, when at first she had suggested that he bring Evelyn over for a bridge game.

"Was he excited or anything that night? Did he show any signs of being nervous?" Hamilton asked.

"That is what I marvel at. He was just as natural as could be. We stayed at the house about fifteen or twenty minutes and then went to the Hester Theater." Gertrude related how they had to stand while awaiting the start of the second show at nine o'clock. She told of their midnight snack at Maggi's Restaurant and their decision to attend the San Jose State–Cal Aggies game Saturday afternoon.

"And you cannot think of any time when there was anything said about money?"

"No."

"Who paid for the tickets for the ball game?" Buffington inquired.

"No one. My father gave us complimentary tickets."

"Who paid for the tickets for the show last Thursday night?"

"My husband paid for mine, and Mr. Holmes paid for his wife. We always did that."

"Did Jack ever discuss this Hart case at all in your presence?" Hamilton wanted to know.

Gertrude recalled Holmes's visit the previous Monday afternoon, when he had agreed with her and her mother that "only the lowest kind" of person could have kidnapped Brooke Hart. "He did not seem to be overly anxious about it, but he talked about it naturally."

"Did you ever notice anything about Holmes to make you feel he was of unsound mind?"

Gertrude pondered the question. "He was a very nervous boy."

"Have you ever thought he was a little weak in the mind?"

"He has been very erratic."

"And was he calm the night of the kidnapping, when you went to the theater?"

"Very calm."

"Did he ever talk to you about this Mr. Thurmond?" Buffington inquired.

"Never mentioned him."

"Did you know Thurmond or anything about him?"

"I just found out today I know his family, but I did not know him personally."

"Did you know that he and Thurmond were running together?"

Gertrude described the one time she had met Thurmond, on South First Street the Saturday before the kidnapping when Holmes had introduced his cruising companion as "my friend Harold."

"Did they say where they were going?" Buffington asked.

"No, we only talked a minute. I did not even recall his name."

Hamilton changed the subject again to test Gertrude's consistency by replowing ground already covered. "Did Mrs. Holmes say anything to you this morning about getting a lawyer for Jack?"

"The lawyer was with her."

"And he took a statement from you?"

"Yes."

"Did he tell you not to answer any of our questions?"

"No. He told me not to say much because of the publicity, but he did not tell me not to say anything."

"What time was he at your house?"

"At seven o'clock this morning."

"Do you know his name?"

"I do not. We were in bed at the time," Gertrude answered in a quaint non sequitur.

"Did Holmes tell you where he had been the night of the ninth?" Hamilton asked, seemingly as an afterthought.

"No."

"Did he tell you that he had gone someplace and just got back?"

"No. You see, the Holmeses were not late when they came over, and he only remarked that his father and mother were at his house visiting, and he said he left them sitting there."

The hour was late when the interrogation ended and Gertrude rejoined her father in the outer office.

The interrogators' seeming solicitude for her privacy—their concern about causing "hard feelings" on the part of her husband—turned out to be a pose. No sooner had Miss Ghetti completed her transcript of the session than Emig released it to the press.

Most newspapers ran every word, and every reader now knew what Buffington and Hamilton had sensed from the beginning: Gertrude's affidavit, especially what she said about the time of Jack's appearance on her doorstep, could pose serious difficulties for his prosecution—if anyone heeded her. But no one was going to heed her. In the court of public opinion, Jack Holmes and Harold Thurmond already stood convicted, with no venue for appeal. It was obvious, Emig insisted, that Holmes had set Gertrude up as his alibi witness and carried off his crime at breakneck speed to make the alibi work.

While Hamilton and Buffington had been grilling Gertrude, Emig had been questioning another woman in another room nearby—the ex-fiancée who Thurmond said had ruined his life by marrying another man. She had made a startling revelation: After the kidnapping, Thurmond had come pleading that she provide him with an alibi. She had refused.

Thurmond's ex-fiancée was luckier than Gertrude Estensen. Emig withheld her identity from the press, and her name would never appear in the annals of the Hart case.

14

The Search

To accommodate their pile-driving barges, the builders of the San Mateo Bridge had dredged a deep channel, wider than the bridge itself, as they worked their way across the bay. By the time lawyer-yachtsman Marshall Hall had spent days dragging this trench for Brooke Hart's body, he was certain the underworld was using it as a convenient watery grave.

His grappling irons had recovered—besides parts of automobiles and countless pay telephones with their coin boxes broken open—at least one piece of human flesh, too fresh to have been Brooke's.

"I was always convinced, and I am now, that that bridge is a dumping place for bodies," Hall said fifty years later. "There was another body there [besides Hart's] that we just didn't look into."

Hall and his crew arrived at the bridge at sunrise on Thursday, November 16, and for the first ten hours were frustrated by lack of equipment. His yacht, the thirty-three-foot *Mermaid*, was a pleasure craft not fitted out with grappling gear. Not until a San Francisco Police Department boat and a seventy-two-foot Coast Guard cutter arrived in late afternoon did dragging begin. It was decided that the *Mermaid*, the smallest and most maneuverable of the three craft, should furnish the platform for the drag men.

"They gave me two police inspectors with Irish names, O'Malley and O'Flaherty, who were supposed to be expert drag men; they had found lots of bodies," Hall recalled in 1983. "So I had them, and I had one or two coast guardsmen, and I had my own two fellows—a pretty good crew. And we started to work."

It was tedious, laborious duty. Every square foot of the bay's bottom alongside the bridge had to be dragged, in swaths eight feet wide and up to half a mile long, with stops for everything on which the grappling hooks snagged. The *Mermaid* was too small to haul up heavy objects without heeling over, so with each major discovery the drag lines had to be passed to a winch-equipped truck on the bridge deck.

Thursday evening, working in the dark, Hall's crew brought up the first promising item, a strip of white cloth with thin purple stripes. It was not too different from Brooke's shirt fabric, according to his published description.

About eleven o'clock, with the tide coming in fast, the drag lines suddenly tautened, and one of the police inspectors called, "Stop, stop! I've got something." As Hall cut his engine, the tidal current hit the powerless *Mermaid* broadside and slammed it against the bridge supports, snapping off the mast, and the impact threw O'Malley and O'Flaherty overboard.

"Fortunately, with her mast gone, the boat could go underneath the roadway part of the bridge, and we picked up the inspectors on the other side," Hall related afterward. "Otherwise we'd have been in serious trouble." When the boat returned to recover the unknown underwater object, it could not be found. The tide, not the darkness, forced the suspension of dragging for the night.

Having read in Thursday's paper that two Hart case suspects were in custody, Evelyn Ridley in Oakland finally summoned the courage to mail the letter she had written three days earlier to Alex Hart. It described chillingly ("terrible to hear") the distress calls that had attracted her husband Vinton and his partner, Al Coley, as they gathered driftwood from the mud flats below the San Mateo Bridge on the night of Brooke's disappearance.

Mrs. Ridley sent her letter in care of Chief Black, who received it Friday morning. He passed it on, not only to Alex Hart but also to Emig (who had been in private possession of the same information since Sunday but had failed to follow up). Black also gave the Ridley-Coley story, for the first time, to the newspapers, which seized on the problems it created for the district attorney. It immensely compounded his difficulty in putting together a kidnap-murder chronology that a jury could believe. If Holmes had tarried at the bridge until anytime near 7:25, when the distress calls were heard, could he really have driven more than thirty miles back to San Jose, fetched Evelyn and the Estensens, and arrived early for the nine o'clock show at the Hester Theater? Emig declined to discuss the time discrepancies when reporters quizzed him about them.

The Ridley-Coley account posed an additional enigma, centering on the shots Thurmond had fired at Brooke Hart's flailing form—or rather at the place where he heard a "gurgling sound" from the water. Both kidnappers said the gun had been discharged several times; yet the wood gatherers had heard no gunfire.

No one was watching the operations at the San Mateo Bridge more closely than Earl Warren, the Alameda County district attorney who stood ready to prosecute Holmes and Thurmond for murder if the Santa Clara County kidnapping case went awry. From his office in Oakland Warren dispatched four investigators to join the growing army of searchers for Brooke Hart's corpse. He also passed the word to Sheriff Mike Driver, his henchman, to go all out on the case.

One of the sheriff's men at the bridge was Vince Strobel, the constable for Eden Township, a sizeable area taking in the desolate lowlands at the bridge's east end. On Friday, with the tide ebbing, Strobel walked slowly out along the span, peering over the rail, studying the terrain below. Suddenly he nudged his partner, Grover Mull: "Look!" He pointed to a concrete block and a coil of wire, exposed and plainly visible on the mud flat from which the water had receded. Removing his shoes and tying a rope around himself, he went over the side and recovered the objects.

Weighing twenty-two pounds precisely, the block met every specification mentioned by Tony Carvalho, who had sold three of them to Thurmond about November 1. Likewise, the wire matched that which Dominic Condensa had sold, ostensibly to Thurmond, at the Vargas store. Within hours of Strobel's discovery, Hall and his *Mermaid* crew brought up another block farther offshore. Wire was still threaded through its holes, as Thurmond had described. A small bloodstain found on the bridge rail nearby confirmed Thurmond's guess that this was where Brooke had been tossed over the side.

The discoveries attested to a furious struggle that the athletic and muscular Hart boy had put up after hitting the water. Although stunned and bleeding, possibly from bullet wounds as well as his head injury, he had managed to break free of his bonds and cast off the weights.

The Hart case came close to claiming two more lives during the Friday search. Two of Warren's investigators from the Alameda County district attorney's office, Oscar Jahnsen and George Henningsen, sank to their waists in underwater mud before extricating themselves and crawling ashore.

By evening the endurance of the dragging crew was nearing its limit, as the tides and winds punished the search vessels, slamming them against the bridge fender and into each other.

"We can't stay with this battering," one of the police inspectors said. "We've got to get out of here." As operations were suspended for the second night, the weary officers glumly contemplated the long cruise back up the bay, against the tide, to home port in San Francisco.

"Why go all that way?" Hall asked. "Why not go into Redwood City?"

The Redwood City anchorage was only a short cruise across the bay, near the west end of the bridge. The inspectors, who seldom sailed south of the San Francisco city limits line, were strangers to the South Bay and astonished to learn that it had navigable ports.

"Redwood City? Is there water in there?" they asked, incredulous.

"Well, 10,000-ton ships go in there," Hall informed them. "You ought to be able to."

"Do you know the way in?"

"Sure."

Hall proposed that they all sail across the bay, tie up their boats, and find a good restaurant. The inspectors offered to buy dinner.

"So anyway," Hall remembered, "I led the way into Redwood Creek. The damned fools kept their searchlight right on me, on the back of the pilot house, and they had a hell of a time seeing where I was going. But we got up to the dock finally."

After the docking, one of the mates paid the young lawyer a compliment that he would still cherish as among the finest in his life, after a half century of professional, juridical, and civic honors.

"By God, Hall," the man said, "you are a master mariner of the bays, rivers, sloughs, marshes, and mud flats."

Back in San Jose, in the white mansion on The Alameda, the ailing Nettie Hart still refused to accept the fact of her son's death. The agony of uncertainty filled the house. So for humane reasons as well as the state's evidential needs, the weary searchers returned to the bay Saturday morning. Discouragement had set in; Brooke had been dead for eight days now, and the tides and currents could have easily carried his body to the open ocean beyond the Golden Gate. Moreover, a ten-foot man-eating shark had recently been caught in the bay, and others had been sighted.

A lab report had come back on the bit of purple-striped fabric that the grapplers had brought up Thursday night; it was not part of

Brooke's shirt, as first thought, but more likely a rag used by a boat crew for engine wiping.

Two Oakland divers, W. B. Townsend and G. E. Kimble, were now added to the dragging crew, as operations moved to deeper waters about seven tenths of a mile from the Alameda shore. With their air hoses connected to a hand pump aboard the *Mermaid*, they stalked the bay floor, watching for clues and making sure the grappling hooks had firm grip on objects taken to the surface.

Airplanes added a vertical dimension to the search. Emig enlisted a Palo Alto pilot to fly over the drag area in the hope of spotting Brooke's body from the air. Another pilot, skimming the water at a twenty-five-foot altitude two miles from the bridge, reported seeing what looked like a body, but surface crews sent to the spot found nothing. Reports of a floating "gray form" prompted a reconnaissance off the Berkeley shore about nineteen miles north of the bridge, but the object turned out to be an automobile gas tank embedded in the mud. Other false alarms were set off by frolicking sea lions.

There remained the slimmest of possibilities that Nettie Hart was right, that for some unfathomable reason Thurmond and Holmes had made up their stories out of whole cloth, and Brooke still lived. Every day, among the huge volume of benevolent and malevolent mail pouring into the Hart home, came unsigned letters telling the family that such was the case. Telephone calls from persons unknown sounded the same theme. Emig and Vetterli deemed these messages deliberate efforts to confuse the family and discourage vigorous prosecution. Yet the annals of crime since the time of Genesis were filled with reappearances of the presumed dead; Joseph had reappeared as governor of Egypt after his envious brothers sold him into slavery and counterfeited his demise by drenching his coat in goat's blood.

With Sunday's dawn came an invasion of the search area by the curious on weekend excursions and amateur searchers lured by a false rumor of a $1,000 reward for Brooke's body. Ten highway patrolmen were dispatched to keep bridge traffic moving.

George Henningsen, recovered from his close call in the bay-bottom quicksand Friday, was back reconnoitering the mud flats Sunday with Joe Brandon, another of Earl Warren's investigators. As they tramped along, their eyes were drawn to a mud-covered object on the ground, determined later to have been 976 feet north of the bridge and 171 feet from the shoreline. It turned out to be a man's hat, size seven, of gray felt with black band and a two-inch, welt-edged brim. Torn and shrunken, it had probably washed ashore with the tide. The partially detached sweatband bore an almost-obliterated, gold-stamped Brookhart label, with the words "Made Exclusively for L. Hart & Son Co., San Jose, Cal."

Alex Hart broke into tears when Emig showed the hat to him. Louis Rossi, the men's wear buyer, examined it and said, "It's Brooke's, beyond a shadow of a doubt. Only two dozen hats like that have been sold."

Three hundred feet from where the hat was found, searchers discovered four Shell Oil Company coupon books bearing stains which appeared to be blood. One bore a signature rendered illegible by the water. Brooke Hart had used such books; an Associated Oil Company courtesy card had been in his wallet when it was found on the tanker.

Another find, on the bridge itself, was part of a pair of eyeglasses that could have been Brooke's. Interest flagged among the searchers (except the greedy amateurs), however, as belief grew that the body would never be found. One deputy sheriff conjectured that everything retrieved so far might have been planted. "The body may be hidden somewhere else," he told a *Chronicle* reporter, "and the cement blocks, the pieces of wire, and the other exhibits placed where they were for the purpose of confusion."

Emig considered the deputy's hypothesis absurd, but having no better idea, decided to confront Thurmond with it.

"Harold, if for any reason this story you've been giving me is a phony, tell me now," he pleaded. "Think of the Hart family. They're taking this terribly hard, this thing you've done to them, and they just want to give their boy a decent burial."

Breaking down in tears, Thurmond raised his hand: "I swear to God, sheriff, I've told you the truth. We threw him off the bridge."

On Monday morning, as the fifth day of searching began, a crewman on a barge six miles away, off Steinberger Slough on the west side of the bay near Belmont, noticed a piece of cloth floating in the water. It turned out to be a pillowcase about fourteen inches square. By now everyone who read the newspapers knew that Brooke Hart had been hooded with a pillowcase while riding to his death, and the barge man turned his find over to Emig, who showed it to Thurmond. No, Harold said, it was not the pillowcase he had slipped over Brooke's head. That one, which he had taken from his nephew's bed, was easily twice as large.

By now, the sheriff felt like a commuter, making daily runs to San Francisco with items for the quivering Thurmond to identify. In Thurmond's tear-filled eyes, Emig had been transformed from captor to protector, and to curry favor Harold was cooperating without stint. On Tuesday Emig showed him a gunnysackful of suspicious items from the garage of Holmes's now deserted house on Bird Avenue. Among them were a firebrick wrapped in a woman's silk stocking and a dirty bath mat embedded with particles of concrete. Thurmond identified the brick as one that he had left with Holmes before the crime, with the idea of using it as a weight for Brooke's body. But in the end, obsessed with the need for a heavy anchor, he had rejected it as too light. As for the bath mat, he had never seen it before.

Meanwhile the matter of the pillowcase was taking a bizarre turn. The sheriff's investigators, tracing its "C–352" laundry mark, found that it belonged to Brooke's Santa Clara University chum, actor Jackie Coogan.

Coogan, whose 1920 portrayal of "The Kid" had made him the movies' first child superstar, was now nineteen. He was popular on the SCU campus, where they made him a cheerleader and exploited his talent in the school's famous Passion Play. Because he was a friend of Brooke Hart, the detectives curiously reasoned now that his pillowcase must fit into the kidnap puzzle somewhere, despite Thurmond's statement to the contrary.

Summoned to the sheriff's office, Coogan said his pillowcase had been stolen two months earlier. On Saturday, September 23, he had taken it to the Santa Clara-Cal football game at Berkeley, traveling by way of the San Mateo Bridge, which carried much of the traffic between the two campuses. He had intended to use the pillow slip as a face shield, but he had left it in his car. "When I came out of the stadium, it was gone," he told the investigators. Since that time he had had no further occasion to cross the bridge.

Emig's daily quiz sessions with Thurmond, while producing little in the way of usable evidence, paid an unexpected dividend by confirming a hunch of Chief Black. Within hours after the kidnappers' arrests, Black had begun to wonder whether they had pulled the earlier hijack-holdups of M. J. Michel and J. W. Scott. It seemed more than coincidental to him that Michel and Holmes had been employed by the same company, Union Oil, and Scott worked for Shell Oil, where Holmes supposedly had a new job lined up. Moreover, Holmes's black Chevrolet answered the description of the car used in the Michel hijacking. The two holdups had netted almost $1,400 in cash, and it was after the second one that Holmes had begun dickering for Frank McKee's boat, which had an asking price of $1,500.

When Emig asked Thurmond about the hijack jobs, he freely confessed both, accurately portraying Holmes as the mastermind. A $220 wad of bills he had been carrying when arrested was part of the loot, he admitted.

"Jack told me everything to do," he said. "After each holdup I drove to where he was waiting for me and we split up the money." Thurmond also directed the sheriff to the cache of checks and coupons taken in the two robberies, under a culvert near the San Jose city limits.

"What did you do with your share of the money, Harold?" Emig asked.

"Spent it. Gave some to my father." Thurmond forgot to mention that some had gone for note payments to his ex-boss at the service station, Francis Wyatt.

When Holmes was asked about the hijackings later, he clammed up. "I've talked too much already," he said.

No one welcomed Thurmond's admission of the holdups more than one Henry Gear, * who was already in the city jail, charged with both of them. Earlier Scott had identified Gear as the hijacker, but in the wake of Thurmond's confession, he was uncertain which suspect had robbed him. Michel, however, did not equivocate.

"That's the man!" he exclaimed, pointing to Thurmond's bulging neck muscle in a photograph. "I'd know that neck muscle in a minute."

On Monday afternoon, with hope of finding Brooke's remains all but abandoned, officers of four counties gathered in Redwood City to figure out their next move. Emig presented the most imaginative idea: rig up a dummy of Brooke Hart's size and weight, tie a couple of concrete blocks to it, and throw it in the water to see where it might drift in the currents. This experiment led to a theory that Brooke, who had been tossed off the north side of the bridge, had

* Fictitious name.

been swept back under it to the south. A fleet of small boats fanned out there, covering a large area to which the dummy drifted. The results were nil.

At Monday's meeting further plans were laid for thirty officers to reconnoiter every foot of the bay shoreline, and for scores of small boats to comb the bay's entire southern arm systematically.

Since Sunday, Navy searchlights had been in use to keep operations going at night, and on Tuesday the Navy Department authorized full commitment of other facilities. All day long the Navy blimp J-4 floated in the mists over the search area, with observers in the gondola training powerful glasses on the water and mud flats below. They spotted nothing.

No help was turned down. Chief of Police Charles Scudero of Pittsburg, a little town at the mouth of the Sacramento River, joined the search with a grappling device he had used to recover fifty-seven drowning victims. George E. Mitchell, a retired sea captain from Capitola on the coast, showed up with a new kind of recovery net which he had used with great success. Mayor Angelo Rossi of San Francisco ordered his fire department to join the effort with a large hydraulic pump, to stir up the loose mud from the bay bottom and dislodge the body if it was stuck there. Marshall Hall's friends in the South Bay Yacht Club sailed out from Alviso to reconnoiter.

From time to time there were flurries of excitement. Near the place where the pillowcase had been recovered, searchers found what seemed to be human lung tissue, but it proved to be part of a lamb carcass from a slaughterhouse two miles away.

The dragging crews at the bridge site recovered a man's shoe and a light-green sock, which were taken to Emig's office in San Jose for viewing by Mrs. Cohn, the Hart family friend from Stockton. She emerged after twenty minutes dabbing her eyes with a handkerchief.

On Tuesday, the grapplers brought up a fifth Shell Oil Company coupon book near the shoreline a thousand feet north of the bridge. Its stains could have been oil or blood or water discoloration.

About sixteen miles to the north, the much more impressive, high-level San Francisco-Oakland Bay Bridge was under construction. On Wednesday night a worker on that job gazed down from high above the water and noticed what seemed to be a floating body. Six other workers confirmed the sighting, and a major search operation was launched by San Francisco and Oakland police boats and airplanes. Nothing of importance was found—the searchers reluctantly concluding that the body, if such it was, had been carried away on the outbound tide.

More bloodstains, up to an inch in diameter, were discovered late Wednesday on the San Mateo Bridge parapet. From directly underneath them, a few minutes before midnight, grapplers brought up the third of the three concrete blocks that Thurmond had purchased. Still clinging to it after thirteen days of tidal action were strands of blond hair. These were sent to Dr. Frederick Proescher, the Santa Clara County criminologist and pathologist, for analysis. Deputies paid a discreet visit to the Hart home to obtain hairs from Brooke's hairbrush for comparison.

On Thursday, on one of the barnacle-encrusted pilings supporting the bridge, Henningsen and Mull made a grim discovery. Above the waterline, the barnacles were clawed and broken. Unquestionably they marked the place where the bleeding Brooke Hart, fighting desperately for life after casting off the blocks that were supposed to sink him, had clung to the piling until his grip failed. A diver worked long into the night combing the bay floor directly beneath, but without result.

As the days passed, the investigators remained troubled by the odd mystery in the wood-gatherers' report: Why had Ridley and Coley clearly heard Brooke Hart's calls for help, but not the shots that Thurmond had fired at Brooke in the water? It was a small inconsistency, but one which might be exploited in court to discredit the confessions.

Finally, on a hunch, Emig sent a team of deputies to the bridge to replicate the ballistics of the crime under atmospheric conditions approximating those of November 9. This experiment worked better than his simulation of Brooke's body. From the place where the bloodstains had been found on the bridge rail, one of the deputies shouted for help, as Brooke had, and was clearly heard at the spot where the Ridley and Coley had been working. Then he fired a pistol, similar to Thurmond's .41, back toward the shoreline, and that report carried strongly too. But when he turned the muzzle away from shore and fired downward as Thurmond had, the water soaked up the sound, and the men on shore heard nothing at all.

By now, everyone at the bridge site was sure the body was forever lost. Was the search a failure? Had the marathon of selfless effort gone for nought? Many who were imperfectly schooled in the law thought so, believing homicide could not be legally established without a corpse. Even the *Chronicle* shared this assumption, reporting on Thursday morning, "It is generally admitted that the murder angle of the case depends upon the finding of the body of young Hart."

Aboard the *Mermaid*, newly minted lawyer Marshall Hall knew better. At Stanford he had learned the distinction between a corpse and a corpus delicti. By now he felt that the prosecutors had enough evidence—the blocks, the wire, the hat, the shoe and sock, the strands of blond hair—to sustain a murder prosecution without a body, even if the confessions were recanted. So believing, Hall pulled the *Mermaid* off the line and sailed her back to Alviso.

District Attorney Thomas shared Hall's knowledge of the law and his opinion. Yes, he told reporters, recovering Brooke's body was desirable but not essential. He was certain he could obtain convictions whether or not Brooke was found.

Alex Hart would not accept the pessimism about the recovery of his boy's remains. On Thursday evening he went to his desk and composed a stilted, formal statement for release to the press:

> My sincere and earnest desire is to locate and recover the body of my son, Brooke L. Hart. . . .
> Therefore, with a full measure of appreciation for the splendid efforts of all who have thus far interested themselves in this search, I desire to offer at this time a reward of $500 for the recovery of the body.

Alex specified that the payment of the money, either to one person or a group, would be up to a committee consisting of Emig, Black, and the coroner of the county in which the body might be found. The sum he offered—half the amount that had been rumored five days earlier—was not niggardly. At the depth of the Great Depression, $500 was half a year's pay for many men.

15

Fury Rising

G. Logan Payne, the publisher of the *Evening News*, was still sulking because only a handful of readers had seen his "Human Devils" editorial—his outpouring of rage on the afternoon after Holmes and Thurmond were arrested. He had finished it so late that only the last few papers off his press had carried it. So now, two days later, he decided to run it again, in full. He filled a big block of Saturday's front page with it, under an editor's note saying it was reprinted in response to popular demand. Each reiterated phrase was a call to arms, crafted to inflame: "If mob violence could ever be justified it would be in a case like this. . . . It [the Hart family's grief] would have made you feel like going out and committing a lynching yourself."

Day by day now, the city's mood grew meaner. *Chronicle* reporter Leo Raridan had caught it the morning after the confessions.

"The word of the murder fell like a thunderbolt," he wrote, "and on the heels of the stunned realization came a wave of intense anger. Groups collected on the street, their faces grim. In hotel lobbies, cigar stands, people gathered to talk it over." In step with the anger marched fear, lust for vengeance, jitters, sullen suspicion, and paranoia.

Not least among the paranoids was a San Jose woman who, after comparing the "o's" in reproduced ransom notes in *True Detective* magazine, leaped to a conclusion that the Hart and Lindbergh kidnappers were the same. She fired off the first of three long letters, marked

"Personal," to apprise J. Edgar Hoover of her discovery, admonishing him to "please act secretly" on it.*

Hoover responded with a polite acknowledgment—which he would regret. The woman took it as her commission to forge ahead as his partner, on the trail of not just a kidnapper but a whole gang. She plunged into the case with the zeal of Nancy Drew, perceiving clues everywhere. Everyone became a suspect. She undertook a surreptitious surveillance program, shadowing people all over town and recording their license numbers, to be checked out with the Department of Motor Vehicles.

For reasons unexplained, she took down the license of a car she saw "circling around the business district about dark." It was a sedan, but the DMV mistakenly reported the number belonged to a roadster. "Will you please have this checked?" she instructed Hoover, giving him the name of the registered owner. "I believe it has a very definite bearing on the case."

Next the woman noticed a large automobile, perhaps a Packard, with either British Columbia (B.C.) or District of Columbia (D.C.) license plates. Four boys were riding in it, and as she watched, two of them "got out and were acting funny." Certainly this was suspicious, she confided to her FBI pen pal, because she had read about a Packard seen in New Jersey the night the Lindbergh baby vanished.

Near the car she had observed a "heavyset, swarthy man with a bleached blonde," and she deemed them "most significant." She had also seen a "fleshy light-haired man" in the phone booth in Tuggle's Drug Store, from which one of the aborted ransom calls to Alex Hart had been placed. It was obvious, she told Hoover, that this man was "the head of the ransom plot that included Thurmond and Holmes."

"I believe that if you will take time to consider the contents of this letter, you will be fully repaid for the search," she assured the FBI chief, adding a mild complaint, "It does not seem right that one woman should bear the burden of it when the government has so many to help."

Alas, a few days later the woman wrote again, confessing to Hoover that her investigative zeal had led her astray. She had just discovered that the Packard with the D.C. plates, which had worried her so, belonged to a former local congressman, Arthur Free.

She had not given up, however. Now she was trying to find out if

*The woman's name was still blacked out when the FBI released the letters fifty years later under the Freedom of Information Act.

Holmes or Thurmond had passed any of the Lindbergh ransom bills in San Jose, but her banker and the post office were uncooperative about telling her their serial numbers. Would Hoover please look into this "while everything is quiet and these people are not suspecting they might be watched?"

The woman was also curious about a certain run-down apartment house in her neighborhood. The owners had begun expensive repairs just after the Lindbergh ransom was paid. Very suspicious.

She had never believed the Lindbergh baby was dead, the woman informed Hoover, and twice lately near Fourth and Julian streets she had observed a short man, "either a Dain [sic] or a Swede," with a "pale baby of the type and size of Lindy." Having seen some "moovies" of the Lindbergh baby earlier, she wrote that the infant in San Jose had the same "peculiar twirk of the eyes."

The tormented Hoover responded that her observations were receiving "appropriate consideration."

An important ingredient of San Jose's obsession with the Hart case was grief. Genuine grief, for thousands of San Joseans had known Brooke Hart, and as *Chronicle* reporter Raridan put it, "His ready smile and wide acquaintance had stippled the community with friends."

Another *Chronicle* writer, Carolyn Anspacher, found that the grief "hung like a pall over Hart's Department Store." Of the 200 employees she wrote, "Their movements were automatic, their speech subdued, their throats tight with the strain of holding back emotions. Many wept openly and were not ashamed."

On Sunday, November 19, prayers were offered in most San Jose churches for the repose of Brooke's soul and peace for his family. Several of the pastors, in wrathful sermons, anathematized the taking of life for gold.

From throughout the nation and abroad, messages of condolence continued to arrive at the Hart mansion. From France came a cablegram signed "Clemenceau," a son of the World War I premier.

Nowhere—neither in street talk nor news reportage nor official action—was the legal presumption of innocence accorded even lip service. The confessions of the prisoners were taken at face value; prospective efforts to repudiate or mitigate them were dismissed out of hand.

The San Francisco District Federation of Women's Clubs called unanimously for speedy punishment. This put the San Jose Women's Club on an uncomfortable spot, for Holmes's mother and one of Thurmond's sisters were among its members. Nevertheless, the San Jose group adopted a companion resolution commending the police and urging "swift, sure justice" for the murderers. It was softened only by a "whereas" clause expressing sympathy for their families.

News publisher Payne, his fury unabated, thundered away in another editorial on Tuesday, November 21:

Let's Show Speed!

Holmes and Thurmond, having seen their lawyers, are already seeking to repudiate their confessions. In spite of this, the necessary legal steps should be gone through swiftly, and they should be tried, sentenced, and hanged in the shortest possible length of time. . . . One reason crime has the upper hand in America is the slowness and uncertainty of our trials. Let's set a world speed record in this case.

Lynch talk was cheap, but readers of Tuesday's *Chronicle* learned that the vigilante activity in Santa Clara County had solid substance. The newspaper did not sensationalize its report, which was buried on page 4, possibly because the crucial material was presented without quotable sources. The reporter wrote:

It was revealed that definite reports of a movement among Santa Clara groups to take the law into their own hands and deal swiftly with the accused killers had been received during the last 24 hours from numerous sources. . . .

"If you try to get those prisoners out of the San Francisco City Prison, they'll never reach San Jose alive," was the gist of one message known to have been received by Sheriff William J. Emig and some of his deputies.

Some of the more hot-headed among the leaders of the lynch movement, it became known, even advised trying to get the prisoners from the city prison.

Anger was especially rife among Brooke Hart's friends at Santa Clara University, and the school newspaper, *The Santa Clara*, was moved to run a formal denial that the lynch plot was being nurtured on the SCU campus. Yet such an allegation would become a lasting part of the Hart case folklore. Fever ran so high that Father Cyril

Robert Kavanagh, who taught philosophy, warned that any student who attended a lynching and by personal will approved it would be morally guilty of murder, a sin avenged by Heaven.

The same edition of *The Santa Clara* carried an editorial headed "Prompt But Just Retribution," which, although written by a student, was taken to reflect the stance of the school's Jesuit fathers. After renouncing lynch law as a "horrible travesty on justice," the writer declared the lives of Brooke Hart's murderers must nonetheless be forfeited, and asked:

> Why should it take longer than two weeks for these culprits to be tried, convicted, and executed? In England and Canada that would be considered ample time for the state to perform its duty.

Bill Emig did not need the *Chronicle*, *The Santa Clara*, or any other newspaper to tell him his town was a tinderbox. Threats and warnings were pouring into his office by the score—by mail, telephone, and word of mouth. So far, despite all the headaches, the Hart case had been a personal political triumph for the first-term sheriff, who like Thomas would be facing the voters for reelection in 1934. A *Mercury Herald* headline the day after the suspects' arrests read "Hart Kidnapping Solution Adds to Emig's Laurels," and the article declared that few California peace officers had "acquitted themselves more creditably."

Emig was acutely aware that the lynching threat contained the seeds of his downfall. To lose his prisoners to a mob would be a disaster; yet, the business and political establishment, whose support he needed, was heavily enlisted in the forces of drumhead justice. He had reason to be thankful that Holmes and Thurmond were fifty miles away in San Francisco, and he was in no hurry to bring them back.

Sharing his reluctance to have them returned were the eighty other prisoners in his jail. The crowd outside made them nervous, and the lynch talk terrified them. No inmate was more frightened than Ray Sousa, whose murder trial was currently in progress in the courthouse across the alley.

Sousa was a twenty-three-year-old Portuguese ranch hand who, back in August, had been caught poaching on Charlie Kuhn's ranch in the hills near Evergreen, southeast of San Jose. In the ensuing altercation he had shot and killed Kuhn's foreman, Leonard Ramonda. He admitted the shooting, claiming self-defense, but was charged with first-degree murder, and the state was asking the death penalty. Kuhn was a popular and influential rancher, and feeling against Sousa was running high. Neither in brutality nor premeditation nor evil purpose did Sousa's crime compare with the murder of Brooke Hart, but he was under no illusion that a lynch mob bent on redress of homicide would heed such petty distinctions.

But Emig, his own wishes and those of his prisoners notwithstanding, could not stall forever about returning Holmes and Thurmond to Santa Clara County. Once he signed a complaint, they were entitled to arraignment within a "reasonable time," generally held to be forty-eight hours. Normally they would be arraigned in the justice court in the hall of justice, a homely sandstone building about 100 yards north of the jail, diagonally to the rear of the main courthouse. The sheriff, however, told reporters he might have them arraigned in their cells instead, to avoid exposing them to a hostile crowd during an open-air transfer. This was so radical that the *News* took pains to assure readers it was not illegal.

Emig's wish to move slowly was shared by Herbert S. Bridges, the deputy district attorney to whom Thomas had assigned the major burden of preparing the state's case.

"I'm going to take every legal delay with the arraignment," he said. Bridges's concern, however, was with tactics rather than security; he still hoped for the recovery of Brooke Hart's body, to strengthen the state's position, before he had to go into court.

Thomas, formally announcing his intention to demand the death penalty for both defendants (a foregone conclusion), resolved to use every advantage the law gave him. He was wrestling with the tactical question of whether to seek indictments by the grand jury or, alternatively, to proceed on the basis of a complaint signed by the sheriff. By coincidence, Santa Clara County had just empaneled its new, 1933–34 grand jury only five days after the arrests. Consisting of eighteen men and one woman nominated by the superior court judges, it represented exclusively the conservative agricultural and mercantile establishment. An insurance broker, C. L. Snyder, was the foreman.

By law, grand jury proceedings took place behind closed doors, with no cross-examination of witnesses. By choosing the indictment route, Thomas could take his case directly to trial in the superior court, avoiding early disclosure of his evidence and strategy at a preliminary hearing in the justice court. An incidental benefit would be to eliminate the need for transporting the kidnappers back and forth along the exposed 300-foot route between the jail and the hall of justice.

In the jurisdictional morass of the case, prosecutors of all agencies reached agreement on a quadruple strategy to eliminate the slightest chance that Holmes or Thurmond could beat the rap, either by acquittal, dismissal, or legal maneuver: In Santa Clara County, Thomas would bring the main charge of kidnapping, invoking the new Little Lindbergh Law, tougher than the murder statute. In Alameda County, where Brooke's body would presumably turn up if found at all, Earl Warren would stand by with murder charges in case the San Jose prosecution blew up. As further backup, U.S. Attorney McPike would have the suspects indicted on at least four federal extortion counts. Finally, to forestall any effort to free them on habeas corpus before the Hart case charges were filed, Thomas stood ready to sock them with other kidnapping and robbery charges arising from the Michel and Scott hijackings.

If the prosecution was in ferment, the defense was in disarray. The murder partners, who from the start had tried to stick each other with the main guilt, continued to go their separate ways. It was now clear they would enter the courtroom as bitter foes. By conicidence, both men's lawyers showed up at the San Francisco City Prison at the same hour on Sunday, November 19, but they saw their clients separately and did not meet.

Ira Langdon, the Stockton attorney Evelyn Holmes had retained for her husband, appeared at the prison at midday.

"Have any charges been filed against my client yet?" he asked.

"No," the jailer replied. "We've just got him 'en route to San Jose.' "

Langdon asked to see Holmes, who was wolfing down a plate of pork and beans in his cell.

"Tell him to wait till I finish my lunch," Holmes instructed the jailer, and went on eating.

Having already disclosed Holmes's intention to repudiate his confession, Langdon dodged questioning by newsmen.

Thurmond was visited Sunday by two sisters and his brother Roy, bringing with them Napoleon J. "Nap" Menard, a feisty young San Jose lawyer who had achieved recognition defending a cop killer. He was closeted with Harold for an hour.

"I don't know just now what my move will be," Menard told reporters afterward, in an uncharacteristically restrained statement. "I believe I should wait until after some of the feeling dies down."

The Hart home, with its echoes of the Petit Trianon, was one of the most handsome homes in San Jose. (*Alex Hart, Jr.*)

The Hart family, gathered c. 1927. Left to right, Aleese, Jeannette, Alex, Sr. (in cap), Alex, Jr., Miriam, Nettie, and Brooke. (*Alex Hart, Jr.*)

The last portrait of Brooke Leopold Hart. (*Hart Family Collection*)

Jane Hammond, a student at San Jose State and Brooke's girlfriend at the time of the kidnapping. (*Delores Hammond*)

A student-sales promotional event at Hart's Department Store, probably in the late 1920s. Left to right, an unidentified man, Ray Renwick, Pearl Humphreys, Brooke Hart, and Louis Rossi. (*Louis A. Rossi*)

Jack Holmes. (San Francisco
Chronicle)

Evelyn Holmes with her
children, Joyce and David,
Christmas 1930. (*David
Holmes*)

Gertrude Estensen, the
"other woman" in Jack
Holmes's life. (San Jose Mercury News)

Harold Thurmond, af-
ter his arrest, with Sheriff William J. Emig (left)
and FBI agent Reed E.
Vetterli. (San Francisco
Chronicle)

San Francisco police sergeant Walter Descalso displays a concrete block and wire retrieved from San Francisco Bay after Brooke Hart's murder. (San Jose Mercury News)

California governor James "Sunny Jim" Rolph, Jr., whose inflammatory pronouncements before and after the lynching won him censure—and applause. (*California State Library*)

Duck hunter Leonard Dalve, with the body of Brooke Hart, on a San Francisco Bay mud flat. Fourteen hours after the body was discovered, the storming of the jail house began. (San Francisco Chronicle)

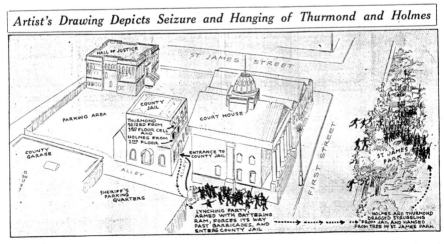

An illustration that appeared in the *San Francisco Call-Bulletin* shortly after the lynching, though out of scale, shows the route the lynchers took. The courthouse dome, which collapsed in 1931, is an anachronism.

An aerial view of San Jose in the 1930s. City Hall and the Police Headquarters are at bottom, just right of center; in the extreme lower right is the Plaza Garage. Hart's Department Store is the long, low white building at far left center, and above it, just blocks away, is St. James Park, the site of the lynching. (San Jose Mercury News)

As photo flashes popped, the mob used a battering ram to break through the hastily secured jail-house doors. (San Jose Mercury Herald *photo by Loris Gardner*)

Thurmond's pants were ripped off by an onlooker. (*Photo by Wilbur Dorn, courtesy of Bob Caya*)

The stripped body of Jack Holmes. (*Photo by Wilbur Dorn, courtesy of Bob Caya*)

The hanging of Harold Thurmond. (San Jose Mercury News)

The mixed reactions to the atrocity: *Baltimore Sun* cartoonist Edmund Duffy won a Pulitzer Prize with an antilynching cartoon, while in California this booklet of "official" photographs of the lynching, complete with a quote from Governor Rolph, was sold to tourists and residents alike.

A reporter asked Roy Thurmond, the pastor from Chico, if he thought Harold was demented.

"Well, a man would have to be either drunk or crazy to do a thing like this, wouldn't he?" the minister answered.

Thurmond had a tearful twenty-minute reunion with Roy and the sisters talking through a wire screen. When it was over, the sisters were outraged that for security reasons, Harold had been denied a razor to shave. "They're trying to make him look like a hardened criminal, which he is not," one of them protested.

The next day Roy Thurmond returned to bring his brother a Bible, which Harold later read for a time.

"What chapter?" a reporter asked the policeman guarding him.

The officer said he wasn't close enough to see.

On Tuesday, November 21, the sheriff's investigators further tightened their case against the suspects. Acting on a tip, they talked to one of Thurmond's neighbors in Campbell, a roofer named E. A. Runnels. The anonymous tipster had heard him say, several days before Thurmond and Holmes were arrested, "A Campbell man who doesn't live very far from here has something to do with the Hart kidnapping."

Under questioning, Runnels explained that he sometimes hung out at the service station where Thurmond had worked. One night a few weeks earlier, before Brooke Hart had vanished, a car had driven into the station with two occupants who engaged Thurmond in earnest conversation.

"When you fellows are ready, I'll take this guy for a ride," Thurmond had called to the men as they left.

Here it was again—the nagging suggestion of at least one other accomplice. If one of the men in the car was Holmes, who was the other?

Nebulous hints of additional accomplices had been cropping up since the investigation began, but in the main Emig had ignored or discounted them. Who were the two "well-dressed men" who had parked their Buick in the alley alongside the department store at 5:45 each afternoon for ten days before the kidnapping? Interest in them had vanished with the arrests of the suspects in custody, whose cars turned out to be a Chevrolet and a Pontiac. Who was the "old man with white hair," who according to some reports had joined Holmes and Thurmond in their orchard rendezvous?

Each time they were asked, the suspects denied having other partners, and the sheriff was happy to take their word for it. He was tying up the Hart case in a neat package, and he did not want anyone yanking on the string.

The press, preoccupied with the confessions, the search for the body, and the lynch talk, had not seriously challenged the sheriff on the matter of other possible accomplices. The newspapers had not known (because Emig had not told them) about Delphine Silveria's tale of seeing five men, not two, transfer a youth from one car to another near her Piedmont Road farmhouse. She had described the second car as a big, dark sedan "about the size of a Buick or a Dodge," but no one had tried to link it with the Buick seen in the alley.

Now, after Emig had been sitting on the Silveria story for eight days, the talkative U.S. Attorney McPike in San Francisco spilled it. Chatting with reporters Tuesday evening, he told them most of what Mrs. Silveria had said and declared he believed it. He said a "nationwide search" was under way for three additional suspects. The disclosure set off a reporters' stampede to Mrs. Silveria's farmhouse, where she and her daughter, who until now had honored Emig's admonition to secrecy, told their story anew with total consistency. It was splashed across the front pages along with their pictures.

Emig was furious. Now he dug his heels in deeper than ever on his assertion that Holmes and Thurmond had acted by themselves. He belittled Mrs. Silveria as an unreliable observer.

Although it was not apparent at the time, the tiff between McPike and Emig put Vetterli on an uncomfortable spot. As the federal prosecutor, McPike was his natural ally, but the FBI agent had a close working relationship with the sheriff and did not want to jeopardize it. When reporters came to him, he threw in with Emig.

"I dislike taking issue with Mr. McPike," Vetterli said, "but I place little credence in Mrs. Silveria's story. It has been completely checked, and we could find nothing to it."

Vetterli's comment to the press was totally at odds, however, with what he had been reporting confidentially to J. Edgar Hoover. On November 13, the day Mrs. Silveria first told her story at the sheriff's office, he had wired the director, "DEVELOPMENTS TODAY INDICATE HART KIDNAPPED BY FIVE MEN DRIVING LARGE BLACK SEDAN BEARING CALIFORNIA LICENSE." In a followup memo he reported, "Close questioning of Mrs. Silveria indicated that she was not endeavoring to furnish any fabricated story, but was apparently telling the truth. . . . Efforts were made to confuse her, but she sticks splendidly to her story." Likewise, Vetterli deemed her daughter, Isabelle, "a very bright and intelligent young girl." He added an additional appraisal betraying his own bias if not the institutional bias of the FBI: "Mrs. Silveria is a Portuguese, but rather intelligent."

As sensational as the Silverias' tale was, events would swiftly push it deep into the shadows. It remains, however, a disquieting footnote to the Hart case. Vetterli's strong belief in the story stayed hidden from public view for fifty years until released under the Freedom of Information Act in 1983.

The San Jose Lions Club had scored a coup by persuading Bill Emig, currently the most newsworthy man in Northern California, to be its luncheon speaker on Wednesday, November 22. The sheriff, a member of the club himself, knew that most in his audience wanted Holmes and Thurmond strung up. Very likely some of the vigilantes planning such an event were present. Emig began on a modest note, minimizing his own role in the kidnappers' capture and commending the work of the FBI, Chief Black, and the city police. Next he gave the Lions a little of the flavor of the search for Brooke's body, going on out on the bay. Then, choosing his words carefully, Emig struck a fine balance between reassurance, warning, and appeal:

> We are determined that the kidnappers be dealt with for their crime under the law and in the courts of this county. The atrocity of the crime has aroused the whole community, we know, but we are prepared to resist any attempt of those who may propose to take the law into their own hands. . . . I bespeak your cooperation and ask that you urge the cooperation of others to the same end. The law is adequate to deal with this crime. The most effective deterrent to crimes of this nature will be prompt and vigorous prosecution under the law, and that we are determined to have.

Emig did not tell the Lions that even as he spoke, his jail was receiving additional tear gas canisters, rifles, revolvers, shotguns, and riot guns, plus hundreds of rounds of ammunition, in readiness for a siege. He took comfort in the knowledge that his nineteenth-century bastille was built like a fortress, with brick walls up to three feet thick.

* * *

It was a quarter to two when the sheriff got back to his office, after his speech. On his desk was a message that Fred Thomas had called. "Urgent," it said. It took Emig only a minute to return the call.

"Yeah, Fred?"

"McPike's gotten the jump on us, Bill,"

"Oh?"

"Yeah, he took the case to the federal grand jury in San Francisco this morning. The kidnappers were indicted less than an hour ago. Seven counts of extortion each, under the Lindbergh Act."

"We'd better get going then."

The federal indictments specified, against each suspect, three counts of using the mails to obtain ransom, three of using the mails to threaten bodily harm, and one of conspiracy "with other persons unknown." Already newsmen were conjecturing that the latter count connoted official knowledge of additional accomplices. The charges carried maximum punishment of 122 years in prison and a $40,000 fine for each kidnapper. Bail for each was fixed at $50,000.

To reporters, McPike reiterated that he did not intend to process these charges, but to hold them in abeyance pending the state prosecution. But Thomas and Emig, determined to bring the suspects to justice in San Jose, were not placing blind trust in that. Time had run out on the idea of seeking state indictments from the new county grand jury, which had not yet held even its organizational meeting. Emig would have to sign the kidnapping complaint himself.

"I've got the complaint ready. It's over in the Justice Court waiting for your signature," Thomas told the sheriff.

"Right."

It took Emig little more than a minute to walk to the chambers of Justice of the Peace Chester W. Moore in the hall of justice, where he signed the one-page document. In wooden legal language, it charged Holmes and Thurmond with violation of Section 200 of the California Penal Code, in that they did "willfully, unlawfully and feloniously seize, abduct, conceal, kidnap, and carry away an individual, to-wit, Brooke Hart, a human being, with intent to hold and detain said Brooke Hart and thereby to commit extortion and to exact from the relatives and friends of said Brooke Hart money and other valuable things."

No sooner had Emig scrawled his signature at the bottom of the complaint than Moore issued felony warrants for Holmes and Thurmond, refusing to fix bail.

At about the same hour, two United States marshals showed up at the San Francisco City Prison. Armed with bench warrants issued pursuant to the federal indictments, they demanded custody of the kidnappers.

"Sorry," the jailer told them. He had orders from Captain Dullea to release the pair to no one but Emig, who had brought them to San Francisco in the first place.

For reporters covering the case, the fast-breaking developments lent new urgency to a question they had wondered about for the past five days: When would Thurmond and Holmes be returned to San Jose? They asked Emig once more. He gave them a quizzical stare and said nothing.

IV

RETRIBUTION

16

In the Grim Bastille

A little after 10:30 Wednesday night, eight hours after Emig had signed the complaint, Holmes and Thurmond were removed from their eighth-floor cells in the San Francisco City Prison. In shackles they were led to a little elevator and taken to the garage below, where four cars waited, each equipped with a machine gun and shotguns and stocked with tear gas.

The convoy had assembled in strict secrecy. Reporters had been tipped that the sheriff intended to bring his prisoners home, but they had agreed to withhold the story until the transfer was complete.

At 10:45 the cars pulled away from the prison and snaked southward in the dark, through the peninsula suburbs, on the lightly traveled road to San Jose. Thurmond rode in the back seat of the lead car, between two deputies, with Emig driving and Chief Black beside him in front. Next came an automobile carrying three San Francisco police inspectors. Holmes was squeezed into the rear of the third vehicle, between two San Jose police officers. Another San Francisco car, with two more inspectors, brought up the rear. All the officers carried side arms.

When the caravan reached Santa Clara, about three miles from its destination, Emig pulled off the highway and phoned ahead to make certain there was no breach of security. All was well. The convoy resumed its trip and rolled up outside the great steel-clad doors of the Santa Clara County Jail just before midnight. Reporters and cameramen stood off to the side, and only two or three other persons were present. As the cars stopped, the officers riding with the prisoners leaped out with sawed-off shotguns drawn and gas grenades ready.

Thurmond was sobbing as he emerged from the lead car and was whisked inside the building. Holmes, retaining his swagger, glared at the newsmen and grunted, "Huh! More damned publicity."

Precisely at twelve o'clock the suspects were locked in their new cells—accommodations whose former tenants' names were household words in the county. Thurmond was given a third-floor room previously occupied by David Lamson, a Stanford University Press executive convicted of bashing in his wife's skull and now on San Quentin's death row.* Holmes was placed in a second floor cell, the former quarters of Howard Springer,† whom Emig had sent to prison for stabbing his aunt to death. Both cells had newly changed locks.

In the week since the suspects had been caught, the *Mercury Herald* had been San Jose's foremost voice for moderation in dealing with them. Moderation in this case was a relative term; all it meant was that the newspaper did not want them lynched. Its position, which doubtless reflected its readers' consensus, was that the two men should be hanged as soon as possible, but after a trial, not a necktie party. Thursday morning's issue carried an editorial headed "Let There Be Reason," but it could not have been timed for less effect. The news that the kidnappers were back in town filled the paper, totally submerging the editorial. Anyway, the town was in no mood for reason.

Outside Emig's office window, in the alleyway separating the courthouse from the jail, the throng grew during the morning. In itself, this was neither surprising nor alarming; like every city in 1933, San Jose had hundreds of idle men who gravitated to any source of diversion, companionship, or excitement. This was not a mean crowd, Emig decided.

Within the press corps rumor ran rife, however. First came a report that a third arrest was due momentarily. Then, after Emig slammed shut the jail's doors and mounted a machine gun inside (precautions unprecedented in anyone's memory), word circulated that a lynching party was already on the way. Orders came down canceling all deputies' leaves and trebling the jail's defense force. When reinforcements arrived a few minutes after noon, the doors were opened only a few inches to admit them.

---

*Lamson's conviction was overturned on appeal, and he was ultimately freed. Later he had a productive career writing for national magazines.
†Fictitious name.

The crowd doubled in size during the afternoon. By nightfall it had reached 200 and was still growing. Visitors were admitted until 11:00 P.M., subject to close scrutiny, but after that hour only deputies passed through the doors, after being identified through a peephole. Newsmen were denied their customary easy entry.

With Holmes and Thurmond back in San Jose, the reporters began getting heat from their city desks to find out when and where they would be arraigned. No one had the answer. Only one thing was clear: neither the state nor the defense wanted to rush things.

Late Thursday afternoon J. Oscar Goldstein, a new attorney for Harold Thurmond, showed up at the jail to meet his client. Goldstein was from the little Northern California town of Chico, where Roy Thurmond, who had retained him, was the pastor of the Assembly of God. Nap Menard, the lawyer previously hired by Harold's sisters, had faded from the scene.

After talking with Thurmond for ninety minutes, Goldstein told the newsmen he would stay on the case despite a tide of opposition from people in San Jose. The implication was that Menard, who lived and practiced in San Jose, had been unable or unwilling to take the heat. Goldstein wanted to delay his client's arraignment at least until Monday; not only did he need time to prepare, but also, he wanted to let the city "cool down."

"Will you use an insanity defense?" a reporter inquired.

"First I have to find out if my client is insane," the lawyer parried.

District Attorney Thomas was happy to accommodate Goldstein about delaying the arraignment. Still hoping Brooke Hart's body would be found, he agreed to put off the proceedings for at least another week.

Alerted by Goldstein's remarks, Emig and Bridges moved quickly to knock any insanity defense on the head. To examine Thurmond they brought in a noted psychiatrist, Dr. J. M. Scanland, the superintendent of Agnews State Hospital, an asylum for the insane north of Santa Clara. Thurmond, just finishing a large wedge of apple pie, cowered as the doctor entered his cell, a large one some fifteen feet square. As Scanland began his questioning, the prisoner sat with downcast eyes, making barely audible responses.

"Tell me how you got here," the doctor asked, as Emig took a seat on the prisoner's cot, listening attentively.

"My brother told me not to talk about the case."

Thurmond's reluctance took Scanland by surprise, not to mention the sheriff. Nonstop talking had been Harold's delight until now. Probably his new lawyer, as well as his brother, was responsible for his new attitude.

"That's perfectly all right." The doctor quickly backed off and switched to general, nonincriminating inquires, made in a quiet, casual manner. Seeming greatly relieved, Thurmond gradually loosened up, and most of his answers were straightforward.

Reporters intercepted the psychiatrist as he left the jail after half an hour. Was Thurmond crazy?

"No, his responses to my questions were prompt and lucid," Scanland replied. "They were those of an entirely normal person. He struck me as a man almost sick with fear and remorse, but sane." Remembering the pie, the doctor added an afterthought: "Regardless of how he might have felt, there was nothing wrong with his appetite."

To corroborate Scanland's opinion, the prosecutors also asked "Doc" Proescher to interview the kidnappers.

Dr. Frederick L. Proescher, a well-known courthouse character, was a large man—a ramrod-straight, militaristic Prussian—who wore many hats. The newspapers customarily referred to him as a "world-famous pathologist and criminologist," and his presumed expertise in several other disciplines was often invoked in criminal cases too, always for the state. He spoke with a German accent which he used to good effect on the witness stand. Under questioning by friendly prosecutors, he had excellent command of English, but during cross-examination by the defense, his accent would grow increasingly thicker and more guttural to the point of unintelligibility.

Proescher was deemed a specialist in forensic evidence; it was to him that Emig had turned over the blond hairs found clinging to the concrete block from the bay. By virtue of a stint of epilepsy research at the Agnews hospital, he also held high repute as an "alienist"— that being a loose generic term for someone deemed qualified to distinguish legally between the sane and the insane. Years before, Proescher had established a ghoulish alliance with law enforcement. At Agnews he had presided over a laboratory full of pickled human brains, and from time to time his experiments were impeded by a shortage of cadavers. He routinely solved the problem by putting out an SOS to the highway patrol for a "fresh young head." The patrol always delivered.

It was in his alienist capacity that Proescher was now called upon to examine Holmes and Thurmond. True to the district attorney's hope and confident expectation, he concluded that both were "perfectly normal."

"Holmes was the more intelligent of the two," he reported. "His motive was clearly for the money. . . . Thurmond had no motive; he was merely the tool of Holmes's intellect."

While the doctors were probing the kidnappers' psyches, Ray Sousa's murder trial had been building toward its climax in the courthouse across the alley. On Wednesday the jury had heard an impassioned clemency plea by the young farm worker's lawyer, Elmer Jensen. Thursday morning had been filled with the district attorney's closing argument, demanding the noose, and the jurors had begun deliberations at twenty minutes past noon. Almost twenty-eight hours later, late Friday afternoon, they returned a verdict of manslaughter, carrying a maximum sentence of ten years in San Quentin.

With luck, trespasser Sousa might even get off with a short jail term and probation for taking the life of Leonard Ramonda. But Jensen, who had sought a clear acquittal, announced he would seek a new trial anyway, and failing in that, take an appeal to the state supreme court. Sousa was returned across the crowded alley to the uneasy confines of Emig's heavily guarded bastille to await sentencing set for Tuesday morning, November 28.

The search for Brooke Hart's body, a heroic effort draining the manpower and money of four counties and the State of California, could not go on forever. Moreover, as the weekend of November 25–26 approached, a special problem loomed. On Saturday in Palo Alto, Stanford University would host the "Big Game" against the University of California, and the San Mateo Bridge was the most direct route there from the UC campus in Berkeley. All day the span would carry a heavy traffic of students and boosters, making impossible the continued direction of the search activity from its deck. At sundown Friday it was announced that the official search was being abandoned.

"We are convinced that the body of Hart is not near the bridge," said San Mateo County Sheriff J. J. McGrath. "It now appears he struggled free of at least one of the weights fastened to him and perhaps the second one also. If this is true his body probably floated away from the bridge and may now be anywhere in the bay."

So on Saturday the orderly search effort of the past nine days gave way to a free-for-all of ill-equipped amateurs tramping the shorelines and grappling in San Francisco Bay's mud, shallows, and depths.

Saturday morning's *Chronicle* did nothing to calm the restiveness of Emig's prisoners. On Tuesday the newspaper had handled its thin report of an organized lynch movement gingerly on an inside page, but now the story was beefed up and moved to the front page under the byline of reporter Royce Brier. There was still no attribution other than "reliable sources," but Brier wrote without equivocation that an "old-time California vigilante committee" was forming. He presented much plausible detail:

> Already between 60 and 70 San Jose citizens have signed [a] secret agreement and stand ready to take "adequate action" against the kidnappers and slayers of the San Jose youth. . . .
>
> The committee was formed with the greatest care and secrecy. Only citizens whom leaders of the movement felt could be implicitly trusted were enlisted in the committee organization.
>
> Working quietly, the leaders in the movement approached likely candidates and sounded them out.
>
> If the candidate evinced sufficient interest, he was given a password with instructions to see "so-and-so" at a certain place at a specified hour. If he passed inspection at the second meeting, he was then sent to a third man, who presented him with a written agreement to sign.
>
> The agreement in itself is ostensibly innocuous and pledges the signers merely to see justice done in the Brooke Hart kidnapping and murder.
>
> It is understood that no action will be taken by the committee, however, unless and until the body of the slain youth is recovered. This precaution leaders feel is absolutely necessary before any action by the committee could be justified in the eyes of the public.
>
> Details of the committee organization have been carefully kept from William J. Emig, the Santa Clara County sheriff, although talk of a "necktie party" is coming more and more into the open on San Jose streets.

So here was a grand conspiracy of homicide in the heart of Emig's territory, common knowledge to his peers and even to an out-of-town reporter. Yet the knowledge was being withheld from the sheriff by conspirators who were his friends, supporters, and usually his allies. There could be only two reasons for this: to shield the conspirators and to afford Emig what a later generation of politicians would call "plausible deniability."

Even as Brier's story was hitting the streets, the vigilantes were meeting anew—not all together, but in small cells. At that point their plan, as Emig feared, was to strike when the kidnappers were taken out of the jail for arraignment.

"We intended to mask and to take the two from their guards as they made their way to court," said one of them later. "We were going to whisk them out in the country, talk to them a short time for additional details of their confessions, and then hang them."

Who were the vigilante leaders? Not the town ruffians.

Fifty years later Louis Rossi, who was invited "not once but several times" to join the cabal but refused, said, "They were men from all walks of life. There were students from various universities; there were men from various fraternal organizations; there was no one particular group. . . . They were all friends of Brooke Hart."

Ten to twelve men, most of them younger than the thirty-five-year-old Rossi, attended most of the meetings. Rossi absolved the University of Santa Clara of orchestrating the conspiracy. It "definitely" came into being off campus, he said, while not ruling out the participation of SCU students as individuals. Apart from their convoluted pledging procedure, mainly designed to weed out informers and the faint-hearted, the vigilantes made little serious effort to keep their enterprise secret.

"All 'inside' San Jose knew of it, and knew the names of most of the pledge-signers," Brier wrote.

Rocky Santoro, then a truck driver and later a *San Jose Mercury News* photographer, was tuned in on the preparations.

"I knew it [a lynching] was going to happen," he recalled. "They had the word out—a bunch of businessmen downtown, the Emig gang, the politicians. It was just rolling, rolling, rolling."

Another who knew was Joe Colla, a thirteen-year-old schoolboy who had a downtown shoeshine route. His elite clientèle included the courthouse crowd, the sheriff, a lot of lawyers including Louis Oneal, most of the First Street merchants, and the pimps, bookies, and gamblers on Post Street. They all talked freely in front of him and even used him to carry messages. Now, as the boy watched little groups of his clients repairing quietly to the Oyster Loaf and Maggi's restaurants and to the Elks Club, he understood fully the grim business they were conducting. Otto Hellwig, an iron foundry owner and political insider, told him exactly what was in store for Holmes and Thurmond three days before it happened.

Long afterward, from the vantage point of retirement after a long career as a San Jose city councilman, Colla remembered, "It was all over the street that they were going to lynch those guys. You know, the storekeepers would tell their employees. It was just like a loud-speaker going over."

But San Joseans who were not insiders and did not read the *Chronicle*—and that was most of them—had little inkling that the lynch talk was more than idle gossip. The San Jose papers were keeping the lid on. The *News* reported vague "mutterings of lynch plans . . . in stores and pool rooms and on street corners," but with no backup. The cautious *Mercury Herald*, on this very Saturday when the *Chronicle* was detailing the conspiracy, lamely told its readers, "Faint rumblings of a possible lynch plot persisted yesterday, but nothing definite could be uncovered." Like the sheriff, the *Mercury Herald* was being kept in the dark by the local gentry.

Publicly, Emig belittled the reports of a disciplined lynch movement, professing total confidence in the safety of his prisoners. Repeatedly, since Holmes and Thurmond had been returned to San Jose, Reed Vetterli had offered FBI help for their protection, but the sheriff had declined it. His private attitude, however, was not so sanguine. The ubiquitous Al Jones was chatting with him in the jail yard about ten o'clock Saturday morning when a deputy came out of the building with a message.

"Sheriff, the governor is on the phone."

Emig had been trying to get through to Governor Rolph in Sacramento for a couple of hours, seeking assurance that the National Guard would be ready to defend his jail if need be. He excused himself and took the call in the jail office, as Jones watched through a glass partition.

This was the same Al Jones who, a decade earlier, had dined at Lillie Thurmond's table while courting her boarder, Natalie, and talked about racing cars with her dullard teenage son, Harold. It was the same Jones who in the mid-1920s had almost gotten himself brained repossessing Jack Holmes's automobile. Since that time he had become the ultimate political hanger-on, gravitating to holders of power both in San Jose and Sacramento and making himself useful wherever he went. While working in the state treasurer's office he had befriended Rolph and was soon being invited along on the governor's out-of-town trips as a sort of court jester. In San Jose he was politically ambivalent—a friend of both Emig and his hated predecessor, George Lyle, who had issued him a special deputy's badge.

Watching through the plate glass as Emig talked with Rolph, Jones could hear neither end of the conversation, but after hanging up, the sheriff said, "Well, Al, I can't expect any help from *him*."

Later that day the governor received and rejected out of hand a second appeal—from another source with vastly different motivation—for National Guard assistance.

Maurice Holmes, the shaken father of cocky Jack, had decided his son needed a more aggressive lawyer than Ira Langdon, the Stockton attorney retained by Evelyn. He went to see Vincent Hallinan, a fiery young barrister in San Francisco. In Hallinan's office, Maurice produced a packet of small bills totaling $10,000—a stupendous sum for a man of ordinary means to have scraped together in 1933—and offered it as a retainer for his son's defense. Hallinan accepted the case and placed the money in his office safe. His first move was to pick up his phone and place a call to Rolph.

"Governor," he said when Sunny Jim came on the line, "I have been retained to represent Jack Holmes in San Jose. As you know there's a lynching threat down there, and if there is violence, I want my client protected. We may need the militia."

"I won't accommodate you, Mr. Hallinan. If they lynch those fellows, I'll pardon the lynchers," Rolph retorted.

"Well, that's a hell of a thing for the governor of a state to say," Hallinan exploded. "You're supposed to enforce the laws."

"I'm sorry, but I have to leave now." Rolph hung up the phone.

Word that he had turned down the pleas for troops quickly became public and got on the news wires. Reporters caught up with the governor in Los Angeles to ask about it.

"Let the sheriff handle the situation," Rolph said. "He can appoint as many deputies as he wants. I'm not going to call out the Guard to protect the kidnappers who willfully killed that fine boy. Let the law take its course."

By now, the Hart family's ordeal had touched news readers around the world; incoming mail at the mansion on The Alameda reached a tremendous volume, from strangers and friends throughout the United

States and abroad. There were offers of money, which Alex declined. Well-wishers sent handcrafted gifts, prayers, religious charms, and sacred objects of all faiths—an outpouring far beyond the ability of the distraught family to acknowledge. Along with the gifts and condolences came sinister messages from cranks, the depraved, the cruel, the sadistic, the unscrupulous, and the greedy trying to exploit the family's heartbreak.

So long as Brooke's body was unrecovered, so long as there remained the slimmest chance that Holmes and Thurmond were lying, distorting, or covering up for whatever reason, the Harts remained vulnerable to extortion by impostor kidnappers. Nettie's refusal to accept the fact of her son's death was widely reported in the press and encouraged such adventurism.

Now, some ten days after the Thurmond and Holmes confessions, two new ransom letters turned up in the Harts' mail, insisting that Brooke still lived. Three similar telephone calls, offering to return him for ransom, were taken by Mrs. Cohn. The FBI, which had withdrawn its agents to San Francisco after the arrests, reactivated its investigation on the million-to-one chance that one of the new offers could be legitimate.

Every running news story, no matter how compelling, sooner or later loses its grip on the minds and hearts of a fickle public. Sixteen days had now elapsed since Brooke's disappearance, and the Hart story was approaching that point: The perpetrators had been caught and confessed; the search for the body had been called off; most people thought the lynching threat would fade. In newsrooms around the bay on this Saturday afternoon, editors sensed all this and saved their top Sunday spots for other stories.

Sixteen miles northwest of San Jose in Stanford Stadium, 86,000 fans put the Hart case out of mind to watch Stanford beat Cal 7–3 in the Big Game. The San Mateo Bridge, by which thousands of them had traveled from Berkeley, was now empty of cranes and rescue gear, and the flotilla of search craft gone from the gray waters below.

17

The Discovery

Alameda Creek, a meandering stream that drains the mountainous backcountry of southern Alameda County, empties into San Francisco Bay three miles south of the San Mateo Bridge. Near its mouth it becomes a broad estuary on whose bleak shores, in 1933, stood the building of the Western Gun Club.

On Saturday, November 25, Leonard Dalve and Harold Stephens left their homes in Redwood City and spent the night at the club to get an early start Sunday for a day of duck hunting. For years the two young men had hunted together on the bay, and they knew its every shoal and channel, tide and current, reef, sandspit, and cove. They understood its moods.

A chilling fog blanketed the water when they rose at five o'clock Sunday morning, two hours before sunrise. By 5:30 they were under way in their small rowboat. On reaching open bay they turned north toward the mouth of Mt. Eden Creek, where the ducks seemed to gather, and headed out from the shoreline.

At nine o'clock the fog still clung to the placid surface. Suddenly, as their boat drifted in five-foot shallows a mile off shore and still half a mile south of the bridge, the two men felt a soft thud. Stephens guessed their hull bottom had hit a seal. Then a form, indistinct at first, broke the surface twenty feet away. Dalve was the first to identify it:

"My god, it's a man!"

Dalve, a surveyor, and Stephens, a storekeeper, had followed the San Jose kidnap story with indifference, but both knew instantly they were gazing on the remains of Brooke Hart. They rowed carefully to bring their boat alongside the body, which was horribly decomposed.

Crabs and fish had fed upon it, and from the waist up it was hardly more than a skeleton. Much of the skull was exposed, as was the rib cage. The left lung seemed mostly intact, but the other organs of the chest cavity and abdomen were missing. The face and hair were eaten away. The arm bones were still in the shoulder sockets, but the hands were gone. The corpse was coatless, and there were only remnants of a shirt, but trousers still clothed the lower part. The feet were in bad shape, but socks and garters remained.

"We don't want to lose the head," Dalve cautioned. The neck had been largely destroyed, and the head dangled tenuously from the spine. The hunters feared its fragile connection would snap if they lifted the body into their skiff. Carefully, using a scull oar, they pushed a tarpaulin under the body, folded it over, and lashed a rope around it. Then, rowing slowly, they towed it to a shell-mound jutting out from the shoreline not far away.

While Dalve remained to guard the body, Stephens made his way inland, picking his way across the mud and rocks of the dredgings. The first policeman he encountered, a traffic officer on patrol, took him to a service station from which he telephoned the Alameda County sheriff's office. Deputy Grover Mull took the call at 9:45.

"My friend and I were out hunting ducks near the bridge and we've found something—a body," Stephens told the deputy. "It looks pretty bad."

Emig had awakened with heavy forebodings. His first worry was about the mental stability of Harold Thurmond, whose depression had deepened markedly since Friday. On his early rounds of the jail, the sheriff found Thurmond sobbing on his bunk—now seemingly his full-time occupation. Terror contorted his features, and he made no reply to Emig's hello. Was he contemplating suicide? As a safeguard, Emig decided to give him a cellmate. He chose Russell Easton,* who was awaiting trial for assault with intent to commit rape.

About eight o'clock the sheriff was diverted by another visit from Al Jones. Knowing the governor had turned a deaf ear on Emig's plea for the militia, Jones had another idea for the kidnappers' safety: Remove them from the jail again and hold them for arraignment in someplace like Palo Alto, still within the Santa Clara County jurisdiction but remote from the San Jose hotheads.

Emig did not take to the idea. He had been working most of the

* Fictitious name.

week to bolster the armament, ammunition, fortifications, and defense force of his own jail, and that was where he would make his stand if need be. Moreover he was beginning to relax a little. After the turndown by Rolph, he had asked Chief Black for reinforcements, and the chief had sent over twelve San Jose policemen, who were now on the premises. Jones had to agree that no threat was perceptible on this early Sabbath morning. Scarcely a dozen persons loitered around the jailhouse doors.

At age twenty-seven, Ray Blackmore had been a San Jose cop for four years. When he had first tried for the force in 1929, through regular channels, he had gotten nowhere. Then he had gone to see Charlie Bigley, the city hall boss. Bigley had no way of telling what sort of officer Blackmore might make, but he liked the stocky youth he saw in front of him. Blackmore had played Sunday baseball and boxed a little, and Bigley decided he would be a valuable addition to the police department's ball team. He told City Manager Clarence Goodwin to hire this young athlete, and it was done. As a rookie, Blackmore had spent his share of time pounding a beat on foot, but now he had a coveted assignment, teamed up with Andy Anderson in one of San Jose's first four radio cars—Pontiac sedans with bulletproof windshields.

On this Sunday morning Blackmore and Anderson finished their regular shift at three o'clock. Less than four hours later their captain, John Guerin, called them back to duty, as part of the detail Chief Black sent to beef up Emig's thin forces at the county jail. It was not paid duty; overtime pay was unheard of for city employees. For a meager salary they worked as long as they were told and considered themselves lucky. A little after seven o'clock the two officers reported to the sheriff, parking their car alongside the jail driveway, which ran off North First Street alongside the courthouse. Besides their pistols, they brought a big single-shot tear gas gun with plenty of shells. Soon the city's three other "prowler" cars showed up also, delivering additional reinforcements.

Emig, who wanted to keep his command post in the jail proper, stationed Blackmore and Anderson in his own office in the courthouse. Its windows commanded a clear view of the jail door, and the alley outside was in their unobstructed field of fire. Observing that the area was clear, the two cops settled down to a game of pinochle.

All was still serene when Captain Guerin came by about 9:30 to see how things were going. The city police, although taking tactical orders from Emig, were still under Guerin's command. At that point, Blackmore recalled fifty years later, "It seemed that possibly there were going to be a few people in protest, but that's as far as it would go."

Guerin, a considerate officer who regretted robbing his men of their Sunday sleep, called his detail together.

"I want two volunteers to stick around," he said. "Whoever stays can take tonight off."

Blackmore and Anderson, who were enjoying their card game, raised their hands and offered to remain. Guerin told the rest to go home. It was a bad mistake.

After Al Jones left, a little before ten o'clock, Emig scanned the *Mercury Herald*, noting with satisfaction that the Hart case was cooling off as news. Today's story was played in third or fourth position, the top spot being devoted to Stanford's cliff-hanger victory in the Big Game. Emig was engrossed in the newspaper's account of the action when the phone on his desk rang. He picked it up and from Alameda County heard the voice of Sheriff Mike Driver.

"Bill?"

"Yeah, Mike."

"We've got a body."

In the next minutes, from telephones in or near Emig's office, calls went out along the wires to certain recipients throughout Santa Clara County and beyond. In an inexorable chain reaction, the recipients called others. By 10:15, scores were aware of the discovery of Brooke Hart's wretched remains—the action signal for the vigilantes. By 10:30, hundreds knew; by 10:45, thousands.

Ray Renwick got one of the calls. He and his wife Jeannette, Brooke's third "sister" who had been raised from childhood by the Harts, had taken their small son to Sacramento for the weekend. About midday the phone rang where they were staying.

"You'd better get down here, Ray," said the caller, a red-haired man Renwick knew. "There's going to be a necktie party." At once Renwick climbed into his car for the three-hour drive back to San Jose.

Most who were called had shorter trips. At eleven o'clock, during a break in their pinochle game, Anderson asked Blackmore, "Have you looked out the window in the last few minutes, Ray?" Blackmore did so. The driveway and the area around the jail doors, which had been nearly empty ninety minutes ago, were filling with people. They soon numbered in the hundreds.

"No one was stopping them from going in there," Blackmore remembered later. "No one was restraining their movement. They were getting in there more and more and more, and it was starting to get ugly."

In San Francisco, the *Chronicle* got the word about the body almost at once from a man it had left at the San Mateo Bridge all weekend just in case. The paper's city desk alerted five other staffers remaining on duty in San Jose, who immediately called their well-placed sources on the vigilance committee. Meanwhile the pressmen, stereotypers, engravers, Linotype operators, carriers, and newsboys were called in. To the *Chronicle* editors, at this point, a lynching was not just something that might happen; it was *going to happen*.

Soon, newspaper switchboards all around the bay were lighting up, as citizens sought confirmation of the wildly spreading reports and rumors. *San Jose News* publisher Payne mobilized virtually his whole staff to crank out two extras, although the paper did not normally publish on Sunday. They were bastardized editions with only the front pages bearing Sunday datelines; the Saturday plates were left on the press for the rest of the pages. It mattered not; 12,000 papers were sold right in the town, whose whole population was only 60,000.

In midmorning, recognized by few if any, the forlorn figure of Maurice Holmes moved through the crowd outside the jail. Each time he had tried to visit Jack since his return from San Francisco, he had been turned away by the jailers, but now they let him in. From his second-floor cell, Jack was brought down to the jail office, where father and son talked for thirty minutes. The fifty-six-year-old tailor, looking his son squarely in the eye, asked, "Are you guilty, Jack?"

With the practiced sincerity of the salesman he was, the son returned the older man's steady gaze.

"Dad," he said, "I swear to you I know nothing about this."

Holmes told his father his only connection with Thurmond was in a business deal; he was trying to sell Harold the old car he had driven before buying the new Chevy: "Thurmond was offering $150 and I wanted $200."

With real or feigned confidence, Jack assured his father that he expected to be freed at his preliminary hearing. Maurice, seizing on the words to ease his torment, convinced himself that his boy was telling the truth. He left after handing Jack a pile of magazines. Once more running the gauntlet of the throng outside, he disappeared down the street.

It was nearing midday when five men, incongruously clad in dark suits, hats, and shirts with tightly knotted ties, slogged out across the ooze and seaweed of the shell mound beneath the San Mateo Bridge.

To identify the remains found by Dalve and Stephens, Emig had rounded up Charlie O'Brien and three trusted employees of Hart's store—Louis Rossi, Dale Range, and Arthur Gossling. The body, face down, still lay where the duck hunters had unwrapped it. A large indentation in the right rear portion of the skull was clearly visible.

Rossi, overcome, gazed down on the crumpled corpse. Kneeling, he felt the texture of the gray tweed trousers, which he had supplied from his men's department.

"This is Brookie all right," he said softly.

Enough of the shirt was left, too, to enable him to identify it. It bore the Arrow label and was of a type that Hart's carried. He likewise recognized what was left of the socks, underwear, red garters, and green suspenders—all from the store.

In the trousers pocket was a trick pearl-handled knife that opened into a pair of scissors. O'Brien, examining it, broke into tears; he knew Brooke carried such a knife, a gift Alex had brought from Europe. He also recognized a gold collar clasp, still clinging to the shreds of the shirt.

At length, litter bearers arrived to remove the body, which was taken to the Pratt-Flierl Mortuary in Hayward and turned over to Alameda County Coroner Grant Miller. Waiting there, having been summoned from San Jose, were Brooke's physician, Dr. Heuschele, and his dentist, Dr. J. R. Conner. Heuschele lifted the right foot of the corpse and pointed to a strip of two-inch adhesive tape still stuck to it—all that remained of the bandage he had placed there just before noon on Brooke's last day of life. Conner, who had taken care of Brooke's teeth since he was eight, had brought along an up-to-date chart of the youth's dental work. After a careful examination, the dentist told reporters, "My chart and the teeth in the body check absolutely. I know the fillings and teeth almost by heart. He had a fine set of teeth."

With identification of the remains certain, three autopsy surgeons took over. Besides the indentation at the rear of the skull, they found a fracture of the right temple and a wound on the top of the head. Any one of the three injuries might have caused death. The decomposed legs bore lesions that might have been bullet holes, but X-rays found no bullets in the corpse.

While the grim labors of the doctors proceeded, the news that the Hart boy's body was at the undertaking parlor spread quickly through Hayward. Several hundred persons gathered outside, talking in hushed tones.

The autopsy told Emig that both killers, in their efforts to impute the major guilt to each other, were erring or lying about how their victim had been killed. Jack Holmes had not hit Brooke over the head with a brick, as Thurmond said; nor had the boy's head struck the concrete of the bridge, as Holmes said. The skull fractures were characteristic of injuries left by the butt of a revolver. Brooke Hart had been pistol-whipped, by which kidnapper it was impossible to tell. As the autopsy ended, Miller announced he would hold an inquest within a few days.

By an exceptional coincidence of timing, at almost the same hour that Dalve and Stephens had spied Brooke's body, an Oakland man named Elmer Murdock had fished his missing coat out of the bay, off Oakland Airport. The bay's capricious currents had carried it eight miles from its wearer. The sleeves were inside out, attesting to Brooke's heroic struggle, even with his skull crushed and his lifeblood draining away, to shed all encumbrance and save himself.

During the return from their dismal mission to Hayward, Emig and his passengers contemplated anew the flash-point anger abroad in San Jose. Rossi decided it was time to let the sheriff know bluntly what the vigilantes had in store.

"Bill, I want to tell you something," he said. "They are going to break into your jail tonight, and they're going to capture the kidnappers, and they're going to hang 'em across the street in St. James Park."

"Oh, Louie, that's impossible," Emig protested. "That jail is like a fort."

"Do me a favor, Bill," Rossi persisted. "Believe me for once. Have the deputies guarding those prisoners put their guns away, to avoid bloodshed."

The FBI's Vetterli, riding alongside Emig, spoke up.

"Bill, you listen to Louie Rossi," he said quietly. "He knows what he's talking about."

Before leaving for Hayward, Emig had instructed Undersheriff Earle Hamilton to strengthen further the jail's fortifications. Now, returning in late afternoon, the sheriff found the driveway off First Street blocked with a truck, and a big sedan obstructing the alley from St. James Street. Flimsy barricades of planking, laid across sawhorses, had been erected in front of each vehicle, perhaps thirty-five feet from the jail doors. Six state highway patrolmen, sent as shock troops, had taken up posts outside to keep the still-growing throng behind the barricades. With relief Emig perceived that the crowd's mood was still light, even jovial. Blackmore, taking a break from the pinochle game, was bantering with the demonstrators from the corner window of the courthouse.

But not much later came a harbinger of trouble, when O. M. Ennis, the advertising manager at Hart's store, approached the barricades afoot. At the store Ennis was a genial favorite who sang and played the banjo at company parties; he had been a speaker at the big September banquet marking Brooke's accession to the vice-presidency. Now, utterly grim, he acted in defiance of a warning from Alex Hart that any employee taking part in an illegal demonstration would be fired.

"You'd better lay down those guns when we move in," Ennis warned the officers. "You know what's good for you. We don't want to see any of you fellows hurt."

In sum, it was the same advice Rossi had given Emig on the ride back from Hayward. But at the barricades it became confrontational and threatening, and Ennis was hustled into the jail to be grilled. Did he belong to the reported vigilance committee? He refused to answer. Finally Emig intervened and released him, telling reporters he was "unduly excited."

Beyond the jail and its environs, the airwaves were feeding the city's excitement. About three blocks south of St. James Park in a storefront building adjoining the First Baptist Church were the studios of San Jose's only commercial radio station, KQW. First Baptist—ironically the church to which Harold Thurmond belonged—had acquired the 500-watt station in 1925, adapting its call letters to a new meaning, "King's Quickening Word." After a year the church sold the outlet but retained a close relationship with it—an affiliation still evident in the peculiar architecture of the church building. Above the main entrance, where the steeple ought to be, rose instead the spindly girders of the KQW antenna. Now in 1933 the station was owned by Fred J. Hart (unrelated to the department store family), an energetic and sometimes combative Farm Bureau leader.

Ordinarily KQW offered serene Sunday fare built around the First Baptist services, but today, as the afternoon wore on, the aroused Fred Hart aired bulletin after frantic bulletin: THE CROWD IS GATHERING! . . . LYNCHING! . . . TONIGHT IN ST. JAMES PARK! Other stations took up the cry, and late in the day traffic thickened on all highways as people piled into their cars and headed for the jail. From San Francisco and Oakland they came; from Gilroy and Morgan Hill and Salinas, from Santa Cruz on the coast. These were not the purposeful vengeance seekers of the vigilance committee. These were ruffians and red-necks, the curious and the thrill seekers, the sadistic, bullies who relished the rare opportunity to kill with impunity.

Among those who heard the radio bulletins and reacted was Anthony Cataldi, an Italian boy from a ranch near San Jose, who would play a unique role in the events to come. Barely turned eighteen, Anthony was a bright, rambunctious youth, and not a little precocious, having successfully eloped twice before his eighteenth birthday. His father's lawyer was currently in process of having the second marriage annulled.

On this gloomy Sunday afternoon, under skies the color of lead, Anthony rode into town with a friend—a glib, hot-headed older man in the produce business. They parked on First Street and went from one jammed tavern to another (technically speakeasies since Prohibition still had nine days to go), drinking as they went. Blown-up photos of Brooke Hart's crab-eaten body were already being passed around in the bars, the still-wet prints having been spirited out of local newspaper darkrooms. Anthony was caught up in the frenzy. Late in the day he and the older man joined the growing throng in the jail driveway. It was still an amorphous crowd.

"There was no leadership at all," Anthony remembered much later. Hisses and catcalls flew back and forth, but without sting, against a background of wisecracking and laughter. It was too tame a scene for the booze-flushed produce dealer, who at length shouted out the word that had, until now, gone unshouted:

"Hey! Why don't we *lynch* 'em?"

The yell galvanized the crowd, which responded with a cheer. The jeering took on a sharper edge.

"Has anybody got a rope?"

Anthony knew where to get one. "Can I borrow your car?" he asked the produce dealer, who handed over his keys.

The youth drove home and went to his father's truck, where there were a couple of three-quarter-inch hemp ropes used to tie down loads, each thirty to forty feet long. He took both and returned to town, arriving outside the jail just at dusk.

Duncan Oneal, the actor-handsome son of boss Louis Oneal, had spent the weekend tranquilly, far from the disquiet of downtown San Jose. He and his surgeon friend, Dr. Cletus Sullivan, had relaxed with their wives at the Oneal ranch atop the mountains to the west.

A rugged, rangy man, Duncan had gone to sea after finishing high school and put in a stint as a deckhand before going on to college and Stanford Law School. Now, at age thirty, he was rising in his father's firm with the expectation of one day heading it. He had no personal stake in the Hart case, in which his father was so deeply involved, but like thousands of San Joseans he was close to the events and knew several of the main characters. Brooke Hart had been his Delta Sigma fraternity brother, though they had gone to different schools; Duncan's wife and Thurmond's sister Hazel, both schoolteachers, were close friends.

Now, as he drove the weekend group back into town late Sunday, Duncan was drawn by his law practice into the thick of the commotion at the jail. He had a client there, an insurance adjuster accused of fraud, and he needed to talk to the man about his arraignment, set for Monday morning. Still clad in jeans and boots, he left his wife and the Sullivans in the car, not far from the jail, and worked his way through the crowd. At the barricades and at the great doors he was recognized and passed through. Inside, he and the adjuster went over what they would do the next morning and then said goodbye, little guessing how soon, where, or under what circumstances they would next meet.

The young lawyer would long remember the bunker atmosphere inside the jail. Every available deputy was there, happily with little to do as yet, and a crap game was going in the booking room.

"The temptation was a little too much for me," Duncan recalled later. "I had a few bucks in my pocket, so I got in the game long enough to lose my money, and that didn't take long. Then I went back to the car and drove home. We dropped the Sullivans off at their residence."

Sometime after five o'clock, the phone rang in the sheriff's courthouse office, still occupied by Andy Anderson and Ray Blackmore with their deck of cards and their enormous stock of tear gas. Blackmore answered. It was Emig, calling from the jail across the alley.

"Come on over for a bite to eat, Ray," the sheriff said. "You can take a sandwich back to Andy."

Blackmore, Anderson, and Emig knew each other well, having been fellow officers on the San Jose police force before Emig's election as sheriff. The invitation now, however, was motivated by more than Emig's concern for the welfare of the other two. He knew of their acquaintance with Holmes, from their beat-cop days, and he wanted Blackmore to chat with the kidnapper for awhile. Maybe the reticent Holmes would break down and let something slip—something that would be useful later in court.

It was ironic that Emig chose Blackmore rather than Anderson to try this gambit. One of the few job matters on which Anderson and Blackmore differed was Emig's competence; Anderson considered him a good officer, while Blackmore thought him a political cop and publicity hound.

Blackmore was still appalled at the way Emig was dealing with the crowd. The barricades were much too close to the jail door. Behind them the driveway was now jam-packed with probably 500 people who should have been restrained far back, away out on the street. Still others were filling the park across the street. Altogether, the crowd was now approaching 2,000.

"The mob should never have been allowed to gather in the first place," Blackmore said half a century later, several years after he had retired as San Jose's chief of police. "Emig really wasn't a good policeman. He was good to the kids, but to be sheriff I think he lacked a whole lot."

Putting aside his doubts, however, Blackmore enjoyed dining with Emig on fare prepared by the jail cooks. As they ate, he urged the sheriff to hang tough with the mob: "Let's beat 'em tonight, Bill. Hold 'em tonight and show 'em you mean business. Otherwise you'll need police here every time you take those guys to court."

Emig nodded but vetoed the idea of a showdown by force.

("What I said didn't sway him," Blackmore opined later, "because he was told what to do."

Who told him?

"I believe he was told by close friends of Brooke Hart. I'm surmising—but there was influence there.")

After a quick supper, Blackmore went upstairs to talk to the kidnappers. Thurmond was whimpering in the corner of his cell, but Holmes was still trying to show a little swagger.

"Looks like a necktie party, Ray," was his greeting.

"Well, Jack, we're going to do everything we can," Blackmore told his old friend, "but I can't guarantee we can hold that mob."

"Thanks, Ray."

"I don't know if you're going to live or die, Jack. Do you want to talk about this thing?"

"No, I'd rather not."

Blackmore did not press the matter. He turned and left, returning across the alley with Anderson's sandwich in his hand.

In late afternoon a hearse brought Brooke Hart home to San Jose for the last time. At six o'clock his body, in a sealed coffin, arrived at the elegant establishment of undertaker Amos O. Williams, who was also the Santa Clara County coroner. Emig, briefly visiting the Hart residence to inform the family, received a tearful plea from Nettie Hart, begging him to let her see her son once more.

"I want to touch his head again," she said.

"Please don't try, Mrs. Hart," the sheriff told her. "Remember Brooke as you last saw him."

Later, Rossi got a call at home from the anguished mother.

"Oh, Louis," she said, "you have full-dress suits at the store, don't you?"

"Yes, Mrs. Hart, I do."

"I'd like to have Brooke dressed in a tuxedo. Will you please see that it's done?"

Rossi, lacking the heart to tell honestly the state of Brooke's remains, said, "OK, I'll take care of it." He went to the store, chose a tuxedo from the rack in his men's department, and delivered it to the Williams Mortuary.

In Eden Township, not far from where Brooke Hart's body had been found, constable Vince Strobel and his wife had returned home at midafternoon from a weekend boat trip on the Sacramento River.

Their small son Billy, who had been left with a babysitter, came running to meet them, wide-eyed.

"Daddy," he yelled, "they're going to hang those men in San Jose. You're supposed to call Mr. Swain right away!"

Strobel was the officer who had lowered himself over the side of the San Mateo Bridge to recover the first concrete block and the coil of leftover clothesline wire. He went to the phone and called Alameda County Undersheriff Frank Swain, his superior.

"Get ready," he was told. "Somebody will come by to pick you up."

Deputy Grover Mull soon appeared at Strobel's door. Skipping supper, they sped to a designated rendezvous point on the main street of Centerville, a village about sixteen miles north of San Jose.* Arriving before dark, they found themselves in a game of hurry up and wait. Three patrol cars with ten or twelve officers were formed up ready to go, but a few men had not yet reported, and Swain, in command, would not leave until all of them came. Five hours would pass before the cars moved out.

Emig was now soliciting reinforcements from all sources, including a second contingent from the California Highway Patrol. The chief of the patrol, E. Raymond Cato, was tracked down to—of all places— the Louis Oneal ranch, where he was spending the evening as a guest. Cato ordered deployment of ten additional men to bolster the sheriff's roster of eighteen deputies. The ten represented the patrol's entire force in Santa Clara County—except for one man; specifically exempted from muster was officer Mel Kent, the ex-brother-in-law of Harold Thurmond.

Pondering the admonitions of Rossi and Ennis, Emig at some point early in the evening arrived at his most controversial and fateful command decision. As he prepared for whatever siege might come, he faced a dilemma that was moral, political, and legal as well as tactical. The "book" told him to use whatever force was needed— lethal firepower if necessary—to repel any assault on his jail or threat to the prisoners in his custody. But among the people likely to be storming his barricades, he knew, were citizens of good repute, leaders of the town. Others in the mob would be mere youngsters—the cream of the student body at the Jesuit college in Santa Clara. Was he going to fire on these people to save temporarily the skins of a couple of

---

* Now part of Fremont.

207

cowardly killers? And even if he gave the order to shoot, would his men obey?

After reflection Emig commanded, "Put away your guns." This would be limited war. In retrospect, many would plausibly deem Emig's no-guns order the key to all that happened thereafter. Would he later regret it?

"Absolutely not," said his daughter, Florence Emig Wheeler, in 1988.

"We confidently thought tear gas would do the work," the sheriff averred after the fact, in a signed article in the *News*.

Undersheriff Earle Hamilton supported his decision.

"We had enough guns to kill a thousand people in that mob," he said, "but we didn't want to do it."

The hotheads besieging the jail were of all ages, but youthful in the main. Loudmouthed drunks set the tone, but there were also many sober couples with not a few children—little girls with rolled stockings, a small boy carrying a dog. It was a strangely formal crowd; casual wear for men had not yet come into its own in the 1930s, and wherever men went—even to a lynching—they wore business suits with vests, felt hats, and neckties.

With darkness, the scene became eerie in the pale saffron light of a lone incandescent bulb above the jail door. The crowd grew in stridency as its numbers increased. Fear grew among the inmates. If the mob broke in, was anyone safe? Ray Sousa felt terror in the pit of his stomach; everyone in town knew he had killed a man and gotten off lightly.

So far the mob showed no sign of being organized; it remained a loose, unregimented rabble. But small happenings told Emig that the disciplined vigilantes were on the sidelines, waiting to take command at the propitious moment. As he wrote later in the *News*, his jail was "spotted on all four corners—watched by groups of men whom my deputies recognized as having been around for days, 'casing the job' as the criminals say." For this reason, Emig at this point decided not to risk spiriting Sousa out of the building.

About six o'clock Santa Clara County Coroner Amos Williams received an ominous telephone message: "Have a hearse in St. James Park at eleven o'clock tonight to pick up Holmes and Thurmond." The caller refused to give his name.

Eleven o'clock! The secret was in the open now, on the streets. Anthony Cataldi knew, as he made the rounds of the bars, when the big push would come, and he passed the word as he went.

Eleven o'clock! The word reached the *Chronicle* office in San Francisco four hours ahead of time, and Assistant Managing Editor Lyn Fox, in charge, strengthened his early edition stories. His reporters in San Jose staked out a phone in a garage near the park, with orders to hold the line open at all costs.

From the courthouse corner office, Blackmore watched the crowd grow ugly. Not long after dark the jostling began. Some of the men up front rolled away the truck that was blocking the driveway. Deputies quickly rolled it back into place as the mob jeered.

"Come on, boys, let's go in and get 'em," yelled a youth in his teens, standing on the roof of a shed overlooking the driveway. He was dragged down by officers and taken inside the jail.

A few minutes before nine o'clock a sudden push from somewhere in the rear of the mob had a massive domino effect, sending the front ranks crashing forward, splintering the wood of the barriers. The shouting took on a throaty, menacing tone. Ten or fifteen officers behind the barricades locked arms, and momentarily their swaying line halted the crowd's plunge toward the jail doors. For a few seconds, it seemed that the line would hold.

Then came a sudden, sharp report.

"A man by the name of Lowell, a deputy sheriff, threw the first gas—a little hand grenade of gas," Blackmore would remember forever after. "And why he did it, I don't know."

18

The Gallows Trees

The noise of the tear gas gun bounced off the walls of the jail and the courthouse. The vapors settled over the front ranks of the mob—a corrosive, clinging miasma that smelled like almonds. Those nearest the jail were blinded as hot, salty water poured from their eyes. They coughed, wheezed, and choked as their mucous membranes were seared and the fumes penetrated their lungs.

The throng, thus challenged, was transformed. Until now it had been a rambunctious rabble; suddenly it was a surly wounded beast, speaking with a terrible voice. Ray Blackmore remembered the noise as "just a steady roar, louder and louder." To an *Oakland Post-Enquirer* writer, it was "a growing murmur like the sound of the surf." Joe Sabatte, who heard it from afar, called it an "eerie wail." A light breeze carried it two miles to the southern edge of the city, where a twelve-year-old girl heard "a frightening voice roar—you knew it was people yelling, roaring and screaming."

The mob reeled backward as the first gas shell exploded. Half a dozen deputies, led by Joseph Walsh, charged out of the jail to pursue. When fists landed in Walsh's face, he fired another shell at his attackers, point-blank. Other deputies lobbed gas grenades from the jail windows, as did Blackmore and Anderson from their post in the courthouse. Momentarily it appeared the siege had been broken.

"That's the end of it," someone said, as the ringleaders staggered in retreat. But within seconds new leaders appeared and reformed the ranks. Blown by uncertain winds, the gas was a treacherous weapon that blinded the officers as well as the rioters. One of the first bombs, fired from an upper jail window, exploded in front of Highway Patrolman Nick Ladner, and a piece of the wadding zapped into his upper right arm, inflicting a painful burn and laceration. Gushing blood, he was taken to San Jose Hospital.

A cry of "Lynch 'em, lynch 'em!" went up, and then, from far back in the crowd, a menacing chant in the relentless cadence of a drum, full of anger and vengeance:

"Brook-ie HART! . . . Brook-ie HART! . . . Brook-ie HART!"

Again and again, louder and louder.

Overlooking the scene from the roof of the jail garage, a cameraman set off a charge of old-fashioned flash powder. As a perfect circle of smoke rose from his flashgun, somebody yelled, "There's the noose!" Momentarily the gas was forgotten as all eyes turned to the gracefully rising smoke ring.

In St. James Park a red-haired youth about seventeen, in cords and a blue sweater, who said he was a student, now took command. Wild-eyed, he brandished a crowbar.

"Are there men with guts enough to follow me in and get those sons of bitches?" he shouted. Half a hundred frenzied demonstrators, most in their late teens or early twenties, fell in behind him, following him across the street to reinforce the flagging assailants of the jail. Highway Patrolman Ben Torres tried futilely to arrest them, firing tear gas into their midst.

"Get some water," shouted the redhead. Someone rigged a garden hose to a faucet on the courthouse lawn, and each time a bomb was tossed, it was doused.

A new post office, which would be a handsome edifice of glazed terra cotta with a red tile roof, was under construction next to the courthouse, and now its piles of stored masonry and hardware became an arsenal for the mob. A hurled brick hit the jail with a loud smack. Within seconds, the defenders came under a steady barrage of rocks, tiles, brickbats, cement chunks, and pipe fittings. The missiles clattered against the old brick walls and clanged against the window bars. An exultant roar went up as a window shattered. Rocks smashed into several cars parked along the driveway. In the melee three shots were fired into the jail's second-story windows, fortunately hitting no one. The marksman, using a rifle, was spotted far back in the crowd but never identified.

With the windows out, the rioters adopted a new tactic. Whenever a gas bomb landed among them, they threw it back into the jail, where the fumes quickly built to several times their outside concentration, blinding the defenders.

In the courthouse across the alley Blackmore and Anderson re-loaded their tear gas launcher. "Raise the window, Andy," Blackmore said, "and I'll blast 'em. Then pull the window down quick before the gas rolls back in on us." The crowd sensed what the two policemen were going to do, and as the window went up, a salvo of missiles sailed in. Blackmore began to bleed from a chin wound. The two cops, who had joshed fraternally with the demonstrators all day, had now become their enemies.

Unlike the jail, which had become a fortress, the courthouse afforded scant protection against invaders. Not wanting to be killed with their own pistols, which they were forbidden to use, Blackmore and Anderson took the elevator to the third floor and hid the weapons in an empty office. They had barely come down when the building went dark, as someone cut the wires. A minute earlier they would have been trapped in the elevator. Back at their post they tried the phone on the sheriff's desk and found it dead. For the rest of the night, they would be on their own, out of communication with Emig's command post in the jail, just a few feet away.

From his vantage point in the window, which was eight or ten feet off the ground, Blackmore could identify the mob's ringleaders. They would advance to the front, provoke each confrontation, and then fade away when new gas volleys were fired.

"It was right at a time when communism was feared," Blackmore remembered later, "and our thoughts were, 'Well, they're probably part of the commies trying to cause trouble.' " To his partner, Blackmore pointed out the redhead. "I don't know if I'm coming out of here or you're coming out of here, Andy," he said, "but if it gets down to a hand-to-hand battle, that's the guy I'm going to get."

On the fringes of the crowd, watching the action as it grew, stood those who had met twenty-four hours earlier and laid the plans to grab the kidnappers at their arraignment. Unlike the roughnecks in the thick of the fray, these disciplined vigilantes were reponsive to a commander—a man issuing directions from behind a mask. One of them, a young San Jose businessman, would explain to reporters the next day, "Some of those not in on the plan started the show last night. We heard about 6 o'clock that some rowdies had gathered at the jail. We went down and found that the crowd was talking a little of lynching but was interested mostly in harassing the officers. I believe that if the first gas bomb had not been thrown, the rowdies soon would have tired of tossing rocks and gone home. We had been standing on the sidelines up to that point, but we decided that with the help of the rock throwers we could storm the jail and get our business over with right there."

A heavy volley of tear gas from inside the jail won a momentary respite for its defenders, as the nauseous rioters fell back across the street and into the park to regroup. About 9:30 their push resumed, accompanied by a new shower of rocks and broken masonry. The barrage was so lethal that it drove the officers still outside the jail to take cover within—all but Torres, who braved the missiles to grab up gas grenades that had fallen short and hurl them into the mob. Blackmore and Anderson kept shooting gas, momentarily raising their window a few inches each time. Suddenly a flying tile fragment shattered the glass.

"Well, Andy, we're gonna gas ourselves," Blackmore told his partner as the fumes poured back in on them.

Up to this point the battle had been fought in the pale light of the lone bulb over the jail door and a floodlight mounted on the corner of the courthouse. Now: *Ping!* Again: *Ping!* Well-aimed chunks of tile took out both sources of illumination. Suddenly the area, as one San Josean would recall, was as "dark as the inside of a cow." The blackness, cloaking the attackers in anonymity and confounding the defenders, was pierced only by the smoky, bluish explosions of the gas bombs and the sporadic silver splotches of light from photographers' flashguns. The *Chronicle*'s Brier called the scene a "blue nightmare." With the lights out, the roar took on a meaner guttural tone.

Behind the drawn blinds of the white mansion on The Alameda, a mile and a half west of the jail, Alex Hart went quietly about the business of arranging the last rites for his fallen firstborn son. In a general way the family knew a tide of vengeance had risen in the city, but they had insulated themselves from the ugliness. Nettie Hart was still ill; Miriam and Aleese, caring for her, were reading the newspapers only superficially.

Early in the evening someone—it may have been Jay McCabe—telephoned and told Alex that control downtown was passing to the rioters. Alex in turn called Emig with a message to relay to the mob.

"Please, please tell them they must not be violent," the father implored. "I'm sure the courts will give the kidnappers their proper punishment. I am so overcome with my own grief that I cannot think of that other terrible thing. My sympathy goes to the families of these two men."

Nothing in the record indicates that Alex's words ever reached the mob, or that they had the slightest effect if they did.

With new crank calls and threats coming each day, fear still lingered in the Hart home. Nettie had become frantic about the physical and emotional well-being of her impressionable youngest child, and now sole surviving son, thirteen-year-old Alex, Jr. To shield him from whatever trauma might lie ahead on this Sunday evening, she decided to send him across town to stay with her sister, Belle Fowler. It was a decision which, for reasons she could not foresee, she would regret.

St. James Park was filling rapidly now. Hundreds of autos loaded with the concerned and the curious, responding to KQW's incessant stream of inflammatory bulletins, converged there and disgorged their passengers. How many? No one knew. Most newspapers would use crowd figures of 5,000 to 15,000. The FBI would guess 3,000.

To one first-year law student at Santa Clara University, the radio bulletins amounted to a straight-out invitation: "Come on down, come on down, everybody!" Newscaster Sam Hayes, whose "Richfield Reporter" program from Los Angeles was standard fare for millions up and down the West Coast, featured the lynching on his ten o'clock show as an event in progress. Hayes, whose style was heavily dramatic, was at that time "the hottest thing in radio," his son Ron recalled in 1989. "He whipped a lot of people into frenzy. Whatever Sam Hayes said was the most exciting thing they ever heard in their lives. I guarantee you Dad would motivate those people."

Al Jones, who had been at the jail earlier when all was quiet, remembered later how "the thing exploded" after Hayes's broadcast. "I would guess that within half an hour there were 3,000 cars down there," Jones said. "They were parking in the middle of the street."

For a week Santa Clara University had been denying accusations that its campus was a hotbed of vigilante ferment—and at the same time striving to squelch the lynching sentiment that did in fact exist there. A warning of expulsion for anyone participating in such an event had come down, but not all of the school's 450 students, most living on campus, were intimidated. Among those who left their dorms and headed for the park were Bob Carlton,* a tall, blond boy from Oakland who boarded at O'Connor Hall, and Brooke's friend, the former child actor Jackie Coogan.

All day, in the governor's mansion at Sacramento, Sunny Jim Rolph had been keeping track of the San Jose disorder with regular telephone reports from his lieutenants in the area, especially Highway Patrol Chief E. Raymond Cato. Rolph was scheduled to leave by plane shortly before midnight for a western governors' conference in Boise, Idaho, but about nine o'clock, with events rushing toward their climax, he abruptly canceled his flight.

"I want to be on the job," he told reporters. But his concern, we know, was not to use the militia as peacekeepers; rather, it was to make certain such action was not taken. Under the state constitution, Rolph's gubernatorial powers would pass to Lieutenant Governor Frank Merriam the instant his plane left California air space, and Merriam, who coveted Rolph's job, would jump at any chance to embarrass him. Who knew what he would do if Emig asked anew for the National Guard?

Here we must digress into a gray area of educated conjecture, essential to a critical evaluation of much that follows.

It is a matter of record that Cato, a crony of Rolph's, served as his "eyes and ears" during the lynching. And as we have already seen, he was operating at least part of the time from the mountain ranch of Louis Oneal, Rolph's friend and Emig's mentor. That is where he was found late in the day when Emig appealed to him for reinforcements.

Let us now consider this in conjunction with another circumstance disclosed in 1989 by Oneal's namesake grandson, Lou Oneal, and unknown publicly in 1933. The grandson told the author it was his understanding, based on knowledge within his family and law firm, that throughout the lynching his grandfather had a phone open from the ranch into the jail. He could thus stay atop the crisis and possibly counsel Emig.

One must ponder, therefore, whether the governor in Sacramento likewise had simultaneous knowledge of the events taking place and the decisions being made. Could he have taken part in the decisions?

*Fictitious name.

If his observer, Cato, was reporting from the ranch on one phone while Oneal was talking to Emig on another, is it not reasonable to ask whether such was the case? The reader is not asked to accept this as fact, only to keep in mind this possibility as Rolph's role in subsequent events develops.

As ten o'clock neared, the early shows ended at four movie houses down the street from the park, and hundreds of departing theatergoers, hearing the din, headed there. At the American Theater the projectionist flashed a slide on the screen telling the audience the lynching was about to start, setting off a surge toward the exits. To *Mercury Herald* reporter John V. Young, emerging from another of the cinemas, the noise was "strange and frightening . . . a kind of keening that stirred a primeval tingling on the back of my neck."

John Sepulveda, one of the Milpitas ranchers who had first spotted Brooke Hart's roadster, had taken his family to the California Theater that night. When they emerged he knew instantly what was happening. As the shrieking assaulted his ears, he seethed with excitement and started walking his family in its direction. At the park he led his wife and three small children to a statue of President McKinley directly across from the courthouse. Leaving them seated on the sculpture's pedestal, he made for the center of the action.

Now the casualties were mounting faster among officers and civilians alike. The rain of rocks, bricks, tiles, and gas bombs, unabated for an hour, had turned the alley outside the jail doors into a fearsome no-man's-land. Patrolman Torres suffered deep burns as a gas grenade exploded, and an object of some sort clipped the abdomen of Patrolman Elliott Marrs. Another struck the arm of Ralph Jordan, a correspondent for International News Service. The scalp of a man named Carson, a cook in a San Jose restaurant, was split open by a flying brick. A druggist, Earl Johnson, was badly gassed. As the missiles flew, Highway Patrolman John Sansone made himself one of the heroes of a night that would have few. Braving the barrage, he rolled his motorcycle into the county garage, where he broke out his first aid kit and set up an emergency station, treating all comers.

In the midst of the battle, jailer Howard Buffington had another concern. A canary fancier, he kept a pair of prize birds in the identification room, into which the gas was now seeping. Surely they were going to die. He took time out to lift their cages down, move them into a tiny storeroom nearby, and slam the door. He could only hope for the best.

Cut off in their courthouse outpost, Blackmore and Anderson were ironically unaware of what by now was widely known on the street—that the vigilantes had set an eleven o'clock H-hour for the lynching. During a lull at ten o'clock, however, there appeared beneath the policemen's window a man Blackmore recognized as a fruit and vegetable shipper close to Charlie Bigley, the city hall boss. Blackmore was still a cog in the Bigley machine.

"I've got a message from the leaders, Ray," the shipper said. "They're going to bust in right at eleven. They don't want you fellows to get hurt, but if you get in the way, they're not going to be responsible. They're absolutely going in. They just wanted to warn you."

Blackmore contemplated the man across the windowsill.

"OK," he replied, "but we're not going to quit."

Long afterward a reporter asked Blackmore why he hadn't backed off after this friendly warning.

"Well," he said, "you're a different animal, I guess, to be a policeman in the first place."

A little after ten o'clock the vigilante leaders huddled and sensed that the insurrection had reached a stalemate. Rocks and bricks could drive the jail's defenders inside but could not make them open the doors. Now was clearly the time to move into the final, decisive phase of the battle.

The word was passed. Imperceptibly the mob at the jail doors thinned out, as the red-haired youth withdrew, leading about forty of his followers to a rendezvous spot in the park. After a few minutes in council they quietly filtered back across the street, in twos and threes, to the post office construction site.

Since early in the evening, Deputy Sheriff William McCaffrey had manned a telephone in a tiny, airless room off the jail office, putting through Emig's calls for reinforcements. At first the lack of ventilation was a blessing, affording protection from the fumes that saturated the rest of the building. Then a rock hit the window of the little room, and the gas poured in. Fighting nausea and blindness, McCaffrey nevertheless remained at his post for two more hours, seeking help from police, fire, and sheriff's departments for miles around. Finally overcome, he had to give it up and run for clean air.

One of the few civilians inside the jail was Hugh Center, a principled young lawyer in the Oneal firm and a friend of Emig. Earlier in the evening, knowing the sheriff was in trouble, he had gone to the jail to help out. Now, with McCaffrey out of service, Center took over a phone booth the newsmen had been using outside, near the courthouse back door, and carried on the solicitation of reinforcements.

In his desperate straits Emig was acutely aware of the grudging stinginess of the City of San Jose, especially Chief Black, in giving him help. Anderson and Blackmore were still the only San Jose policemen on the scene (others having been sent home early that morning), although the riot was raging in the heart of the SJPD jurisdiction, building toward a grim climax on city property in a public park. Now, with his jail a shambles, Emig decided to try the San Jose Fire Department.

"Please! Bring your hoses over and soak these bastards," he begged the captain on duty in the main firehouse, only a block away.

"Sorry, sheriff, I can't authorize use of the apparatus for that purpose. Somebody might cut the hoses."

So, the fire department was as reluctant as the police force! Were the orders coming from city hall? Emig tried to go over the captain's head, placing calls to Fire Chief Charles Plummer and City Manager Goodwin. Neither could be located.

Finally, at 10:20, after canvassing Palo Alto and Santa Clara, Center got a call through to Inspector Clyde Crosswell at the Oakland Police Department.

"Tell the sheriff we're on our way," Crosswell said. But it was figured out later that twenty-seven minutes elapsed before Oakland's convoy, with twelve men under Inspector William F. Kyle, rolled away on the forty-four-mile trip to San Jose. The cars, with sirens blaring and red lights on, were loaded with guns, clubs, tear gas bombs, and other riot gear. About the same time they left the Oakland City Hall, a patrol wagon carrying fourteen officers and a car with two inspectors and a tear gas cargo left San Francisco.

Meanwhile the Alameda County sheriff's deputies who had gathered at Centerville before dark remained parked by the road after almost five hours—sixteen miles north of their prospective destination, the jail in San Jose.

* * *

Outside the jail now reappeared the two-score rioters who had retreated earlier to the park with the red-haired youth. They suddenly emerged from the shadowy depths of the post office construction site, carrying two battering rams of heavy steel pipe. Each was probably twenty feet long and six or eight inches in diameter, weighing several hundred pounds. One had a huge cast-iron "T" fitting with a two-foot crossbar at one end.*

Peering from a darkened jail window, Emig watched the pipe bearers moving into position. All hope of holding out against the mob now deserted him. He knew the war was lost.

For Louis Rossi, it had been a long, punishing day. He had endured the agony of identifying Brooke's corpse, made his impassioned entreaty to Emig to avoid gunfire, and dealt with Nettie's plea that her son go to his eternal rest in a tuxedo. Now, as he sat by the radio in his little home on Iris Court, physically and emotionally drained, the phone rang. He answered and heard the voice of his neighbor George Millard, the *News*'s cigar-chomping police reporter. Millard, an insider who carried a pistol and often accompanied the cops on raids, lived close by, but he was calling from the jail.

"Louie, they're getting ready to hang the sons of bitches. Come on down and watch. Bring your wife."

Impossible, Rossi replied; they couldn't leave Beverly, their small daughter.

"It's all arranged," Millard said. "I just talked to my wife. She's on her way to your house and take care of Beverly."

About that time Mrs. Millard showed up at the door, and the Rossis climbed into their car and headed downtown. Rossi drove slowly; he did not want to reach the park before the lynchers had completed their work.

"I wanted proof that I wasn't one of them," he later explained, "because I would naturally be the first one under suspicion."

From the hurricane's eye outside the jail, the storm was washing across the city, state, and nation. Word-of-mouth contagion of excite-

---

* At the time of the lynching, there was no public suggestion that the pipes were other than regular construction materials for the post office. In 1985, however, a San Jose man who was a teenager in 1933 told the author of seeing the fabricated rams cached at the site earlier by young men he believed to be Santa Clara University students. This observation could not be corroborated.

ment, as the ghastly drama unfolded, now brought on a crisis in the San Jose telephone office. Thousands of calls lit up the switchboards as people phoned each other with lynch talk, and long-distance lines were overloaded by newsmen flashing the story all over the world. At ten o'clock twenty extra-duty operators were added to the force, and until 1:30 each handled some 200 calls an hour. To callers who could not reach the jammed switchboard of the *Mercury Herald*, the operators read the latest lynching bulletins.

With their battering rams, the rioters took undisputed possession of the rubble-strewn area outside the jail, which a short time before had been no-man's-land. The men with the crossbar-ram made the first lunge at the doors—a clumsy, ill-coordinated thrust that bounced off the steel sheathing. Thrown off balance, they fell back momentarily.

Suddenly, atop the low roof of the jail garage, appeared a man with a handkerchief mask—the de facto vigilante leader who until now had exercised remote control from the sidelines. Now he jumped to the ground and took active command at the rear end of the ram.

Other vigilantes also wore masks, not just for anonymity but also to filter the fumes. The sheriff's men, without masks and nearly sightless, went on hurling their grenades at targets they could not see. (Later they would plead gas blindness when asked to identify the lynchers.)

From his place in the phone booth, Hugh Center watched the insurrection with dismay and loathing. Suddenly he charged out of the booth in a futile one-man stand against the mob, trying to disrupt it until the promised arrival of the San Francisco and Oakland reinforcements. Pulling an unsuspected .45 from his pocket, he attacked the men wielding the pipe, one by one, with its butt. Taken by surprise in the dark, they fell like tenpins. Finally one of them realized what was happening and smashed the lawyer over the head with a brick.

A member of the battering ram crew was truck driver Rocky Santoro, a man irresistibly drawn to any scene of violence, disorder, bloodshed, or fire—an affinity that would later make him one of San Jose's most visible news photographers. Like many of Emig's friends, he carried a "special deputy" badge, a strictly honorary but politically helpful item. Ironically, Santoro had also been issued a key to the doors he was now trying to break down, and it was in his pocket. Trying to use it now would have been futile, however, because of the steel reinforcing bars inside.

"I got my belly full of gas, and I smelled it for two weeks afterward," Santoro remembered later. "Eight or ten men at one time were on the ramrod. They'd drop off, and someone else would pick it up. It was crazy, but you get pushed and pushed and pushed, and you just keep going."

Many of the jail's attackers were strangers to each other. Most, but not all, were young. Fraternal organizations were well represented. *Mercury Herald* reporter Young saw "a frightful number of presumably decent citizens turned into a pack of hyenas. They were all kinds— well-dressed businessmen and housewives, students, bums from the slums, professional people of all races and nationalities."*

"We had Italians with hot blood," recalled another spectator. "These guys were very passionate; they are very emotional, OK? What happened that night was that emotion took over the goddamn reason of these people."

Anthony Cataldi, the teenager who had brought the ropes, took a position up front on the battering ram where he could be first through the doors. Ernest Sauliere, the Hart family's former chauffeur and the father of its unofficially adopted daughter Jeannette, was there. Nearby was his son, Frank Sauliere, a volatile young man in his twenties and something of a local celebrity—reputed to have been the youngest soldier in the AEF during World War I, at age twelve or thereabouts. Bob Carlton, the blond SCU junior from Oakland, took a handhold on the battering ram. So did a teenager named Ray Loren.†

Agnew Shea, a twenty-four-year-old East San Jose rancher who had gone to SCU with Brooke Hart, was in the thick of the action. So was Paul Maggi, whose South First Street restaurant was rumored to have been a vigilante meeting place (and, ironically, where Holmes had taken his wife and the Estensens for their posttheater snack on the night of Brooke's murder). Also identifiable were a man who had a South First Street men's store, a physician, another restaurateur, an auto dealer, and a couple of brothers who ran a garage.

The lynchers were getting jumpy now, as word filtered through the mob that the San Francisco and Oakland police were on their way. Whatever was going to be done had to be done fast. The masked leader braced his ramming crew for a second assault on the doors, this time a mighty heave-ho with the whole crew charging in unison. The ancient portals yielded ever so slightly. A shrill, gloating rebel yell went up:

"Yeeoweeeeeeh!"

---

*John V. Young, *Hot Type & Pony Wire* (Santa Cruz, Calif.: Western Tanager Press, 1980).
†Fictitious name.

Then, a gasp. Suddenly, behind the bars of his open third-floor window the ashen face of Harold Thurmond appeared, a contorted mask of terror, despair, and confusion.

"We're coming to get you," someone shouted at him.

"We're going to get Cocky Jack, too!" yelled another.

Thurmond slammed the window shut and disappeared.

Still under a heavy gas barrage, the rammers now coordinated their attack with the man holding the water hose. Each time they fell back, he would drench the area, scattering and settling the vapors so that the big pipe could be carried forward again.

Inside the jail the tear gas was running low. And now, momentarily, Emig faced a new threat even more ominous than invasion. By telephone or messenger—it is unknown which—he was warned that the mob had obtained a box of dynamite from an orchard outside of town.

"Bring 'em out or we'll blow the jail to hell," came the ultimatum.

A girl in a fur coat—a blonde in her twenties—moved to the front of the mob. Her eyes flashed as she beckoned the rammers on, exhorting them to a final assault: "Get 'em, go get em! More cops are coming."

"Don't let a girl outdo us!" a man screamed. With everyone along the pipe straining, it was heaved into the doors a third time, and they gave way with a thunderous crash. A roar went up, and the screeching mob surged into the jail like water into the hold of a torpedoed ship. Anthony Cataldi, barely eighteen, and Ray Loren, seventeen, raced to be first over the threshold—a distinction each would later claim.

The bomb threat was now academic. "Come on, Emig, give the bastards to us!" someone yelled.

In the courthouse across the alley, Blackmore and Anderson had run out of gas too. Blackmore looked at his watch. It was precisely eleven o'clock.

Emig had two final duties to perform before capitulating to the mob. As the invaders swarmed into his building, he bounded upstairs to the third floor and transferred Russ Easton, Thurmond's cellmate, to another cell close by. No need for a suicide watch now. The sheriff did not want Easton taken, either by mistake or because of excessive zeal on the part of lynchers, who would feel righteous stringing up an additional man accused of a sex crime.

The sheriff also had to find out, now or never, whether anyone had helped Holmes and Thurmond with their crime. Such a suspicion was still widely held. Emig did not share it, but it haunted him nonetheless. Moreover, a strange new rumor was making the rounds, although without substantiation, that Holmes and Thurmond had abducted Brooke originally as hired guns, to collect debts he had run up at a local gambling joint. If so, Emig needed to know who did the hiring. He confronted the white-faced Harold alone in his cell after Easton had been taken out. The kidnapper shuddered convulsively at the clatter of the invaders.

"Sheriff," Thurmond whimpered, "are they going to take me out and hang me?"

Emig spoke slowly and deliberately, looking squarely into the eyes of his prisoner:

"Harold, it looks as if we can't hold out. I'm doing my best, but I'm afraid you may not have long to live. There isn't much time to talk. I'm going to give you a question, and I want you to tell me the truth. This is your last chance. Was anybody else in this thing with you and Holmes?"

Thurmond raised his hand and, with tears streaming from his eyes, said:

"Before God, Sheriff, Holmes and I were alone on this job."

Still more of the thrill seekers and the curious were converging on downtown San Jose. For one privileged group, however, the park per se was not the destination; Elks Club members headed for their squar-ish building on St. John Street facing the park. From the upstairs windows, the lodge brothers would have an unmatched grandstand view of the town's retribution to the murderers. Among the Elks so privileged was Ray Renwick, Brooke Hart's unofficial brother-in-law, back from Sacramento.

Deputy Paul Arnerich was just inside the jail doors at the instant they buckled. Alone, he met the invaders head-on. He tried to argue with them, but the tide swept him out of the way.

"They were as polite as could be to me," he said later. "Why, a lot of them called me by name."

The jail's entrance corridor, a passage some twenty feet long, led to another door, with steel bars and heavy wire mesh, leading in turn to the inmates' quarters. Again the mob brought the battering ram into play and with one mighty lunge ripped this inner door from its hinges. Crashing to the floor, it struck Deputy Joe Walsh, breaking his finger.

For all his loudmouthed bravado, Anthony Cataldi was "scared stiff" when the inner door gave way. "They'll get us inside and lock us up for good," he thought—but he stayed with the mob. Not so Bob Carlton, the SCU student from Oakland who had helped wield the ram. He was so terrified by what he had done that he turned, split from the pack, and slunk out of the jail to lose himself in the crowd.

With the last barrier gone, twenty or thirty of the invaders started up the narrow, dingy, wooden stairs leading to the second- and third-floor cells. Blocking the staircase were Undersheriff Hamilton, Buffington, and Deputy John Moore, in phalanx for a final stand.

"Don't do this, boys," Buffington pleaded. The mob attacked him with fists, knocking him down, and then kicked him in the stomach. In the fight, Hamilton's hand was cut.

"Who's got the cell keys?" one of the leaders demanded. Moore said he didn't know, but they didn't believe him. Pushing him into a corner of the stairwell, they choked him and went through his pockets until they found his key ring, which they seized.

Emig had just left Thurmond's cell and started down the stairs, and he met the mob head-on as he rounded the turn at the top of the lower flight. He still had one shell in his tear gas gun, which he fired point-blank.

"You're not going to get them, men," he shouted.

"We'll get them, all right," one of the invaders retorted, taking a roundhouse swing at him. At this instant someone put out the lights in the stairwell, and a melee broke out in the dark. Emig felt a pipe slam into the back of his head. He fell and rolled down the stairs, wrenching his back.

Anthony Cataldi, carrying the ropes, was the first to reach the second floor. From cell to cell the mob went, looking for Holmes. Finally someone spotted the glint of his cell's new lock, which was the giveaway. The leaders tried the keys on Moore's ring, one by one, until one of them worked. As they burst into the cell, it seemed empty, but a man of truculent mien and cruel features, clad only in an undershirt, was found in the toilet enclosure.

"Holmes?"

"I'm not Holmes." the occupant shouted, throwing up his arms. "I'm Jack Pearson from Evergreen."

"Let me see him," said a man who pushed forward. "I can tell." Someone beamed a flashlight at the prisoner.

"The hell you're not Holmes. I've seen you too many times to forget that face," said the identifier, swinging a hammy fist that cracked the prisoner on the jaw. "Got anything to say, you son of a bitch?"

"Nothing."

Other lynchers jumped the kidnapper, smashing in his nose and knocking him to the floor, out cold. Then they picked him up and slapped him back to consciousness.

"Who else was in this thing with you?" they demanded—the same question Emig had put to Holmes's partner.

"Nobody but Thurmond."

Another fist floored Holmes again. When he struggled to his feet, the next man hit him, and it went on that way, the lynchers taking turns. Finally, as he lay unconscious a second time, they picked him up, propped him against the wall, slipped Cataldi's rope around his neck, and pulled him down the stairs headfirst, his face bumping the treads until it was bloody.

With Holmes in hand, the lynchers quickly located Thurmond's cell on the northeast corner of the jail's third floor. By appearing in the window earlier, he had made it easy for them; he might as well have drawn them a map. In less than a minute they found a key that fit his cell's new lock.

Thurmond was trying to hide in the shadows near the ceiling of his tiny toilet stall, suspending himself from an iron grating above the water box. Wedged between the walls of the stall, his head against one and his feet against the other, he clung to the grating with clenched fingers. "Like a treed raccoon," the *San Francisco Call-Bulletin* said. Unlike Holmes, Thurmond was fully dressed.

"Get out of here. I'll kill all of you!" he screamed at the top of his voice as the invaders entered.

"He was plum crazy," a member of the mob said later, "trying to climb the walls like a monkey. He was squealing and leaping about, and I had to chase him and pull him down."

Soon Thurmond's scream turned to a whimper.

"Don't string me up. For God's sake, don't string me up!" he pleaded again and again, in the last words he ever uttered, amid nonsensical gibbering. His face was white, his mouth twitched, his eyes stared wildly. As he crashed down from his hiding place, his head struck the floor or the toilet seat (the stories differed), and he was knocked unconscious.

"Wait a minute, boys," someone cried out. "The bastard doesn't deserve it, but we ought to pray for him before we take him out."

In an exceptional scene, five or six of the lynchers fell to their knees amid the bedlam and began to pray for Thomas Harold Thurmond's soul.

"Dear Father," intoned a man holding a rope, "forgive this sinner. . . ."

"Never mind, he's going to hell anyway," another lyncher interrupted before the prayer got any further, and a drunk in the party shouted, "Amen, Brother Ben!" The prayer session broke up. Someone produced bricks to hammer in Thurmond's skull, but another man objected: "Don't kill him here. We promised the crowd we'd bring him outside."

Rising, the kneelers looped a rope around Thurmond's neck, grabbed him by the arms, and walked him down the stairs. He was still out cold, and mute, as he stumbled along between them.

For the other inmates, the invasion of the jail was a nightmare. With a crazed mob like this, was anyone safe? A few prisoners took advantage of the chaos to bolt for freedom. Most, tear-gassed and terrified, cowered in far corners of the building. Some hid under their bunks. Others cried out, "Don't take me!" A snitch identified Holmes to the mob leaders. Jack McCoy,* a young black man awaiting sentence for molesting several women, dropped to his knees to pray.

Ray Sousa was frightened with cause. Many San Joseans deemed his manslaughter conviction for shooting Charlie Kuhn's ranch foreman a slap on the wrist, and now the mob, having taken Holmes and Thurmond, demanded Sousa also.

"Let's polish Ray off, too," cried one of the lynchers, and part of the gang headed for a certain third-floor cell where they figured out he was. Lying on his bunk, he could hear them yelling for him. He pulled his blanket over his head and lay there trembling.

Now Buffington, having risen from where he had been dumped in the stairwell, ran to Sousa's cell and took a stand before the door, shedding angry tears.

"You've gone mad," he shouted at the mob, in a voice that carried throughout the building. "This man has been tried by a jury. Let the law take it's course. Don't let another man's death be charged to you when you answer that last roll call!"

The lynchers, confounded by Buffington's vehemence, backed off. But as they moved on, one of them struck him on the head with some blunt instrument, from behind, and he fell to the floor with a brain concussion.

A wild cry went up from the mob outside as the invaders emerged from the jail dragging the kidnappers. Holmes was the first delivered

---

*Fictitious name.

to the bloodthirsty thousands. In the chill night air he regained consciousness a second time and resumed his ferocious fight for life. Grasping at the feeblest of straws, he tried a new alias.

"You've got the wrong man!" he screamed. "My name is Johnson."

"You're Holmes, all right," said a man who knew him, "and you're going to die."

"All right, all right, I'm Jack Holmes, but for God's sake give me a chance to explain my part in this thing."

The lynchers responded with taunts and tore away the last shreds of his undershirt, leaving him naked except for his socks and right shoe. Then, in a flying wedge, they propelled him down the driveway toward the park—a distance perhaps the length of a football field. One of them loosened his noose to keep him from strangling before he reached the gallows tree. His premature death by error would not sate the mob's lust. This drama had to be played to its end.

As Holmes was pulled feet first down the rubble-strewn concrete, the lynchers jumped on his face, taking turns. As he lay on the ground, writhing, a fist struck him full on his nose, which began to spurt blood.

Thurmond, carried along behind Holmes, still showed no sign of consciousness. This was disconcerting to the mob.

"We don't want to hang a guy when he doesn't know what's happening to him," a spectator complained. "Shake him out of it."

One who doubted that Thurmond's unconsciousness was genuine was Anthony Cataldi, who lifted the kidnapper's eyelids and thought he detected a flicker.

"Wake up!" someone shouted into Harold's ear, and someone else kicked him. But whether or not he was faking, the efforts to rouse him were futile. His limp form, clad in a brown coat and trousers over a light-colored shirt, was moved swiftly along the driveway by a dozen businesslike lynchers, who overtook the violent cluster around Holmes.

With the mob's frenzy totally focused on Holmes and Thurmond, Undersheriff Hamilton decided it was the right moment to activate a plan that had taken shape in his mind. On the north side of the jail, around a corner and out of the mob's line of sight was a small door used for deliveries to the kitchen. From within, Hamilton cautiously opened it a crack and, upon ascertaining that he was not under surveillance, beckoned to a figure following behind. Mingling with the crowd, Hamilton and his companion, who was attired as a woman, walked five blocks to a designated spot where Deputies Elmer Trousdell and Leland Calice waited in a county car. Calice gunned the engine as the "woman," whom no one had recognized as Ray Sousa, climbed in, to be sped to the safety of the San Francisco City Prison.

At the end of the fifty-mile ride, the trembling Sousa hugged his deliverers as a lost child hugs its mother. Deposited in a San Francisco cell, he tested the bars and grinned upon finding them solid. He begged to be taken to state prison right away without the formality of sentencing.

"Tell my attorney he's fired," he said. "I don't want a new trial. I never want to see San Jose again. All I want is to get over in San Quentin where they can't lynch a fellow." Jubilant in his safety, he turned to a photographer nearby, who was focusing his camera: "Sure you can take my picture. I'll stand on my head, hang onto the ceiling, or pose any way you want."

About the same time Sousa was being spirited out of the jail's kitchen door, another inmate was taking flight out the unguarded front door, under his own power.

Lawyer Duncan Oneal, whose late afternoon visit to his jailed client had cost him his ready cash in the crap game, had gone home and retired early. Then his phone jangled, and he again heard the familiar voice of his weekend companion, Dr. Cletus Sullivan. The doctor was excited by the nonstop radio bulletins describing the pitched battle in progress where it had seemed so calm a few hours earlier.

"Let's go back down and see what's doing, Duncan," Sullivan said. "Get your clothes on, and I'll come by and pick you up."

Miraculously, the two men found a parking place on First Street only a block and a half from the jail. Nearing the lockup on foot, Duncan was startled to spy his client, the suspected embezzler, running up the sidewalk toward him. As the man passed, Duncan grabbed him.

"Where the hell do you think you're going?"

The man was shivering with fright.

"Mr. Oneal," he said, "that mob pretty near took me. My wife is over at the YWCA, and I just want to go and tell her I'm all right. I'll come back."

"Well, you damn well better. You're in big trouble if you don't."

The client was sincere, as he proved the next morning by showing up for his arraignment at the appointed time.

With the buckling of the jail doors, Ray Blackmore and Andy Anderson considered themselves liberated from the asphyxiating confines of their post in the courthouse. Their tear gas was exhausted; the battle was lost. They were tattered, shaken soldiers of a defeated army. They found seats on a running board of their police car, which was undamaged and still parked beside the driveway, down which the lynchers at that moment were hustling the kidnappers to their doom. The mob no longer perceived the San Jose officers as a threat, and its hostility to them had vanished.

"Don't hurt the police," a leader commanded. "They're only doing their job, OK?"

The men dragging Jack Holmes paused when they reached a point opposite the two exhausted cops, to display their quarry triumphantly from a distance of a few feet.

"Well, we got 'em!" someone in the mob gloated.

Suddenly, from afar, Anderson and Blackmore heard the shrill blast of a police whistle. Until now they had believed themselves the only San Jose policemen in the neighborhood, but they were wrong: Officer Mike Guerin—brother of their captain, John—had remained throughout the lynching at the intersection of First and St. John, a stone's throw away, directing traffic!

"If the sky had fallen," the *Chronicle*'s Brier wrote, "that policeman would still toot his whistle. . . . He kept on sending 'em down First Street by the courthouse."

Blackmore and Anderson gazed after the lynchers jostling the kidnappers into the park. At the First Street curb a parked automobile blocked their path. They did not detour; they bodily threw Holmes over the top of the car and picked him up on the other side.

Emig, ignoring his concussion, forlornly followed the mob across the street. Supported by Highway Patrolmen Torres and Ray Barry, he pleaded with the lynchers to surrender their prisoners. In reply, they turned on him and beat him. A rock struck his jaw.

In the park the mood was buoyant. Some who were there had witnessed the lynching of the Howard Street Gang in Santa Rosa thirteen years before, and that had been a grim show. By contrast, this was a Roman circus—a hundred performers cheered by a bloodthirsty audience of thousands.

The inflamed group with Holmes in tow reached the park a few steps ahead of the dozen-odd men pushing Thurmond along. But at their destination, the latter went about their work with cold efficiency, and Thurmond died first. They carried him straightway to a mulberry tree near the park's southwest corner, across from the Elks Club and Trinity Episcopal Church. The red-haired youth tightened the rope around Thurmond's neck and tossed the loose end over a sturdy low limb.* Flashlights, arc lights, and spotlights from cars illuminated the grisly scene. There was little commotion. Somewhere in the throng, the ignored voice of an elderly clergyman moaned, "Wait, men, wait! . . . Don't become murderers! . . . Don't hang a lifeless man!"

Hugh Center, Emig's wounded lawyer friend, mingled with the lynchers, trying anew to sabotage their undertaking. Each time the redhead threw the rope over the limb, Center would throw it back. Finally he gave up, but as he made his way out of the crush, he clung to the rope and reeled it out behind him, snarling the lynchers and forcing them to disentangle themselves before proceeding. His tactics bought only a moment's time, and the delay made the crowd surlier.

"Remember Brooke Hart!" an onlooker yelled.

When the Thurmond rope was finally ready, a youth in his early twenties shouted, "Let him have it!" With all hands pulling, the kidnapper was hoisted in lurches. At the first jerk upward, his legs went stiff and his eyes opened. From the mob came a throaty cheer. When Thurmond's feet were four or five feet off the ground, one of the leaders commanded, "Hold him there, Red." The time was 11:20.

A young girl with a maniacal laugh addressed the dangling form: "How do you like it, you bastard? How do you like it up there? We like it. Oh, we like it, you bet! We put you there and we'd put you there again."

The crowd took up the chant: "How do you like it? . . . How do you like it? . . . How do you like it?"

A youth pulled the pants off the kidnapper, exposing his genitals.

"Come up and see us sometime, baby," taunted a woman in the crowd, mimicking Mae West.

---

*The *Oakland Post-Enquirer* reported that the Thurmond rope belonged to the San Jose Fire Department, and in the *News*, George Millard wrote that the Holmes rope was fire department property. However, Cataldi said later that both kidnappers were hanged with the ropes he brought from his father's truck.

Some women fainted, some wept; one beat her fists on a tree trunk, crying, "Oh, dear God, no, no, no, no!" But other women—housewives, white-haired old ladies, stenographers, coeds, debutantes—jabbed lighted cigarettes at Thurmond's nude thighs. A torch of rolled-up newspapers was set aflame and held to his feet. Someone held a match to his pubic hair, which burned briefly. Young mothers laughed, ignoring their children—hair-ribboned girls, boys in knickers, infants in arms who retched and vomited in horror.

From the multitude the chant of "Brook-ie HART . . . Brook-ie HART! . . . Brook-ie HART!" rose again, exultantly now.

Thurmond's neck was not broken; he strangled to death with convulsions continuing for several minutes, his body bending at the hips with each spasm. His face turned black and his tongue hung out. At last he was motionless, more effigy than man, turning slowly from side to side on the taut rope.

"This saves the county the expense of a trial," somebody said.

Post-Enquirer photographer Howard Robbins was holding his flashlight reflector overhead, about to snap a picture of Thurmond's pendent body, when he felt the cold steel of a revolver muzzle against his neck.

"Don't shoot or I'll shoot," a man at his rear threatened, reaching for the reflector with his free hand and pulling it back over Robbins's shoulder.

While the mob had abandoned its hostility toward the policemen, who were now powerless against it, and while it ignored pencil-and-paper journalists whose stories could be refuted or denied, it still looked on cameramen as a menace. A recognizable face in a photograph could convict a lyncher of homicide. Mob leaders with handkerchief masks went through the crowd smashing every camera they saw and exposing film.

In the crush of the crowd, Robbins could not turn to face his assailant, but he was able to wrench his reflector free. Within seconds a free-for-all erupted between newspapermen and the mob. As the brawl went on around him, Robbins managed to get his picture.

In the park, the Holmes lynchers ran into unforeseen trouble. Nimble teenagers and college youths, assigned to climb trees, could not find a branch that would bear the weight of the husky kidnapper, who continued to scream, thrash, and fight savagely for his life. Several minutes were lost before a limb that seemed sturdy enough was discovered about twenty-five feet up an elm not far from the McKinley statue. The delay made the lynchers anxious, because of garbled rumors racing through the crowd.

"President Roosevelt has just wired the Sunnyvale naval base," someone shouted. "Ten trucks of marines are on the way."

Now in a supreme paroxysm, with biceps bulging and tendons tense, Holmes succeeded in wriggling out of his noose. A leader replaced it, adjusting it snugly,* and the rope, tossed over the high limb, was pulled taut.

"Don't string me up, boys. Don't string me up!" the killer pleaded. "Give me a chance."

In this extreme moment, Holmes got a last fleeting hope of salvation.

"Are you sure that's him?" asked a newspaperman, who had not heard his earlier admission of identity.

"I don't know. Is it?" blankly replied the man fitting the noose.

The mob hesitated. But then, from somewhere in the press of people, a man said, "Yes, that's him. I know him." Holmes's last chance was gone.

"OK, up with him," the man with the noose commanded. The kidnapper, prone at this point, was pulled to his feet—at the very instant a screaming courier arrived from the other gallows tree, some distance away.

"We've strung up Thurmond!" he shouted. "Let Holmes see what we've done to his buddy." The lynchers, taken with the idea, hoisted Holmes to give him a last view of his partner, now dangling from the mulberry tree.

"How do you like it, Cocky Holmes?" they shouted into his ear, using an epithet the newspapers had coined. Then they slackened the rope to let him down, pulled him up a second time, and again dropped him.

"Torture him!" a vigilante screamed.

"Cut him up!"

"Tear him apart!"

"Make him suffer like Brooke did!"

---

*Brooke Hart's college friend Agnew Shea later told Ray Renwick that he was the man who put the noose around Holmes's neck—a role nonetheless doubted by many who knew him. As a cowboy-rancher, Shea was skilled at roping and knotting. He later became a tavern operator on Monterey's Cannery Row. He died in 1977.

Youths swigging bootleg booze from flasks attacked Holmes with clubs and their fists, fingernails, and feet, with no letup. Women lit matches and pressed them against his flesh. John Sepulveda, so close that he could almost touch the kidnapper, thought the mob had "turned to animals . . . lost their whole sense of being human." The sophomoric mentality of the younger thrill seekers surfaced as they broke into football chants: "We want a touchdown!" . . . "Block that kick!" . . . "Hold that line!"

"Hurry!" somebody yelled. "The San Francisco cops are coming!"

The motley throng surrounding Holmes, enraged by his arrogance, was huge compared to that which had lynched Thurmond. Billy Morris, Brooke Hart's first cousin and close friend, was close in. A well-known lawyer, on crutches, was struggling for a place on the rope. There was a huge shirtless man who looked to Marshall Hall "like a bull moose." And a young man coiling the rope was recognized as Jackie Coogan.

"What do you say now?" the mob leader demanded of Holmes.

"There's nothing to be said," he muttered, crumpling to his knees.

"All right. Let him have it," the leader ordered. The men on the rope gave it a mighty yank. Scores of hands pulled slowly, deliberately, until Holmes's feet were fifteen feet off the ground. Even as he rose, screaming with pain, he kicked the air and made two final grabs at the rope above his head, endeavoring to climb it hand over hand. Frantically he tried to slacken the noose and jerk it free of his neck. The mob lowered him, broke his arms, and hauled him up again. The time was 11:25.

A gasp rose as the crowd got its first clear view of the six-foot kidnapper—well muscled, his face a bloody pulp, a score of flashlights playing on his white nakedness. As he lost bladder control, a stream of urine gushed forth, and a cackle of laughter went through the park. Women, some with babies, hugged their men in exultation. Some parents held small children aloft for a better view.

Holmes strangled in midair. He did not convulse as Thurmond had. He was dead within four or five minutes.

"Turn him around. Let us have a look at him," came a shout from the crowd. The lynchers complied. Holmes's face was a cruel mask.

"Well, there won't be any more kidnapping in this county for a long time," said someone below.

Now the hangmen melted anonymously into the throng of onlookers, unchallenged by the law officers watching helplessly from across the street.

* * *

Fifty miles to the north in San Francisco, attorney Vincent Hallinan and his wife were playing bridge with friends that evening. In high spirits, he looked forward to immersing himself in Holmes's defense, a venture that would challenge the outer limits of his courtroom capability. Moreover, he needed the $10,000 retainer Maurice Holmes had given him in greenbacks, now reposing in his office safe. He intended to go to San Jose in the morning to meet Jack Holmes himself.

Sometime during the evening, the radio was turned on and Hallinan caught a few words about the jail siege. He went to the phone and called a friend on the city desk of a San Francisco newspaper.

"What's happening down there?"

"They're taking the kidnappers across to the park right now. Hold the phone."

Several minutes passed before the friend's voice returned:

"It's done. They've strung up both men."

Hallinan returned to the bridge table disconsolate. The noose had cheated him out of a client and a cause. Now he would have to give Maurice Holmes his $10,000 back.

A little after 11:30, the telephone rang in the Hart mansion. Aleese, the younger daughter, answered it and heard the voice of the family's live-in friend and helper, Jay McCabe.

"It's all over with," he said.

"I don't understand."

"Both men are dead."

"*What are you talking about, Jay?*"

"Holmes and Thurmond. They've just hung both of them in the park."

Aleese was astounded. The Harts in their sorrow had kept their radios silent all evening, and the daughters were unaware of the violence set in motion by the discovery of their brother's body. Aleese's first reaction to McCabe's message was horror. Then, as what had happened sunk in, she experienced a vast relief—for her ailing mother's sake, not her own. For eleven days, ever since the arrest of the kidnappers, Nettie Hart had been dreading the ordeal of a trial at which family members, perhaps she herself, would have to appear. "I could never face those people," she had said over and over.

Now Aleese would be able to tell her mother, "Forget it, everything's going to be fine."

All evening long, in the home of Nettie's sister Belle Fowler, thirteen-year-old Alex Hart, Jr., had known much more than his sisters about what was happening. Nettie's purpose, in sending the boy out of the family home, had been to insulate him from ugliness. But in choosing the Fowler home as his haven, she had not reckoned with Belle's taste for adventure.

Unlike the Harts, the Fowlers had kept their radio on all evening and were following every word about the events in St. James Park. Now, as the lynching reached its climax, Belle turned to her nephew.

"Would you like to see what's going on downtown, Alex?" she asked.

The boy, who was not really sure how he felt about it, nevertheless nodded. Belle piled him into her car and headed for the park. The crowd was just starting to break up, and with amazing luck she found a parking place on First Street, almost in front of the courthouse. It was probably no more than fifty yards from where the stripped corpse of Jack Holmes swayed. Harold Thurmond, naked below the waist, dangled in the farther distance. The scene would remain with young Alex forever: two bodies, eerily illuminated by auto light beams, hanging limply amid the greenery with faces plainly visible. The sight made the boy queasy, but half a century later he would still say, "I felt they got what they deserved."

When Nettie learned later of the nocturnal adventure on which Belle had taken her son—the only member of her immediate family to witness the awful retribution to Brooke's murderers—she was furious. A resulting rift between the sisters took long to heal.

When Inspector Kyle's squad of Oakland police finally arrived in the park, a jocular voice in the crowd greeted them: "Well, boys, you're five or ten minutes late."

All that was left for the Oakland officers to do was guard the hanging bodies and joke with the onlookers until the coroner came. Their presence dissuaded a bunch of young drunks who were talking loudly about excising the kidnappers' penises and testicles.

The Alameda sheriff's posse, which had gathered at Centerville before dark, had still been sitting there when the Oakland squad screamed past sometime after eleven o'clock. Not until then did Undersheriff Frank Swain give the command to move out. The sixteen-mile ride to San Jose took about twenty minutes, and on arrival the Alameda deputies, like the Oakland police, had little to do. The whole area was saturated with tear gas, and just walking around stirred it up, Constable Vince Strobel remembered.

San Francisco's riot squad rolled into town with five dozen gas bombs shortly before midnight. The San Francisco officers had known they were too late by the time they reached Santa Clara, where they began meeting cars with obscured license plates, streaming away from the lynching locale.

Ironically, the out-of-town rescue convoys generated new thrill seekers to replace those dispersing. All along the way, their sirens had excited people, many of whom climbed into their cars and fell in behind the police vehicles. The throng in the park continued to be fed too by streetcar passengers. In the gridlock created by the fleeing automobiles, lines of yellow trolleys stacked up on the First Street tracks, disgorging their riders to view the bodies twisting slowly.

Souvenir hunters swarmed around the gallows trees, stripping bark, snapping off twigs and limbs and snatching at Thurmond's remaining garments. The sight sickened a young man in the crowd, a general contractor, who chased one bunch of women predators away.

"Christ sakes, what the hell's the matter with you?" he shouted at them. "Get the hell out of here. Enough is enough!"

Spectators kept filing by to spit on Thurmond's low-hanging corpse. A group of men poured gasoline on it and lit a bonfire below.

"We'll burn you to hell before you have a chance to get there," one of them cried at the dead murderer. The body blazed for a moment when a match was touched to it.

Out of the crowd, supported by a friend, came an aging woman in tears who said she was Thurmond's mother.

"Oh, please don't, please," she begged. "Give him to me. Let me have him now." One of the men kindling the fire roughly shoved the woman aside. She ran away screaming.

The corpses hung from their trees for about forty minutes. It was past midnight when a hearse from the Williams Mortuary inched through the crowd and stopped first beneath the mulberry from which Thurmond drooped. His tongue still protruded from between clenched teeth. The fires had burned away the front of his remaining clothes, but his body was charred only slightly. The noose which had strangled him was amateurish—a simple loop with a slip knot.

The naked, battered Holmes was harder to recover. His rope snagged on the branches of the old elm and it had to be cut, dropping the body to the ground. Holmes's noose, unlike Thurmond's, was an expertly tied hangman's knot, with thirteen turns of the rope. Below the right ear, the knot had snapped his neck, causing his head to sag grotesquely to the left. His mouth and nose were crusted with blood; his eyes badly bruised.

Three deputy coroners recovered the bodies with the assistance of two Oakland policemen and *News* reporter Frank Lowery.

"Throw 'em in the bay and let the crabs eat 'em like they ate Brooke," somebody yelled.

In the hearse the corpses, with the ropes still about their necks, were covered with sheets and placed side by side as the vehicle moved out slowly through the crowd. The men who had recovered the dead rode in silence on the running boards. The mob did not try to follow. At the Williams Mortuary an assistant took custody of the bodies, and the nooses were removed. The pitiful remains of Brooke Hart, which had arrived earlier, lay nearby.

So not much past midnight on Monday, November 27, the killers were reunited on coroner's slabs with the man they had dumped to his death in San Francisco Bay, seventeen days and five or six hours before.

V

AFTERMATH

19

The Next Three Days

Even as the murderers' limp forms dangled on their ropes, reporters in Sacramento made their way to the creaky old Victorian that served California as a governor's residence to solicit the reaction of Sunny Jim Rolph.

He greeted them expansively. He was well prepared, having just been briefed by Cato and Motor Vehicles Director Theodore Roche, and his comment was a bombshell.

"This is a fine lesson to the whole nation," he declared. "There will be less kidnapping now."

A stunned reporter pointed out that the mob leaders in San Jose had left themselves open to prosecution for homicide. The governor's response was deliberate and emphatic:

"I don't think they will arrest anyone for the lynchings. . . . They made a good job of it. If anyone is arrested for the good job, I'll pardon them all."

Rolph defended anew his refusal to send the militia to prevent the hangings: "Well, if the people have confidence that troops will not be called out to mow them down when they seek to protect themselves against kidnappers, there is liable to be swifter justice and fewer kidnappings."

As he went on, the governor warmed to his subject and his ebullience grew.

"I am checking San Quentin and Folsom to find out what kidnappers they have," he said. "I am thinking of paroling them to those fine citizens of San Jose who know how to handle such a situation."

To let the reporters know he was only half joking, Rolph told them he had already determined that Folsom held two men, both from Los

Angeles, currently serving kidnap-extortion terms. He had not yet heard from San Quentin.

In St. James Park, after the bodies were cut down, the mob dissolved silently into the night.

It took three hours to clear the gridlock in the park's surrounding streets. In nearby cafes and taverns, to which the lynchers repaired, the governor's clemency promise quickly became known by radio and word of mouth, producing a sense of relief followed by noisy euphoria. A copious flow of liquor loosened tongues, and men who claimed to have had their hands on the ropes became loudmouthed heroes in the bars. Gaping admirers swarmed around the boasters like groupies around rock stars in a later time.

Exhilarated teenagers, basking in sordid glory, were the loudest. Anthony Cataldi laid an extravagant claim to having organized the whole uprising. Ray Loren told all who would listen that he was the first to enter the jail.

What everyone wanted to know was the identity of the fur-coated blonde who had goaded the rammers into their final, successful assault. One talkative vigilante, recognized as a young San Jose businessman, parried the question.

"She played her part, all right," he said with a quiet smile, "but I seem to forget what her name is." It was the best answer anyone would ever get.

For some, the exertions of the long night were far from over.

At San Jose Hospital a stream of casualties—beaten, burned, or gassed—poured through the emergency room, foremost among them being Emig and Buffington. Emig, who had kept up a killing work pace during the seventeen days since Brooke Hart's disappearance, was admitted to the hospital for nervous exhaustion as well as his back injury and head wound—the latter appearing to be a concussion with possible skull fracture. Soon after his admission, he was sedated by his physician, Dr. H. J. Arnold, and sunk into fitful unconsciousness. Buffington was treated for severe bruises and shock. No-visitors notices were posted for both patients.

Policemen Blackmore and Anderson had been on duty more than sixteen hours when the kidnappers' bodies were driven away in the hearse. Weary and battered, they recovered their guns from their courthouse hiding place, returned to their car, and slowly drove to the police station, where they reported to Chief Black. For a police chief in whose city law and order had collapsed totally, Black was calm and unperturbed. He took only a casual debriefing.

For the newspapermen covering the story, the grueling labor of filing their dispatches lay ahead. Out-of-town reporters converged on the Western Union office three blocks south of the courthouse, among them the *Chronicle*'s Royce Brier, who took over an unused typewriter and began to write. His lead came naturally, easily:

> San Jose, Nov. 26—Lynch law wrote the last grim chapter in the Brooke Hart kidnapping here tonight. . . .

On and on Brier spun his tale with skill, power, and grace, handing his copy to the telegraph operator in short takes. His imagery was gripping, all the way to the final paragraph:

> The bodies hung in the park for almost an hour. Shortly before midnight came squads of San Francisco police officers . . . too late to save anything but the dead clay of the murderers.

Brier's account, set in type as fast as it was received in San Francisco, filled more than 100 column-inches in Monday morning's paper. It would win the year's Pulitzer Prize for reporting and become a standard in anthologies of splendid twentieth-century journalism.

The lynching was a circulation manager's dream. The combined Monday press runs of the San Francisco and Oakland dailies exceeded 1.2 million, double the ordinary production. Street sales set new records everywhere. The *Examiner*'s run was 150,000 higher than usual. The *Chronicle* issued thirteen editions carrying the "EXTRA" plate, with sales shattering the previous mark set by the World War I armistice.

At the Stice residence in Stockton, some eighty miles northeast of San Jose, Evelyn Holmes had put her children to bed and retired Sunday night unaware of the crisis in St. James Park. She had not heard the radio all day.

Early Monday the phone rang, and Evelyn's sister, Beatrice Stice, took the call. From a San Jose friend, she learned what had happened, and it fell to Beatrice to tell Evelyn how Jack had died. The enormity of the tidings so overwhelmed Evelyn that she retained no memory of how she reacted. But her small son David would never forget: "She went completely to pieces."

Whatever family happiness the six-year-old boy and his younger sister had known in their first years of life—and it appears to have been much—was, in David's words, "shattered totally." They would never return to the friendly old Victorian on Bird Avenue or to the school in Willow Glen. Their future and their mother's, which a few weeks earlier had beckoned with security, hope, and promise, was suddenly a void.

In Monday's daylight, Sunday night's battleground stood desolate and drear. Rubble still obstructed the entrance to the jail, nearly every window of which was shattered. The hulk of an automobile stood between the jail and the courthouse, the tonneau filled with bricks and chunks of concrete, the hood and body caved in. The jail's booking room and offices were littered with splintered boards and shards of glass, and records were strewn about. The steel-sheathed doors sagged on their hinges. Half a ton of debris carpeted the sheriff's office, and tear gas clung to everything, the fumes permeating most of the other courthouse offices.

As jail trusties were put to work cleaning up the mess, glaziers began restoring the windows. Ironfounder Otto Hellwig—the same who had told Joe Colla three days earlier that the lynching would take place—was called to repair the doors. The damage looked more costly than it was. After some calling around, County Purchasing Agent Emma Allegrini said $300 should take care of everything. Someone observed, "Well, it's cheaper than trying Holmes and Thurmond would have been."

In his San Francisco office, Reed Vetterli sat down to compose a memo to J. Edgar Hoover, disclaiming any FBI culpability in the lynching. Vetterli was still painfully mindful of his earlier reprimand from Hoover for taking the kidnappers out of jail for questioning. ("If they should be lynched while in our custody it would be terrible.") In the stilted FBI jargon that seemed to be his everyday language, he wrote:

> I desire to advise that while federal indictments were re-
> turned against these subjects [Holmes and Thurmond], sub-
> jects were always in custody of either the San Francisco police

or the sheriff at San Jose, California. . . . In no sense of the word was either prisoner in the custody of the federal government.

In Washington, Hoover received this assurance with immense relief and passed the message on immediately to his nominal superior, Attorney General Homer S. Cummings.

Close to midday, a sheriff's car pulled up outside the battered jail and disgorged the disheveled figure of Ray Sousa, who had almost become the mob's third victim before being spirited away to San Francisco. The heartfelt wish Sousa had voiced—never to see San Jose again—had not been honored, but exceptional arrangements had been made to guarantee his safety as he returned to be sentenced for the slaying of Leonard Ramonda. By stipulation of his lawyer and the district attorney, the sentencing had been moved up a day from the Tuesday time originally set. Sousa was hustled from the car into the courthouse and taken straight to the bench of Judge Robert R. Syer. One minute later he was back in the car, on his way to San Quentin facing up to ten years of incarceration. Never before had a killer left for prison so full of gratitude and relief.

Inevitably, reporters made their way Monday morning to the comfortable cottage on South Eleventh Street where lived the tailor, Maurice Holmes, and his wife Hulda. Maurice spoke for the family. With fatigue and anguish contorting his Scandinavian features, he seemed much older than his fifty-six years.

"Our boy was innocent—innocent, I tell you," he cried out. "We know where he was that night. I can prove almost every minute of it."

The "proof" rested on his steadfast insistence that it had been only seven o'clock on the kidnapping night when Jack arrived home to pick up Evelyn for their movie date with the Estensens. That was at least an hour earlier than possible if Jack's confession was to be taken at face value. According to the confession, seven o'clock was just about the time Brooke Hart was being tossed off the San Mateo Bridge.

"We can prove the stories of that man Thurmond were lies," Maurice said. "They forced my boy to confess something he never did. My boy was accused only by one man, Thurmond, whose family admits he was insane."

Clenching his fists, the old man spoke hoarsely with an intensity showing that he believed all his boy had told him, or at least wanted to. The family, he said, was thinking about suing the governor, the sheriff, and the county. Hulda Holmes, seated on the divan beside her husband, tearfully interrupted him.

"My boy—he never did it!" she screamed. "Couldn't you have seen that? Couldn't anybody have seen it? If it takes until we join him in death, we will prove it to the world."

For the grieving Thurmond family, the burden of meeting the press fell to Harold's brother Roy, the preacher from Chico; his sister, Gail Karnagel; and J. Oscar Goldstein, the lawyer they had retained.

Unlike the Holmeses, the Thurmonds professed no ill will toward the sheriff; they had no plans to sue him or anyone. They offered no claim of Harold's innocence, but handed reporters a statement signed by their mother, Lillie, who they said was in deep shock and could not face the press herself. She fell back on what would have been Harold's defense in court, his purported insanity:

> My son, Harold Thurmond, has been an exemplary young man, always devoted, kind and loving. He was a delicate child, but never showed at any time any criminal tendencies. On the contrary, he was spiritually inclined. He attended church services regularly. . . .
>
> In his early childhood Harold suffered a severe injury to the head, which at the time my family did not consider of importance. Later, however, we observed indications of considerable mental dullness.

Over the past four years, the statement went on, a noticeable change had come over Harold, though he still showed a "kindly, gentle, and religious heart." The family had considered placing him in an asylum, but had dropped the idea, feeling he would improve. Now, however, they were convinced that he "had entirely become deranged and reason had completely left him."

> Our grief is unbearable, and we are all heartbroken beyond expression. . . . In this, our most tragic hour, we are sustained and strengthened by our great faith in God and our abiding loyalty to our religious beliefs. We are further strengthened and comforted by the prayers of countless true and loyal friends.

The family wanted one bit of misinformation set aright. The woman who had begged for Harold Thurmond's body while he hung from the tree, claiming to be his mother, was an impostor. Lillie's doctor would certify that she had been in seclusion at home for the past several days.

Attorney Goldstein, in a separate statement, declared his independent belief that Harold had been "absolutely mentally unbalanced and in every sense of the word insane."

Underscoring the family's good will toward Emig, Roy Thurmond and Goldstein later called to visit him at San Jose Hospital. Told that he could have no visitors, they left a note wishing him a speedy recovery.

Early Monday afternoon, out of respect or curiosity, San Joseans began to gather on the sidewalk in front of the Hart home, along the low hedge that bordered the deep lawn. There had been no public notice of Brooke's funeral, but the arrangements had become widely known by word of mouth. The hearse in the porte cochère had alerted many.

The services, in the mansion's dark-paneled living room, were for the family and a few friends only, but by the time they began at 2:30, several hundred persons stood outside, speaking in whispers.

The rites embraced both Alex Hart's Judaism and Nettie's Catholicism—faiths between which Brooke had never made a choice. Rabbi Karesh, not much older than Brooke and his close friend, officiated, reciting the Kaddish, the Hebrew liturgical prayer for the dead, and delivering a brief eulogy. Father William C. Gianera, who had counseled Brooke throughout his four years at Santa Clara University, also eulogized him, recalling his popularity with teachers and fellow students alike. The priest then offered a prayer in Latin at the head of the closed metal casket, on which lay a spray of roses, lilies of the valley, and orchids.

Six of Brooke's close friends, including Charlie O'Brien, carried the casket out across the lawn, flanked by an honor guard of fifty students from SCU, which had dismissed classes for the afternoon. Sixty-seven automobiles fell in behind the hearse to make up a procession seven city blocks in length, with a highway patrol escort of four motorcycles. The cortège moved slowly eastward along The Alameda and into the business district, taking Brooke for the last time past the department store. During all that had happened, this was the first time its doors had been shut on a working day. All other downtown businesses had closed too.

At Oak Hill Memorial Park, on the south side of the city, the cars wound their way between lawns dotted with marble and granite tombstones and up a winding road to a hilltop where a domed mausoleum overlooked the valley—a view softened by purplish haze in the pale sunlight of this late autumn afternoon.

Nettie Hart, wearing black and heavily veiled, faltered twice as she followed the flower-decked coffin into the building for a committal service in the flower-filled rotunda. Miriam Hart and Billie Cohn supported her.

"Oh, my son, my poor boy," the mother murmured. Alex Hart followed his wife, his drawn face awash with tears.

Subdued yellow illumination from a stained-glass skylight flooded the scene as the pallbearers carried Brooke a last time, from the rotunda to a wide corridor lined with cream-colored marble. As they gently slid the coffin into a crypt in the second tier from the floor, Nettie fainted. Carried from the mausoleum by her husband and a nephew, she was rushed home with a police escort.

The press, tugging at readers' heartstrings, had been obsessed with Nettie's health since the first days after the kidnapping. Her breakdown at the funeral fed the newswriters' orgy of maudlin excess. "Physicians were hurriedly summoned, and it was feared that the relapse might be fatal," the *Call-Bulletin* solemnly reported. The *News* titillated its readers with a comment from Nettie's nephew, Billy Morris, that, "She appears to be losing her mind." The staid *Mercury Herald*, however, assured its readers that Mrs. Hart, after her collapse, was "resting easily" and "bearing up well" at home.

Alex Hart, who had resisted personal publicity throughout his ordeal, poured out his feelings on Tuesday to the *Chronicle*'s Carolyn Anspacher. Her sensitive account of Brooke's funeral in that morning's paper may have led him to grant the interview.

"I was perfectly satisfied that the law should take its course against the two men who killed my son," he told her, "but it brings me some comfort to feel my fellow citizens took violent action because they loved Brooke. I am a believer in law and order and have never tolerated violence of any sort. . . . When I was informed of what was happening Sunday night, I must confess that I didn't know whether to laugh or cry. I was seized with a sort of hysteria that I couldn't control. I had forbidden any member of my family or organization to participate in any kind of violence, and it didn't seem possible to me that the lynching was actually going on. It seemed too remote. I didn't know what to do. As a matter of fact there was nothing I could do. The little word I sent urging the crowd to let the law take its course could not have stemmed that tide of righteous fury, not if it had been amplified a thousand times. You see, I felt it was all rather futile. After all, my boy was dead."

It took less than a day for a new full-blown cottage industry to arise in San Jose: the collection, fabrication, and sale of lynching souvenirs.

Pieces of "the rope" were in heavy demand. As thousands of the curious gravitated to the park, peddlers worked the crowds, selling what were purported to be lengths of the lynching ropes for a dollar a foot or whatever the traffic would bear. Times were hard, and no one knows how many hundred feet of old hemp lines were turned into Christmas money by resourceful entrepreneurs who chopped them into short lengths and sold them to the gullible.

Shreds of Thurmond's trousers and Holmes's undershirt were also prized relics, and slivers from the gallows trees brought money on the streets. Hardly had the hanging ended when enterprising youths severed the lynching limbs, which were cut up and sold for fifty cents an inch.

At Monday night's city council meeting, City Manager Goodwin announced that the trees would have to be cut down because of irreparable mutilation by the souvenir hunters. The *Mercury Herald*, however, suggested that the real purpose was to obliterate the visible evidence of the town's murderous orgy. The elm and the mulberry stood doomed as surely as the killers who had swung from them. Four days later both were felled and the logs distributed to needy families for firewood.

Such obliteration was not universally applauded. In a letter to the *News*, a reader named Thomas Johns proposed naming the two trees "Holmes" and "Thurmond" as warnings to criminals, and mounting on each a metal tablet with a full account of the lynching. "And it may not be inappropriate," he wrote, "to erect a life-size statue of Brooke Hart midway between the two trees. It would have an effect on crime."

Postcards depicting the lynching showed up for sale all over town, as well as a series of "official photographs" in a fold-out mailer. Chief Black, who had sat out the event itself with a dispassion bordering on nonchalance, erupted in outrage upon learning that photos of the bodies were circulating. He declared the pictures "indecent" because of Holmes's nudity and warned that anyone selling them would be arrested. One widely sold postcard, a crude paste-up job in which both kidnappers seemed to hang from the same tree, showed Holmes in three-quarter front view. It appeared to have been retouched to endow him with an enlongated penis, semi-erect.

Black's censorship did not distinguish between front, side, and rear views of the corpses, however, and along with the postcards, he seized all street copies of Monday's *Oakland Post-Enquirer*. This uninhibited Hearst sheet had filled its salmon-pink front page with photos of the slayers dangling on their ropes (Holmes viewed from the rear). Bundles of the papers were rushed to San Jose within hours of the event. Their posted street price was three cents, but newsboys were soon bootlegging them for as much as a dollar. The police confiscated all copies they could find, on the pretext that the boys lacked city licenses. Joe Colla, then thirteen, eluded Black's censorial sweep by taking up a position just outside the city limits. There he sold 300 copies of the November 27 *Post-Enquirer* at prices ranging from a dime to a quarter.

In San Francisco too the lynching pictures were banned. Judge Daniel S. O'Brien gave one man a thirty-day jail term for hawking them, but the sentence was stayed when he demanded a jury trial. Three other men were arraigned on similar charges. From the bench, O'Brien commended the four San Francisco dailies for refraining from use of "ghastly" photos à la the *Post Enquirer*.

Both San Jose papers also withheld such pictures. The *News*, professing a sensitivity not apparent in its earlier "Human Devils" editorial, now used part of its editorial column to explain its decision, affirm its competitive zeal, and extol its own righteousness:

Weren't Scooped

The *News* was not "scooped" on the two horrible pictures of Holmes and Thurmond hanging by their necks in St. James Park. Our cameraman snapped those pictures, just as he did all other phases of the lynching.

The *News*, however, is proud of the fact that it is accepted freely and gladly into thousands of homes where there are children and sensitive women. We did not feel that we could, in good taste, publish these gruesome and horrible pictures. The same view was taken by all the San Francisco newspapers. We understand that one Oakland paper printed the pictures and had a heavy sale as a result. There are some standards of good taste which the *News* would not violate, even in exchange for heavier sales. We are a home newspaper in a city of happy homes, and we would not care to place in those homes pictures as gruesome and horrible as these.

But on the substantive issue of the lynching itself, the *News* was unrepentant. It devoted two columns of Monday's second page to a defensive editorial that stopped just short of canonizing to the lynchers:

SAN JOSE'S MESSAGE TO THE WORLD

In an orderly manner and without any attempt at unnecessary force—and evading any open riot that might occur from too much excitement—a vigilance committee headed by citizens who had given the matter much thought stormed the county jail last night and demanded what they and the general public believed was justice. . . .

There has been a feeling for many months throughout the entire United States that in order to stop the great wave of crime . . . the public must revert to the old days of taking the law into their own hands and in this manner make criminals respect the law. There could be no better way than by a few lynchings, many citizens believed.

San Jose is made up of the finest citizens of any city in the entire United States—peace loving, quiet, cultured people. . . . God-fearing, law-observing, good citizens have been watching these murders increasing and have watched crime increase in this country and from the time this splendid young fellow [Brooke Hart] was murdered this vigilance committee had in mind carrying out what in their minds was real justice. . . .

Many people who don't believe in mob violence will criticize them. The *News* offers no criticism.

Taken together, the *News*'s editorials showed a curious disparity of values: Lynching was acceptable; pictures of it were not.

Among those in the barroom audience of teenage braggart Anthony Cataldi, in the first hours after the lynching, had been United Press correspondent Robert C. Elliott. Intrigued by the youth's boast that he had masterminded all that had happened, Elliott asked him to tell his story in full. Bloated with self-importance, Anthony had needed no persuading. When the boy's "as told to" story moved on the

U.P. wire, the *News* relegated it to page seven under a one-column headline:

YOUTH, 18,
SAYS HE
LED MOB

BY ANTHONY CATALDI
(Copyright, 1933, By United Press)

I was the first one of the gang to break into the jail.

I came to town in the afternoon and saw the crowd and heard that Brooke Hart's body had been found. I decided to organize a necktie party. I went to my father's ranch and got some rope for the hanging.

Then I went all over town in my flivver roadster and passed out the word: "We're going to have a lynching at the jail at 11 o'clock tonight."

As he went on with his blustering account, exhilarated by the telling of it, Cataldi seemed blithely unmindful that he was making serious admissions of criminality, one after another:

I was the first one of the gang to get on the second floor. . . . We took the keys away from the deputies and broke into Thurmond's cell. . . . Two officers identified him for us. . . .

Part of the gang rushed Holmes' cell, and he told us he was Pierce, but we had the goods on him. There was a fellow in the party who knew him and a deputy sheriff also whispered, "Boys, you've got the right fellow." . . .

I knew Brooke Hart by sight but never had spoken to him. I thought that his terrible murder should be avenged. I found that several hundred others thought the same thing.

Perhaps the *News* gave Cataldi's flight of braggadocio its modest treatment because it was not staff produced, but more likely because Jack Wright, the managing editor, recognized it as a piece of adolescent nonsense. He could not have imagined that this story would have more impact in the weeks ahead than anything else in that day's paper.

Wherever he went that Monday, testing the feelings in the town, the *Chronicle*'s Brier found satisfaction, even smugness—not chagrin. At

252

length he sat down at a typewriter and began to put his second-day story together:

> Whatever the world may think of San Jose, this city is of but one opinion—justice was done in last night's lynching. You can't find a man, woman, or child who dissents from the fearful decree of Judge Lynch.
> It is a closed scene, a fallen curtain, in America's drama of kidnapping. Nothing will ever be done about it, unless an effort is made to find the assailant of Sheriff Emig. . . . The immunity of the mob leaders is almost as conclusive as a jury's verdict. . . .
> Brooke Hart is a martyr in San Jose. His death stands for something in the innermost hearts of his fellow citizens. They believe that in avenging his death they have done righteously, whatever others may think.

In a followup dispatch a day after he wrote the foregoing, Brier hammered on the same themes, proclaiming anew San Jose's supposedly unanimous satisfaction with Sunday night's events:

> In the light of the more or less orderly manner in which the affair was conducted, citizens are open in their declaration that they are "glad the sheriff didn't order gun play," and express commendation of his action. . . .
> The vigilantes, who appeared like wraiths in the night to lead the public's protest against legal delays and kidnapping have vanished as they came, their identities sunken forever behind the loyalty of their townspeople.

If Brier's reports were hyperbole, they nonetheless presented a valid reading of major sentiment in political and business circles. The *Call-Bulletin* quoted Chief Black as bluntly saying he did not consider the lynching a miscarriage of justice. The wife of FBI agent Vetterli, writing years later, affirmed that "the act was condoned in the heart of every public official."

With the advantage of a half-century's hindsight, we are justified today in challenging the objectivity of Brier's reportage. To write off the lynching as "a closed scene, a fallen curtain," less than twenty-four hours after it happened, betrayed an unreportorial reluctance to pursue the guilty. Not only did Brier accept without quibble that the lynchers' identities were "sunken forever," he indeed seemed approving. Moreover, it required a far jump away from objectivity and truth for him to write (echoing the News's editorial) of the "more or less orderly manner" in which the hangings were conducted. Transparently if perhaps unconsciously, he had become an apologist for the vigilantes, among whom he had nurtured his trusted and productive inside sources. It was in their interest to stifle public discussion and let the events of Sunday night fade mercifully into history.

But that was not to be—not yet, anyway. Violent passions loosed by those events remained unassuaged, and the strong forces set in motion were out of control.

In the first twenty-four hours after the lynching, little was heard from the thousands of San Joseans who were shocked, horrified, and sickened by it. Then Royce Brier's extravagant, defiant declaration that "this city is of but one opinion—justice was done" became the catalyst that ignited the fury of the dissenters.

On Tuesday the San Jose High School Faculty Women's Club became one of the first groups to rise in anger, disavowing Brier's assessment and resolving, "We abhor the substitution of lawlessness and mob violence for the orderly processes of law." The Women's Christian Temperance Union and the Unitarian Church quickly followed, the latter denouncing the lynching as "a most dastardly act" carried out by cowards of low mentality. Going a step further, the Christian Assembly demanded a grand jury investigation. The First Baptist Church—Harold Thurmond's church—called the lynching a "diabolical bestiality of conduct." Twenty Protestant pastors declared that it forfeited "the progress that countless Christian generations have won by slow stages toward elevating our civilization." One protest group chose the hanging site as its own forum, drawing several hundred persons to an antilynching rally in St. James Park.

Nowhere was the morality of the lynching more passionately debated than at Santa Clara University, because of continuing accusations that it had been fomented there. This charge gained new credence in the first hours after the event, when Undersheriff Earle Hamilton told a San Francisco reporter, "These lynchings were the work of students. Students led the mob, and students actually did the rough work." The Stanford Daily placed full responsibility for the hangings on "a handful of Santa Clara students, roommates [and] buddies of murdered Brooke Hart."

Certainly a few Santa Clara students had abetted the uprising.

Jackie Coogan, the school's celebrity undergraduate, was unmistakably recognized in the park, close in with the lynch crew. And in the next day's news pictures the tall, blond form of young Bob Carlton from Oakland was clearly identifiable on the battering ram. To blame the university exclusively, however, was to ignore the widely known and brazen role of San Jose's downtown vigilantes—essentially the business establishment. Two newspapers, the *News* in San Jose and the *Examiner* in San Francisco, came to the university's defense. The *News* editorially doubted that the mob was "in the faintest degree" university inspired.

As the moral debate widened, the courts and the penal system (which had never been given a chance to work) became the handiest scapegoats for lynching apologists. The *Mercury Herald* gave front-page play to a lengthy statement by a prominent lawyer, Samuel G. Tompkins, assailing the criminal statutes as "woefully antiquated, decrepit and inefficient, and wholly inadequate to protect society from the modern criminal." He held the constitutional guarantee against self-incrimination and the requirement of unanimous juries for criminal convictions to be "absurd." It was scandalous, he said, that penitentiaries offered such amenties as libraries, motion pictures, and recreation grounds, which made a criminal career "rather attractive."

Emig and Buffington were still in shock at San Jose Hospital Monday afternoon, but their injuries did not appear as serious as first feared. The blow to Emig's head had not fractured his skull, X rays showed, and his concussion was mild. He was suffering severe head, eye, and back pains, however, and newsmen admitted to his room found his head swathed in bandages. In their first access to the sheriff since the hangings, the reporters wanted to know why Holmes and Thurmond had not been evacuated through the jail's side door, as Ray Sousa had.

"We did consider it, but we soon decided it was impossible," Emig said. "We took Sousa out while the mob had the kidnappers in the park; we didn't have the same opportunity with the other two fellows. If we had taken [Holmes and Thurmond] out that way, we would have delivered them right into the hands of the lynchers. I suppose we could have taken them out during the day, but I really did not expect serious trouble."

This professed unconcern was hard to square with Emig's repeated entreaties to Governor Rolph, before the lynching, for deployment of the National Guard.

In diametric dissent from his undersheriff's declaration that students had done the "rough work," the sheriff added, "Remember, that mob wasn't composed of kids. There were substantial, gray-haired citizens in that mob."

Emig disclosed he had received numerous telegrams commending his decision not to shed blood, including one from Governor Rolph.

Late Monday, jailer Buffington's wife, Lula, visited him at the hospital, and as they chattered away, he suddenly sat bolt upright in bed.

"My birds!"

It was the first time he had remembered the caged canaries he had stowed away in the tiny storeroom, in his desperate effort to save them from the tear gas. Mrs. Buffington hurried to the jail and found night jailer Al Covey, who opened the storeroom, brought out the cages, and gave the two birds some seed. In a minute they burst into song.

Vincent Hallinan, the San Francisco lawyer who had lost his best-known client to the noose, reentered the picture Tuesday morning. He and another attorney, Nathan C. Coghlan, announced their intention, on behalf of the Holmes family, to sue Governor Rolph and the authorities of Santa Clara and San Francisco counties.

"Every time Holmes had an opportunity to speak unhampered, he asserted that [his] confession was obtained by third-degree tactics," Hallinan said. The two lawyers resurrected Holmes's allegation that his interrogators had threatened to let the mob have him if he did not sign.

In the lawsuit, the governor would be charged with inciting the lynching by his inflammatory statements, and with failure to uphold the law. Negligence charges would be brought against the San Jose and Santa Clara County officials, and the San Francisco police would be sued for letting Emig return the prisoners to San Jose's supercharged atmosphere of hatred and fear. Hallinan intended to name, as well, a large number of John Does, representing the actual lynchers and the police officers who watched them without intervening. Heavy damages would be demanded. The action would be filed in San Francisco, not in Santa Clara County where the lawyers despaired of getting a fair jury. The law afforded that option because San Francisco was the legal residence of Governor Rolph, the lead defendant.

Hallinan's "third-degree" charge brought a prompt counterblast from the convalescing Emig, hotly denying he had employed duress.

"Jack Holmes was guilty," the sheriff insisted. "He was able to supply several details which were missing from Thurmond's confession, and which Thurmond verified when I asked about them. For example, Thurmond did not know the route they had followed [to the bridge]. Holmes supplied it in detail. Holmes told how Thurmond had climbed over the bridge railing and shot into the water. When I asked Thurmond about it, he said he had forgotten to give that point in his story, but admitted it was true."

The *News*, submerging its bloodthirsty instincts, adopted a high-minded tone on its Tuesday editorial page, holding out an olive branch to the kidnappers' bereaved families. In a welcome-back-to-the-human-race editorial that must have afforded scant solace, the paper said, "We would like to make the parents of both Holmes and Thurmond realize that the public holds nothing against them, and that they have the sympathy of all San Jose in this, their great trial." The editorialist went on, "The *News* doesn't want to dwell any further upon this matter and will carry only the essentials of the aftermath news." It was a cheap promise, the essentials themselves promising headlines for months to come.

Because the kidnappers never saw the inside of a courtroom, it fell to Grant Miller, the Alameda County coroner, to conduct the only official public inquiry ever made into the death of Brooke Hart. The inquest was held on Wednesday at the same mortuary in Hayward where Brooke's forlorn remains had first been taken after their discovery.

District Attorney Earl Warren lent the resources and talent of his office to put the evidence together. In a well-structured proceeding, witnesses recited the events in chronological sequence, painting a shocking picture in bold strokes.

As lead-off witness, Louis Rossi told of seeing Brooke leave the store a few minutes before 6:00 P.M. on November 9, to pick up his car at the parking lot. One of the lot's operators recalled watching Brooke's green convertible move down the driveway toward the Market exit, until his attention was diverted just before the car reached the street. The next witness, Deputy Sheriff Felix Cordray, told of the vehicle's discovery on remote Evans Road seven hours later.

Undersheriff Hamilton then read the confessions into the record, and Belle Gallagher, the court reporter, attested to their authenticity.

The inquest's most poignant testimony came from Vinton Ridley, the Oakland wood seller who, with his partner Al Coley, had heard Brooke's distress calls from somewhere offshore beneath the San Mateo Bridge. The cries had ceased after a last desperate plea, "Hurry, I can't hold on much longer," at 7:25, less than ninety minutes after Brooke's abduction.

Several persons who had taken part in the search at the bridge site told of retrieving the concrete blocks, the wire, and the youth's hat and coat.

Two key witnesses established the murderers' premeditation. Tony Carvalho, from California Concrete Products, related anew how he sold three concrete blocks to Thurmond about November 1, dwelling upon Thurmond's quirky concern about their weight. Dominic Condensa, from the Vargas store in Santa Clara, examined the recovered strands of clothesline wire and affirmed that they could have been from a roll he had sold either on the kidnapping day or one day earlier. The purchaser could have been Thurmond; he wasn't sure.

Duck hunter Harold Stephens took the stand to describe the recovery of Brooke Hart's floating corpse on Sunday morning. (He and his partner, Leonard Dalve, were shortly to share the $500 reward Alex Hart had posted for the body's recovery.) Three witnesses—Rossi, Dr. Heuschele, and Dr. Conner—confirmed their identification of the body, and finally Dr. E. E. Hamlin, the autopsy surgeon, described its decomposed state and noted the absence of bullets in it.

When the testimony ended, the coroner's jury took little time in returning its one-paragraph verdict—the same, as to fact, as the drumhead verdict of the mob:

> We find that Brooke Hart died on November 9 from asphyxiation due to submersion after he was first assaulted and cast into San Francisco Bay from the San Mateo Bridge by Thomas H. Thurmond and John Holmes, and we accuse Thurmond and Holmes of murder.

Some San Joseans were loath to grant the kidnappers repose, even in death. On Monday the curious, hoping to view the bodies, had gathered outside the Amos Williams Mortuary—the county's de facto morgue. Rumors that they would try to snatch and mutilate the corpses kept Williams on edge, but the threats never materialized. Even as the authorities were quietly letting it be known that the lynchers would not be punished, they put out the word that ghouls would be prosecuted to the limit of the law.

On Wednesday morning, from the Curry & Gripenstraw Undertaking Parlor on Third Street, just south of St. James Park, came voices raised in an old gospel hymn:

> *In the sweet by and by*
> *We shall meet on that beautiful shore.*

The verses were sung with conviction by friends who had come to bid farewell to Harold Thurmond. The Rev. Andrew L. Fraser of the First Baptist Church officiated. City Traffic Officer Julian Covill stood outside the parlors during the services, on guard against mischief, but there was none.

Another cortège now wound its way through the city and out to Oak Hill Cemetery. Not long before noon, in a grassy tract near the foot of the hill where Brooke Hart slept in his newly sealed crypt, Thurmond's body was lowered into a grave that would never be marked.

Private services for Jack Holmes had been held Tuesday evening in the Williams chapel. A few hours before Thurmond's burial, Holmes's remains had been taken secretly to the crematory of this same cemetery and reduced to ashes.

20

Prosecution and Cover-up

There was born, on the first day after Holmes and Thurmond died, a conspiracy of silence—an unspoken pact shielding the identity of the vigilantes. It would still be honored half a century later.

Early on the evening of the lynching District Attorney Fred Thomas had received a telephone call at home—from whom his family never knew. He left at once for his office in the courthouse, where he stayed the rest of the night.

In the aftermath of the event, Thomas would find himself in the most awkward position of his long career. To many in San Jose, what had happened was a source of satisfaction, even pride; but in the eyes of the law it was double murder, and in the cold light of Monday's dawn the city was full of fear. Businessmen, students, workingmen, housewives, rowdies of a dozen stripes—all had participated in Sunday night's homicidal binge by act or acquiescence. What faced them now? Arrest? Could they go to prison? Only Thomas, who would initiate any prosecution, knew the answers. Governor Rolph's clemency promise alone could not wholly allay the uneasiness in scores of San Jose homes.

Certainly the lynching had devalued Thomas's political stock. As the successful prosecutor of Holmes and Thurmond, he would have been unbeatable in the upcoming 1934 elections, but the mob had stolen that chance from him. Now his clear and unenviable duty was to act instead against the lynchers, and the outcome politically could only be disaster. The vigilantes, most assuredly, were his own friends and backers—respected citizens who had committed two murders condoned by the establishment, popular among his constituents, and endorsed by the governor.

Monday afternoon, reporters beat a path to the district attorney's door to learn what he intended to do. With transparent elation the *News* splashed the answer in fat gothic letters across page one of its "Fourth Extra," on the streets at 3:00 P.M.:

ACTION AGAINST MOB
UNLIKELY, D.A. ADMITS

The story said the ringleaders might face "technical charges of murder," but, "It seemed improbable today that charges would ever be filed."

The headline writer had perceptively read between the lines of a finely balanced statement issued by Thomas. He had chosen his words carefully to preserve his image as a diligent prosecutor, yet also send signals that the establishment had little to fear.

"It is the duty of the district attorney's office," he said, "to prosecute any person against whom charges should be filed. But before charges can be brought, it is necessary that an eyewitness to the lynching be able to identify the ringleaders and swear a complaint. I can't swear a complaint because I wasn't on the scene. . . . I have ordered an investigation into the possibility of identifying the leaders of the mob. If they can be identified and placed in the lynching party by corroborative evidence, they will be charged with murder."

"Corroborative evidence" was the key. But who in San Jose was going to come forward?

In denying his own presence at the lynching, Thomas was essentially truthful. His courthouse office, where he had sat out the battle, was on the third floor, and although its windows overlooked the jail and its driveway, he could scarcely have identified anyone in the dark below. He told the reporters he would talk with Emig about a possible prosecution as soon as the latter was well enough, but he didn't know when that would be. In the same news story C. L. Snyder, the foreman of the county's newly sworn grand jury, was quoted as saying it so far had no plans to investigate the lynching.

Did he expect to indict anybody?

That would depend on what Thomas came up with—but the jury would not even hold its first meeting until Wednesday of the current week.

Apart from anything the district attorney or grand jury might or might not do, Coroner Williams now prepared to hold an inquest into the deaths of the men who were hanged. A crowd filled his office Monday afternoon while a coroner's jury was chosen. The panel, mainly from the business community, included a banker, a bookkeeper, a life insurance underwriter, and the architect of the new post office whose construction materials had supplied the lynch mob's ammunition.

The inquest would take place either Tuesday or Wednesday, Williams said at first, and the *Chronicle* conjectured that the ropes would be brought in as exhibits (to the dismay of many who had paid good money to fast-buck artists for pieces of them). However, the prospect of an early inquest quickly evaporated. On Tuesday morning Williams announced a delay of a few days, until Emig got out of the hospital. Then on Wednesday, he postponed the inquest indefinitely.

Thus the buck was passed, from the grand jury to the district attorney to the coroner to the sheriff—and the sheriff was out of service.

The conspiracy of silence comprised many besides the guilty. The daily press, to be sure, was part of it. This was four decades before Watergate, and no overpowering investigative urge to ferret out evildoers and bring them to justice was felt in the newsrooms and editorial offices. Reporters who sought to identify the lynchers were frustrated. The *News*'s George Millard, during the thick of the riot, had taken cover in the half-built post office long enough to jot down the names of everyone he recognized, but none ever appeared in print. Observing the journalistic mores of the time, editors and publishers were content to handle that part of the story with benign neglect.

A resolve to preserve the vigilantes' anonymity likewise pervaded the ranks of officialdom and of law and order. "Nobody knew, officially, who took part in the lynchings," wrote *Oakland Tribune* reporter Harold J. Fitzgerald in his Monday story, "Not an official could be found today who would say that he recognized any member of the mob, and if spectators recognized any of them they have not reported the fact."* Among the lynchers thus cloaked in anonymity were those who had joshed with Blackmore and Anderson, confronted Buffington at the barricades, and greeted Paul Arnerich by name at the jail door.

Public officials called upon for comment walked a fine political line between lip service to the processes of justice and respect for the vigilantes.

"These two lynchings come as a direct result of the laws of this nation against serious crimes not being adequately enforced," declared

*Copyright 1933 by The Tribune Publishing Company.

262

Earl Warren. "Our government simply has not measured up to its responsibility as far as protecting life and property are concerned . . . I cannot help but believe that if the public were adequately protected against murder and kidnapping, the people would never take the law into their own hands in such matters."

Even within the judiciary, which had been cheated out of its right to hold Holmes and Thurmond to account, the cover-up had its advocates.

"I am for law and order of course," said Judge Fred V. Wood in Alameda County, "but the people are tired of the law's delays. I trust that the San Jose authorities will let the matter drop. The sooner we forget about these lynchings the better."

In San Francisco, two other judges concurred. "While as a jurist I cannot countenance mob rule," said Judge P. Shortall, "as a human being and a parent I feel that if there was ever an exception that might be justified under the moral code, it was in this case." Judge T. L. Fitzpatrick was even blunter: "There was no element of doubt in this case . . . I can only say in my own personal opinion they [the lynchers] did a damned good job."

On Wednesday morning, at about the same hour Harold Thurmond was being lowered into his grave, reporters were keeping a vigil outside a closed door in the courthouse. There the new grand jury was convening for the first time, with the district attorney present. As the meeting broke up, the newsmen converged on the foreman.

"What happened in there, Mr. Snyder?"

"Well, we got organized, and we set up five committees, and we laid out our plans for the year's work."

"What about the lynching?"

"We didn't take up the lynching."

"When will you hold your next meeting?"

"We didn't set a time for our next meeting. I'll call it when the time comes."

"What did Mr. Thomas say about the lynching?"

"He had nothing to present at this time. He's waiting till Sheriff Emig gets out of the hospital."

Much later, when reporters gained admittance to the sheriff's hospital room, they asked him what the next move was.

"I don't know whether any action will be taken or not," he replied. "When I am up and around I'll talk to Fred Thomas and leave it up to him."

*   *   *

For the moment, the sweep-it-under-the-rug strategy seemed to be working. It might have succeeded totally were it not for the outrage of Roger Baldwin, the director of the American Civil Liberties Union, in New York. In his view, Governor Rolph's endorsement of the lynching made it a matter for the ACLU's national agenda. On Saturday, December 2, the organization posted a $1,000 reward for information leading to arrest and conviction of the perpetrators. From Los Angeles two ACLU representatives, A. L. Wirin and Ellis Jones, were dispatched to San Jose to find witnesses. Their arrival emboldened and gave new vigor to the sizeable number of San Joseans—perhaps a silent majority—who were pained, mortified, and angered at the barbarism in their midst.

For the next three days all was quiet. Emig finally left the hospital and returned to the job, and on Tuesday, December 5, he met at last with Thomas to discuss what action, if any, should be taken. When the brief meeting broke up, both men said nothing had been decided. Cryptically, Thomas added that "certain phases" of the lynching would be investigated and announced that he was delegating Deputy District Attorney Herbert Bridges to handle the inquiry.

The *News* quoted Emig as saying, "I don't believe I could identify any leaders of the mob," but he denied saying it in the *Mercury Herald* the next morning. In both papers, the accounts of the meeting were so bland that the town could tell the lid was still on—or so it seemed.

Wirin and Jones remained in San Jose, however, snooping around, and on Thursday, December 7, Wirin went to San Francisco and gave out a sensational story. He told the Associated Press he had identified two of the lynch mob ringleaders, and if the authorities in San Jose would not act against them, the ACLU would turn their names over to U.S. Attorney General Homer S. Cummings. Wirin then left for Los Angeles, and as his train passed through Salinas he tossed another thunderbolt, releasing the text of a jubilant telegram he had sent to Baldwin at ACLU headquarters in New York:

DISTRICT ATTORNEY FRED L. THOMAS OF SAN
JOSE HAS AGREED WITH JONES AND ME, AS REPRE-
SENTATIVES OF THE AMERICAN CIVIL LIBERTIES

UNION, TO INSTITUTE CRIMINAL PROCEEDINGS AGAINST LYNCHERS NEXT TUESDAY. I AM TO SIGN COMPLAINTS.

Wirin also urged Baldwin to wire Thomas congratulations and enlist additional support for him from the legendary defense attorney Clarence Darrow, of the Scopes monkey trial and the Leopold-Loeb murder case, and from Arthur Garfield Hays of Sacco-Vanzetti fame.

The telegram, when made public, took San Jose by surprise and jangled its nerves anew. There had been no prior inkling that Thomas had met with Wirin and Jones, let alone agreed to embark upon a prosecution. Reporters tried to reach the district attorney for confirmation but could not find him. When they reached Emig, he was vague. Yes, a couple of men from the ACLU had talked to him Wednesday night; he hadn't caught their names. They had wanted to know everything about the lynching.

"I told them the whole story as I saw it," the sheriff said. "They thanked me for my cooperation and left. I was not aware that they had conferred with Thomas. I will assist in any way I can with the prosecution of the lynchers."

Newsmen finally caught up with Thomas on Friday. He verified that Wirin and Jones had talked to him, claiming they could identify the mob's ringleaders.

Who were they?

The ACLU men had assured Thomas they had newspaper statements in which the suspects openly admitted their roles. There could be no doubt about whom they were speaking: the two teenage braggarts, Anthony Cataldi and Ray Loren. Cataldi's adolescent blathering in his signed newspaper story was damning on its face. Loren's claim to being the first rioter inside the jail was almost as damaging. Earlier, Thomas had all but dismissed the idea of a prosecution based on the youths' newspaper boasting. Now he said he would issue complaints if Wirin and Jones kept their promise to produce sufficient evidence.

To keep the kettle boiling over the weekend, the ACLU kicked off a statewide series of mass meetings to launch a campaign for a national antilynching law. The first was held Friday night in Santa Barbara, the second, Saturday in Los Angeles.

Wirin and Jones returned to town Tuesday morning, December 12, and went directly to the district attorney's office for what turned out to be an all-day conference behind closed doors. When it broke up in late afternoon, Thomas announced he had filed charges against Cataldi, not for murder, but for violation of the California anti-lynching law. The youth, who had been arrested, could serve up to twenty years if convicted. By now the other young boaster, Loren, had faded from sight, but Wirin and Jones claimed they had evidence against "numerous" other lynching participants.

The district attorney, the sheriff, and the ACLU men briefed reporters on the deal that had been struck. Emig had signed the complaint against Cataldi to hold him pending his possible indictment by the grand jury. Thomas would ask foreman Snyder to convene the panel within a few days to hear the ACLU's evidence against the youth and all other suspects. In Cataldi's case, whatever action the jurors might take would supersede the complaint just issued.

"Governor Rolph may yet be given an opportunity to back up his irresponsible utterance by pardoning all those who are convicted of collective murder," Wirin jabbed.

Emig hinted that as many as six more arrests might be in the offing, but Thomas emphasized anew that he would not charge anyone with lynching in the absence of eyewitness testimony or positive photo identification.

Photographic evidence was feared most by the vigilantes; the perception that cameras did not lie was widely held. The news pictures that had appeared up to now were not worrisome; most were too fuzzy to afford positive identification, and the primitive photoflashes of the time had whitened most faces to unrecognizability. The few clear pictures, such as an eight-column shot of the battering ram crew in the *Post-Enquirer*, were so obviously retouched as to be inadmissible in court. However, the park had been full of photographers snapping away anonymously, and no one knew what their prints might show. One such cameraman, a free-lancer named Peter Pavley, returned to his studio a few days after the lynching to find it burglarized; all that was gone was his St. James Park file.

Predictably, San Jose business and political circles seethed at the ACLU's intervention to compel arrests. Nowhere, save possibly in the Cataldi household, was the fury hotter than in the offices of the *News*, which, if it had not incited the hangings, had condoned them pridefully. Publisher Payne gave vent to his ire in an editorial linking the ACLU with "reds and communists."

*   *   *

Anthony Cataldi spent only five hours in jail before his father's lawyer, Richard Bressani, obtained his release on a $10,000 bond. To reporters, Bressani declared his young client "legally and morally innocent." When word of the youth's arrest reached Sacramento, Rolph's response was unequivocal.

"I have not changed my opinion one iota," he said. "I stand by my original statement. If the boy is convicted and sent to prison, I'll pardon him." However, the case could reach Rolph's desk only *after* a conviction, and in the meantime he would not impede the wheels of justice.

Cataldi's arraignment was set for 10:30 Friday morning, December 15, before Justice of the Peace Chester Moore. It precipitated a barrage of press statements by all concerned.

"How strange it is," Bressani reflected, "that these two representatives of the so-called Civil Liberties Union with headquarters in New York should travel a great distance—but all for pay—to select a schoolboy and make him shoulder the blame for the thousands who were present [at the lynching]."

In San Francisco, California Attorney General U. S. Webb entered the dialogue. He wasted no time in squelching an idea someone had suggested, that he assign a special prosecutor to the lynching cases, relieving Thomas of the need to take action against San Joseans who were very likely his friends. Webb said he had no power to name a special prosecutor unless Thomas asked him to—and the district attorney had no intention of doing that.

Wednesday, December 20, was the first date set by Moore for Cataldi's preliminary hearing. When it came, Deputy District Attorney Bridges moved for a continuance until January 9, because the grand jury still had not acted. Bressani readily assented, and the judge so ordered. It was pointless to press Emig's holding charge against the boy if the grand jury was not going to indict him. When January 9 rolled around, another continuance was granted for the same reason.

On Thursday morning, January 11, the grand jury at last convened, in closed session as the law required, to hear testimony and sift what evidence had been collected about the perpetrators of the "Sabbath lynching," as the newspapers were now calling it. Thomas presented more than twenty witnesses, presumably including those rounded up by the ACLU, over the course of the next five days. On January 16 the jury unanimously adopted its report—one stark, unadorned paragraph:

> Resolved: That the testimony to this grand jury to date is totally inadequate to justify the bringing of any indictment against any person or persons for participation in the lynching of John M. Holmes and Harold Thurmond, and we have therefore failed to bring an indictment against anyone.

The decision drew a rapturous response from the *News*, which praised the jury's "wisdom and courage."

Procedurally, the jury's finding did not quite terminate the case against young Cataldi. The complaint obtained by Emig was still pending, and Thomas insisted on playing out the full scenario.

"If Cataldi is to be cleared of the charges," he said, "he should be cleared through the courts, even though the grand jury failed to find adequate evidence against him."

Anthony's next scheduled court date was only two days away, but Thomas asked a further continuance during which he would reassess the case.

Now, with the grand jury having virtually ruled out additional prosecutions, Coroner Williams at last went ahead with his inquest. The hearing, on Saturday, January 27, was dull until Emig, as the final witness, was set upon by attorneys Alfred Aram and Emmett Gottenberg, representing the Holmes and Thurmond families respectively. The Holmeses, who had openly and vociferously condemned the sheriff from the start, were now joined by the Thurmonds, whose good will toward Emig had clearly evaporated. Gottenberg cross-examined Emig first.

"Now, sheriff," he began, "the prisoners were taken to San Francisco right after their arrest for safekeeping—but later they were left in the jail here when a crowd began to gather and the situation was more serious."

"I took them to San Francisco for further questioning," Emig corrected. "Holmes had not yet confessed."

From the audience Thurmond's sister, Gail Karnagel, spoke up. "You told us it was to prevent a lynching that they were taken away."

"No, it was for further questioning," the sheriff insisted, seemingly forgetful of the elaborate ruse he had employed—having the men don mechanics' clothes—to spirit them out of town.

"You represented things entirely differently to us when we spoke to you in your office," Mrs. Karnagel snapped.

Now Aram took over, demanding to know what Emig had done to

prevent the lynching. The sheriff, his cool demeanor giving way, roared his response:

"I called the San Jose Police and Fire Departments, the Santa Clara Fire Department, the Palo Alto police, the San Francisco police, and even the governor of California. And if you think I could have done more, I'd like to know what it was!"

"You realized that when the men used a battering ram on the door, they were bent on murder?"

"Well, they probably were."

"And you have men who can shoot where they aim. Had these men shot down one or two of the men on the battering ram, do you think others would have come on to be shot?"

"I don't think that would have stopped the mob, and besides, too many innocent people might have been shot."

"Don't you think if one or two had been shot, the trouble might have been avoided?"

"I handled the matter the best I could."

All in all it was a dismal session for the sheriff, but it mattered little. The coroner's jury returned its verdict in fifteen minutes, holding that Holmes and Thurmond died "from strangulation by hanging at the hands of a mob, members of which are unknown." Additionally the jurors found that Emig "used his best judgment in handling the situation."

Two and a half more weeks passed. When Anthony Cataldi's long-delayed preliminary hearing was finally held on Thursday, February 15, it was cut and dried. Deputy District Attorney Bridges moved for dismissal of the charge against the youth, and Judge Moore complied.

Cataldi, who would one day win prominence, wealth, and respect as a San Jose real estate developer, walked out of the courtroom with the burden of legal guilt lifted from his shoulders. He bore a unique distinction as the only person ever prosecuted, however briefly, for the St. James Park murders that had been committed by scores, abetted by hundreds, and witnessed, condoned, and applauded by thousands.

And so the charade ended. Royce Brier had had it right: the vigilantes had "vanished as they came, their identities sunken forever." A curtain had fallen.

The fabric of the curtain—a fabric of secrecy—has been durable and remains so. Nearly six decades after the lynching, only a few of those who conceived and executed it have been publicly identified. The innocent as well as the culpable still honor a commitment not to speak.

In 1983, as the fiftieth anniversary of the event approached, the author was assigned to examine the episode in two retrospective articles in the *San Jose Mercury News* (the two competing papers of 1933 having since merged). I interviewed scores of old-timers with varied insights. Many would tell, often with undisguised pride, of being outside the jail or in St. James Park on the night of November 26, 1933. But only the late Rocky Santoro candidly acknowledged active participation in the events that took place. Most who were close to the events spoke candidly, up to a point—at which they slid gracefully, with the agility of long practice, behind a veil of obfuscation.

San Joseans who remember 1933 remain acutely aware of the fact that in California there is no statute of limitations for murder.

The late Louis Rossi, the last person at Hart's store to say goodbye to Brooke Hart, talked much about the happenings of that year when I interviewed him fifty years afterward. He had warned Sheriff Emig beforehand, bluntly and without reservation, that the hangings were going to take place precisely the way they did. He knew because he had been invited to join the vigilante group "not once but several times."

"What group was it?" I asked.

"Well, that's a good question. I've been asked that question so many times. . . ."

"Are any of them still around?"

"Frankly, I really can't tell you. I don't know." Rossi's expression told me he had gone as far as he intended, but I persisted.

"Do you still remember who they were?"

"I've tried to forget it, and I can't recall."

"You knew who they were, though?"

"Let me say this. I think I knew most of them."

"Did everybody cover up for everybody else?"

"That's right, they did."

"Did you cover up?"

"Certainly I did. I wouldn't give the name of anyone."

"And they're still doing it?"

"Sure they're still doing it—those that are alive."

21

A Storm Across the Land

"All the Californians I have met are going around proud today," crowed Will Rogers in his syndicated newspaper feature the day after the lynching.

At Stanford University a language instructor compelled her students to applaud for one minute in honor of "due justice rendered."

But Heywood Broun, the liberal crusader of the *New York World-Telegram*, wrote, "To your knees, Governor, and pray that your commonwealth be washed clean of this bath of bestiality into which a whole community has plunged."

Within a day Governor Rolph took the place of the lynchers themselves as the lightning rod for a nationwide storm. Western Union wires in Sacramento were clogged with messages of elation or outrage from at least thirty-one states. Jubilantly Rolph announced that in an early count they ran 267 to 57 in his favor, with most of the criticism coming from outside California. Actor Leo Carrillo wired, "Dear Uncle Jim, the entire country commends you for your courageous attitude."

Nowhere was reaction more volatile than in the churches and synagogues. *The Monitor*, a Catholic organ, offered a harsh judgment: "Only God can cleanse the soul from the blot of murder, certainly not Governor Rolph." No one in California public life could take *The Monitor* lightly; it spoke for the San Francisco Archdiocese headed by Archbishop Edward J. Hanna, who wielded immense political influence on Rolph's home turf.

In New York, Rabbi Stephen S. Wise advised Californians to serve an ultimatum: "Resign, Governor Rolph, or be impeached."

Even among the clergy, however, the governor was not without his champions. The Rev. Dr. Henry Darlington, rector of the Protestant Episcopal Church of the Heavenly Rest in New York, wired him congratulations, and Rolph, an Episcopal communicant himself, eagerly released the message to the papers. The rector's comeuppance was not long coming; the next day his superior, Episcopal Bishop William T. Manning, demanded that Rolph publicly apologize or be removed. The chastened Darlington recanted his commendation of the governor, but not before a score of theological students appeared with protest placards outside his fashionable church. In an ensuing melee a woman named Mary Brown was injured, and three pickets were arrested for disorderly conduct.

From other sectors of public life, the lynching and Rolph's attitude drew widely diverse responses. San Francisco's city health officer, Dr. J. C. Geiger, said, "My only comment on the affair is 'more and better hangings,' " and in gang-ridden Chicago, Coroner Frank Walsh seconded the sentiment. A couple of lynchings there, he suggested, "might put some real fear into the hearts of criminals."

The celebrated defense lawyer Clarence Darrow echoed the revulsion of the ACLU: "I am unalterably opposed to lynching. I thought every intelligent person was." William L. Patterson, secretary of the International Labor Defense in New York, declared, "The spread of lynching evidences development of fascism."

Roy Wilkins, assistant secretary of the National Association for the Advancement of Colored People, was similarly impelled to speak out, sending Rolph a blistering telegram. The crime of lynching carried a special repugnance for the NAACP because almost three fourths of all lynching victims were black, and the fact that Holmes and Thurmond were white did not mitigate the offense.

Most of Rolph's fellow governors were restrained in their comments, with such notable exceptions as Floyd B. Olson of Minnesota, who snapped, "If the incident had occurred in Minnesota, I would feel that the state had been disgraced."

For editorial writers across the nation and beyond, the San Jose events provided a field day, an opportunity for effulgent prose, rage, acidulous commentary, and dogmatic pronouncement pro and con. The foreign press leaped at the opportunity to heap scorn on the United States. Sarcasm was the weapon of the *New York Times*:

> "A fine lesson to the whole nation," he [Rolph] calls it. . . .
> A warm-hearted, jovial, glad-handed man, he loves to be popular. If "the people" want to kill somebody, they should be

allowed to do so, and he wants to help in the good work. . . . Governor Rolph insures them protection beforehand, pats them on the back after they have made their kill, longs for more lynchings. Such a governor is a fine lesson to California.

Cartoonist Edmund Duffy of the *Baltimore Sun* drew a damning caricature of Rolph pointing to a pair of corpses dangling from a tree. The caption for the panel, which would win a Pulitzer Prize, was, "California Points With Pride."

In Kansas William Allen White wrote in his *Emporia Gazette*, "Southern governors have the brains to be ashamed of their lynchings, which is more than can be said of Rolph." In the governor's hometown the *San Francisco News* declared the lynching "an orgy of blood lust and savagery, a shocking demonstration of the brute in man breaking through the veneer of civilization. . . . Mr. Rolph must be out of his mind."

Nowhere did the lynching give California a blacker eye than in the nation's liberal periodicals. An article headed "California's Little Hitlers" in the *New Republic*, by Ella Winter, portrayed Emig and the police as the mob's conspirators and sought to identify the lynchers with union busters in a series of 1933 farm strikes. Perhaps the harshest denunciation appeared in *The Commonweal*, whose editors wrote, "If Governor Rolph made the statements attributed to him, he should not only be impeached but incarcerated in an asylum for imbecilic children. A soul which can harbor such antisocial sentiments is a soul devoid of honor, rectitude, and even a moronic sense of responsibility."

Rolph could take comfort, however, from the *Denver Post*, which editorialized, "Millions of red-blooded Americans envy Californians their governor," and from the *Sacramento Bee*, which called the lynching "a goodly and a righteous and a necessary thing."

A Hearst editorial, like much reaction elsewhere, ran toward the schizophrenic: What happened in San Jose was to be regretted, *but*. . . . The writer declared the lynching "impossible to justify," but having said that, found mitigating circumstances:

The lynching in San Jose . . . makes out a case for suspension of judgment. The incident does not mark the collapse or even the weakness of society. On the contrary, it is an impressive social phenomenon, carrying, as the governor of California truthfully says, a lesson. Americans are tolerant and patient under normal circumstances. They do not expect or require the impossible of their officials. They know that a certain amount of crime must go unpunished. But the crime of kidnapping they will not brook. . . . Their anger knows no bounds. Their instinct of self-preservation will obey no restraint.

In the eye of the storm, Rolph carried on not merely with equanimity but with every sign of enjoyment. Like Emig and Thomas, he was less than a year away from a bid for reelection—something he wanted badly. A more conventional politician, having entered the lynching imbroglio, might have retreated quickly to cut his losses. Not Sunny Jim. He had not stumbled into this conflagration; he had ignited it himself, quite deliberately, and having done so he now added fuel to it at every opportunity. Every time a reporter came into view he talked about it incessantly. Articles under his byline appeared in papers from coast to coast. For the North American Newspaper Alliance, he wrote a florid "declaration of war":

> The livid head of crime rears itself in every corner of our nation. . . . The first duty of government is to protect its law-abiding citizens, no matter what the methods or the cost. The criminals have armed themselves. They have made it war, and so have we.*

Decades later Duncan Oneal, who knew Rolph well, would dispute the buffoon image that history has accorded him, averring, "He was not a fly-by-night idiot by a damn sight." Rolph's forte, long before the time of scientific polling, was knowing and pleasing his people, and now he sensed that whatever disparagement might be heaped upon him, he was a winner with the masses.

This governor had been born in San Francisco only a few years after it had been rescued from corruption verging on anarchy by vigilantes honored in history. His instinct told him that now in the crime-ridden depression year of 1933, a time of desperation for many, California's genteel facade masked a broad redneck strain. Kidnapping terrified and enraged people, and they welcomed whatever it took to stop it.

Despite all the drumbeating, the San Jose lynching might have been a three-day sensation, fading quickly in the spotlight, had other events not occurred thousands of miles to the east in Missouri and Maryland.

At almost the same hour Holmes and Thurmond had been hanged,

*Copyright 1933 by the North American Newspaper Alliance, Inc.

a twenty-one-year-old white woman on her way home from a movie in San Jose's namesake city of St. Joseph, Missouri, had been waylaid by a muscular young black man, dragged into an alley, raped, and beaten. Police soon arrested Lloyd Warner, nineteen, who was lynched two nights later. In many ways the St. Joseph lynching was an eerie replay of the San Jose events. A mob of some 5,000 persons, using an iron pipe battering ram, broke into the Buchanan County Jail after a three-and-a-half-hour tear gas battle. They grabbed Warner, beat and stabbed him to death, and then strung up his body and set it afire.

"Many & many a person," reported *Time*, "held Governor James ('Sunny Jim') Rolph, Jr. of California directly responsible for Negro Warner's death." If the San Jose lynching was a lesson to the nation, the magazine commented, "Missouri . . . had been quick to learn."

In St. Joseph, chagrined citizens were only too ready to make Rolph their scapegoat. In the *St. Joseph News-Press*, managing editor Chris L. Rutt wrote, "The mob spirit is latent in every community. When the governor of a great state like California will publicly condone a lynching, we can scarcely expect the man on the street to take a higher moral tone."

Another lynching of a black man, likewise accused of raping a white woman, had taken place in Princess Anne, Maryland, more than three weeks before the Hart kidnapping. Nine suspected lynchers had been identified, but a sympathetic state's attorney had refused to prosecute. After a long stalemate Governor Albert C. Ritchie, the antithesis of Sunny Jim Rolph, mobilized 250 National Guardsmen, who rounded up four of the suspects in a surprise raid. Two days after the San Jose lynching, a pitched battle took place outside a state armory where the four were incarcerated. A thousand rioters trying to liberate them were held off by tear gas and National Guard bayonets, but the next day, amid cheers, a local judge freed the suspects anyway. Afterward the jubilant citizens of Princess Anne, furious at their own governor, wired Rolph in California: "Congratulations on your stand. When you run for president you will have 100 per cent support from the Eastern Shore of Maryland. Please publish."*

Among those who charged Rolph with inciting both the Missouri lynching and the Maryland uprising was Walter White, executive secretary of the NAACP and author of a definitive 1929 book on lynching, *Rope and Faggot*. White announced that the NAACP

---

* Ironically, Ritchie's resolute action against the Maryland lynchers left his career in a shambles. Before that time, the square-jawed, owlish governor had been widely regarded as presidential timber.

would lead a new effort to pass a federal antilynching bill, to be introduced in January by Senator Edward P. Costigan of Colorado.

Two American presidents and the English House of Commons were about to enter the controversy, not to mention Hollywood's "blonde bombshell," Jean Harlow. Miss Harlow told reporters that her friends in the film colony, always vulnerable to kidnapping, were "resting more easily" since the San Jose hangings.

Santa Clara County's best-known resident in November 1933, was the former president of the United States, Herbert Clark Hoover. He had left the White House only eight months earlier, turned out of office by Franklin D. Roosevelt and blamed by many for the hard times that had overtaken the country. Now, lonely and embittered, he brooded in his hilltop home overlooking the Stanford campus at Palo Alto.

Immediately after the lynching Hoover had declined comment, in keeping with a policy of silence on public affairs which he had adopted upon leaving office. Two days later, however, he broke the silence for the first time, lashing out not at a Democratic antagonist but at Governor Rolph, a fellow Republican. Hoover was among twenty-five persons who issued an unforgiving blast at both the lynching and the governor—an exceptional document because its originators, a strange-bedfellows lot, represented California's top leadership in commerce, labor, industry, religion, politics, and academe:

> The very spirit of government has been violated and the state has been disgraced in the eyes of the world by a brutal outburst of primitive lust for vengeance. . . . The mob could have been restrained if assistance had been given to the local officers; unrestrained, the lowest passions were unleashed to leave their degrading mark on every participant and to bring humiliation and shame . . . which the whole state must share.
>
> This humiliation and shame is intensified by the laudation of the mob and its actions. More than this, such laudation, particularly when coming from the chief executive of the state, undermines the very foundations upon which the state and all civilized society is built.

The statement was released from the offices of the San Francisco Chamber of Commerce. Besides Hoover, its signers included Dr. Ray Lyman Wilbur, president of Stanford University; Archbishop Hanna,

Rabbi Irving Reichert, and secretary Paul Scharrenberg of the California State Federation of Labor.

When reporters confronted Rolph for his reaction to the censure, he had none, but by the next day he was ready with a delayed riposte, tweaking Hoover in a sensitive spot. He harked back to the summer of 1932, when Hoover had used the Army to evict the ragtag "Bonus Expeditionary Force" of World War I veterans from the nation's capital.*

"Look at the mess we got into when troops were called out in Washington against the bonus marchers," Rolph said. "Men with guns and bombs were sent out to attack good American citizens—our World War veterans who fought for us."

The governor's thrust infuriated Hoover, who interrupted his Thanksgiving observance to accuse Rolph of gross ignorance of the facts.

"Not a single shot was fired," he said, "not a single person was injured by the troops called out in Washington. The troops ended the bloodshed which was then in progress through conflicts between rioters and police. The issue here is plain and not to be obscured by such misstatements: The governor has been advocating lynch law. It is subversion of the very spirit of organized society. It is un-American and is a reflection on the State of California."

No one wanted Rolph punished more than did novelist Gertrude Atherton. Censure by the ex-president did not satisfy her; she wanted the governor chastised by the incumbent, Roosevelt. A telegram to FDR, signed by her and others, asked him "as the leading citizen of the United States" to issue the rebuke. Roosevelt semicomplied, choosing the Federal Council of Churches of Christ in America as his forum. In an address to the council, which was in session in Washington, he condemned lynch law as a "vile form of collective murder [and] a deliberate and definite disobedience of the commandment, 'Thou shalt not kill.' " Avoiding mention of Rolph by name, the president went on to comment pointedly, "We do not excuse those in high places or low who condone lynch law."

The answer to crime, FDR said, was "quick and certain justice" through the judicial function. (At that moment a task force in his

---

*Some 20,000 jobless veterans converged on Washington, D.C., in the spring of 1932 demanding immediate payment of their World War I bonus. On July 28, two of them were killed in a clash with District of Columbia police, and Hoover ordered soldiers under General Douglas MacArthur to evict the marchers. MacArthur moved in with a thousand soldiers and burnt their shantytown. The bonus was finally paid in 1936.

Department of Justice was at work on a comprehensive program to combat kidnapping and extortion. Among its ideas were universal fingerprinting, federal licensing of cars driven across state lines, a tripling of FBI personnel, firearms regulation, and abandonment of the unanimous verdict requirement in criminal trials.)

All over America politicians, bureaucrats, and special pleaders realized by now there was mileage to be had from the kidnapping-lynching furor. In Sacramento, Assemblyman Roy J. Neilsen announced he would sponsor a bill making the death penalty mandatory for kidnapping, whether or not bodily harm was inflicted.

A Santa Clara University political science professor, Father Cornelius Deenery, complained to the Federal Communications Commission about the role of the "Richfield Reporter" in fomenting the San Jose lynching. With questionable accuracy, he argued that few persons thought of taking the law into their own hands until "a Los Angeles radio station 400 miles away announced a mob was marching toward the San Jose jail."

By now, shock waves from San Jose had crossed the Atlantic and were rippling through Great Britain. An American newsreel company, prevented by darkness and the mob from shooting actual footage of the dangling corpses in the park, had "reconstructed" the scene later and sent the finished product overseas. Showing of the pictures in English cinemas led the *Times* of London to denounce them as a "horrifying manifestation of the growing tendency to sacrifice all decency to sensationalism." The outcry reached Parliament, and Home Secretary Sir John Gilmour drew cheers in the House of Commons when he announced that the newsreel had been withdrawn. The cinemas had acted voluntarily, he said, but "if further experience shows action to be necessary, steps will be taken by His Majesty's government."

Rolph came under new fire daily. Thirty-five professors, attorneys, and clergymen in Berkeley, Oakland, and San Francisco demanded his resignation and set about organizing a statewide coalition to get rid of him. Mrs. Paul Eliel, president of the California League of Women Voters upbraided him for statements "in plain violation of your oath of office, subversive of law and order." An interfaith mass meeting at the City College of New York condemned him for "betrayal of trust." One of the speakers, Dr. Adam Clayton Powell, warned, "If they don't stop the lynching of white criminals, they soon will lynch governors and newspaper reporters and photographers." The National War Veterans Association expelled Rolph from its advisory board, finding him "unfit" to serve. In a sermon to the First Humanist Society in New York, Charles Francis Potter proposed that mob executions be called "rolphing" instead of "lynching."*

Rolph met the torrent of rebuke with his own blend of jovial bluster and self-righteous defiance.

"It's nothing to worry about," he said. "I'm still governor of California, you know. I am the foe of kidnappers and murderers. I am going to do my best to make the hearts of mothers in California happier than they have been since the Lindbergh baby was kidnapped and killed."

Sunny Jim's donning of the crime fighter's mantle was not precisely in keeping with his record. In his three years in office, he had signed 508 pardons, issued eighty-eight reprieves, and commuted forty-nine sentences, setting a California record for clemency. His predecessor, Governor C. C. Young, had signed only eight pardons, six reprieves, and seven commutations in a full four-year term.

Rolph's composure had its limits. His anger flared into view when a rebellion broke out within his administration.

Of all the political plums at the governor's disposal, few were more coveted than the three seats on the State Athletic Commission. These jobs carried clout; the commission exercised sole jurisdiction over boxing and wrestling, and everyone in the fight racket from the pugilists to the timekeepers had to toe its line. One of its more unlikely members was the Rev. Leslie C. Kelley, rector of St. Paul's Episcopal Church in San Francisco, known as "the fighting chaplain." The day after Rolph's clash with Herbert Hoover, Kelley resigned with a scathing statement calling the governor "un-Christianlike" and his attitude "unspeakable."

*The origin of the word *lynch* is uncertain, but it is widely thought to be derived from the name of Charles Lynch, a member of the Virginia House of Burgesses who, without legal basis, harassed and imprisoned Tory loyalists before and during the American Revolution. In its broadest definition, *lynch law* refers to any extralegal act of summary punishment by a mob, but in common usage it means putting to death, especially by hanging.

Rolph was furious. "All fakers are not gone yet," he lashed back, telling reporters that earlier that week, Kelley had come to him pleading for a new term—something he was now unlikely to get.

"It's a fine thing," the governor sneered, "when an Episcopal minister of the church which I attend condemns me when he has begged me to reappoint him. Can you beat that?" Rolph said he would invite Kelley to air his charges in an open hearing. "I am sure a minister imbued with fine Christian spirit would want to explain such public statements."

Sunny Jim was wrong.

"I'm not going to answer his summons," Kelley retorted. "I'm through with him."

Three days before Christmas California had another lynching scare. Feeling was running high in Modesto, the seat of Stanislaus County, against the confessed slayer of a man named Fred Cornwall. When Sheriff Grant Hogan heard that fifteen ranchers had met in nearby Prescott to discuss vigilante action, he acted swiftly to transfer the suspect to the county jail of neighboring San Joaquin County in Stockton, some thirty miles away.

As the last days of December passed, the hurricane of controversy had lost most of its vigor. By New Year's, Sunny Jim Rolph was sure he had weathered it. The old war-horse felt fine and ready to charge into the 1934 campaign—though his friends and doctors were telling him not to.

22

Lingering Doubts

In the more than half century since the Hart kidnapping and the lynching, the facts of the case have become encrusted with misinformation, rumor, doubt, and folklore.

This is not surprising. It arises from the demise of the participants, the dimming of memories, and the destruction of records. In 1981 the San Jose Police Department purged all files on 1933 homicides, and the Santa Clara County sheriff's files are gone, too. Many key exhibits in the FBI's custody were destroyed in 1946, regrettably including the only known transcript of a follow-up interrogation of Harold Thurmond, two days after his capture.

For years the influential Hart family (which has kindly cooperated with the author) vigorously discouraged publicity or discussion that might revive painful memories of the episode. The story was taboo in the San Jose newspapers until the late 1970s.

Not least among the causes for confusion about the case in the public mind is the lynchers' durable pact of silence, which is still honored. Finally, and most importantly, the lynching itself precluded a public trial that would have illuminated many facts now lost to history.

What has appeared in this book so far is fact, as best it can be discerned from admittedly incomplete and imperfect records and memories. But because there are doubts that linger, no examination of the case can be complete without a discussion of certain matters in the realm of conjecture.

The Confessions: Voluntary or Coerced?

From the time that Thurmond and Holmes were caught, as we have seen, they stood convicted in the press and in the eyes of the community. Their confessions were taken at face value.

In Thurmond's case, even his family did not dispute his confession's validity. Holmes's family, however, took every opportunity to proclaim that he had been framed—for reasons never defined. He convinced both his wife and his parents that his confession was a fictitious document signed only after his inquisitors had sweated and tortured him for a sleepless "twelve or thirteen hours," threatening to deliver him to the mob. Whatever the *methods* of his grilling, it could not have been so constant and protracted. He was arrested around 3:30 A.M. and had confessed by early afternoon, with much of the intervening time taken up by his transfer to San Francisco.

For today's discerning inquirer, it flies in the face of plausibility to dismiss the confessions as fabrications out of whole cloth. Thurmond's was witnessed by six officers from three law enforcement agencies, including Sheriff Emig, Chief Black, and Vetterli of the FBI. All these officers except Black also witnessed Holmes's confession. Conceivably (though no clear evidence suggests it) pressures of public opinion or politics might have influenced the local officers to falsify or doctor the documents, but what would have induced three out-of-town FBI men to abet such perjury?

The question of whether the confessions were extracted by third-degree methods is less easily dealt with. The Hart kidnapping occurred thirty-three years before the *Miranda* decision, and certainly no one took pains to read the suspects their rights. To the contrary, Vetterli boasted to J. Edgar Hoover that Thurmond's admissions were "immediately reduced to writing so that we might have a signed confession in our possession before he was advised not to talk any further." Vetterli added that agents questioned Thurmond "most vigorously," but he did not elaborate.

The two confessions are markedly different in format. Thurmond's document, while written in the first person, is couched in stilted law enforcement jargon. Obviously his disclosures, though not necessarily altered in meaning, were recast in "officialese" as he went along. By contrast, Emig's interrogation of Holmes sounds just like what it was: a low-key dialogue between a couple of old friends.

The Holmes Alibi: Two Versions

Had Holmes gone to trial, his attorney Ira Langdon intended to show, if he could, that Jack was at home when the crimes against Brooke Hart were committed. The critical hours that Thursday evening were between six o'clock, when Brooke disappeared, and nine o'clock, when by all accounts Holmes was watching "The Three Little Pigs" with Evelyn and the Estensens at the Hester Theater

Holmes's parents and his wife were equally prepared to confirm his alibi for those three hours, but we know now that had they done so, Langdon would have faced a vexing problem: Their stories, while equally exculpatory for Jack, did not agree.

Maurice and Hulda Holmes told everyone who would listen that they were at their son's house on the kidnapping night to baby-sit their grandchildren while Jack and Evelyn went to the movies. Hulda said Evelyn helped her fit a dress while they waited for Jack to appear, and he showed up at seven o'clock.

What Evelyn would have testified, had she appeared for her husband, did not become public in 1933 because at that time she talked neither to the press nor the authorities, but in 1989 she revealed her story to the author. It follows a materially different scenario. According to his wife, Jack came home from work between 5:30 and 6:00 as usual and was there from then on, the whole time until they left for the show. Moreover, she stated positively, it was *her* mother, not Jack's folks, who baby-sat the children that evening. *The senior Holmeses were not there*; the dress fitting took place on a different night.

A third alibi witness Langdon might have called, had Holmes gone to trial, was Gertrude Estensen. In her statement to the sheriff she said Jack and Evelyn arrived at her home "between 7:30 and 8, possibly a quarter to 8." If believed, Gertrude's declaration would by itself have exonerated Holmes, because the killers, whoever they were, could not have left the San Mateo Bridge much before 7:25 when Brooke Hart's cries for help were heard. Gertrude, a grade school teacher of good repute, could have been a highly credible witness in Holmes's defense. How the prosecution might have rebutted or impeached all this alibi testimony is conjectural.

Over nearly six decades, Holmes's unruffled attendance at the movie on the night of the kidnapping has been accepted as fact, attested to by both Gertrude and Evelyn, and it has kept alive the questions about his guilt. Now, new information comes to light, further deepening the morass of factual contradiction surrounding the events of that evening. In 1989, three years after the death of Gertrude

Estensen, her late husband Leonard told the author he had *no recollection of ever going to the movies with the Holmeses*, on the kidnap night or any other.

"I am emphatic that I never saw 'The Three Little Pigs,' " he added.

So the movements and actions of Jack Holmes on the night of November 9, 1933, remain obscure in the murk of history. But if, as Leonard Estensen belatedly declared, the Holmeses and Estensens did not go to the movies together, what might have been a convincing alibi for Holmes collapses like a house of cards.

Who Really Wrote the Notes?

Other enigmas of the confessions likewise remain unsolved.

According to both kidnappers, the three ransom notes were mainly written by Holmes, using paper, envelopes, and postage furnished by Thurmond. Holmes did the writing, he explained, because "Harold couldn't spell"—a grotesque concern under the circumstances.

Holmes's claim to authorship supported the prevailing view that he was the instigator, architect, and driving force of the kidnapping, and Thurmond his sheeplike follower. The investigators were in for a shock, therefore, when they received the report of the FBI laboratory in Washington, to which they sent the notes for analysis. After comparing them with specimens of both kidnappers' writing and printing, document specialist C. A. Appel concluded that they were Thurmond's work, not Holmes's, "notwithstanding the admissions of the men."

The question of who wrote them was already moot, however. Appel did not report his findings until December 1, 1933, five days after both kidnappers had been hanged.

Other Accomplices: Did Some Go Free?

"Before God, sheriff, Holmes and I were alone on this job."

Harold Thurmond's words, spoken with upraised hand a few minutes before he died, convinced Emig that there were no other accomplices in the Brooke Hart kidnapping.

Not everyone was so easily satisfied. The FBI did not wholly write off the possibility of additional collaborators; the federal indictment of Holmes and Thurmond also named "others not known." On December 13, two and a half weeks after the lynching, agent Ramsey was back in San Jose refusing either to confirm or deny rumors that a third suspect was sought. For several months thereafter, an FBI car escorted

Charlie O'Brien, who was thought to have been an alternative target of the kidnappers, home from his midnight shift at his family's restaurant.

Certainly the preponderance of the evidence that has come down to us validates the sheriff's conclusion that the Hart kidnap-murder was a two-man job. One of Emig's traits, however, was to ignore any evidence not consistent with his mind-set. He dismissed out of hand Delphine Silveria's report that she and her daughter Isabelle had watched five men, not two, transfer a captive who looked like Brooke from a car that looked like Brooke's to another automobile near her farmhouse on remote Piedmont Road. But now we know, from documents obtained under the Freedom of Information Act, that FBI agent Vetterli deemed not only Mrs. Silveria but also her daughter highly credible.

In 1987 Isabelle, then sixty-eight years old and married, was living in Southern California. Contacted by telephone without notice, she instantly recalled the 1933 episode with clarity and related her experience anew, without essential change from what she and her mother had reported fifty-four years earlier. For the author she later drew a detailed map pinpointing the locations of the two cars and the positions of her mother and herself in relation to their house, their barn, their driveway, and the road.

Interestingly, Delphine Silveria described the automobile to which the captive was transferred as a large, dark sedan with a long hood, "about the size of a Buick or Dodge." This was buried deep in the 1933 news reports. But it will be recalled that in the days just before Brooke vanished, a man who worked at Hart's store had noticed a 1931 Buick sedan parked in Lightston Alley each afternoon, just before quitting time. Nothing in the record indicates that the investigators ever connected the coinciding auto descriptions. The Buick in the alley had two unknown men as occupants; whoever they were, it is unlikely that either was Holmes, who drove a Chevrolet, or Thurmond, who used his father's Pontiac.

Another suggestion of a third conspirator and a third car arises from Thurmond's and Holmes's orchard rendezvous on White Oaks Road, witnessed by tree pruners Merle Shaves and Everett Mason. FBI reports indicate Shaves and Mason saw only two men, who arrived and left in their respective cars. Yet inexplicably at least three newspapers—the *News*, the *Examiner*, and the *Chronicle*—reported that a third car of unspecified make was supposedly present, driven by an elderly man with white or gray hair. The papers quoted indefinite sources, ostensibly in the sheriff's office.

Emig dealt with the orchard encounter much as he handled his tip from Mrs. Silveria. "Nothing to it," he told reporters. Actually there was a lot to it. Shaves and Mason supplied the license numbers of the cars they had seen, which turned out to belong to Holmes and Thurmond's father. Emig had possessed this information two days before he arrested the suspects.

Was Brooke a Gambler?

No bit of Hart case folklore has been hardier than the belief held by some that the kidnapping began as an attempt to collect a gambling debt, and that the murder was an unintended outcome. Not a shred of documentation supports this, but the tale must be dealt with because of its durability. While researching this book, the author encountered it repeatedly from widely diverse sources—always hearsay of nebulous origin. Several callers mentioned it on a San Francisco radio talk show in 1989.

The particulars vary with the telling, but the gist is that Brooke Hart had become a heavy loser at one or more of several gambling houses that flourished in and around San Jose with the tolerant acquiescence of the police and the town's political overseers. When there was no move to settle his debt, so the story goes, the gamblers hired Holmes and Thurmond, who dwelt on the underworld fringes, to take Brooke for a ride and scare him or his father into paying up. Having seized their prisoner, the kidnappers supposedly ran amok, killed him, and set about recovering the ransom for themselves. When they were caught, according to the scenario, the terrified gambling entrepreneurs realized that their role as originators of the heinous crime might come to light if the case got to court, with the blame extending to their protectors among the cops and politicians. It was therefore decided at the highest establishment levels that Holmes and Thurmond must never reach a courtroom; lynch law must claim them first.

One researcher who tried to nail down this conspiracy is Edith Smith, an archivist for the Sourisseau Academy, a local history research facility at San Jose State University. In 1971, she sought out the late Gertrude McCabe, surviving sister of Jay McCabe, the friend who managed the devastated Hart family's affairs for a long period after the kidnapping.

In a telephone interview, Miss McCabe told Mrs. Smith an astonishing tale. It was to the effect that the original police documents in the Hart case, possibly including the confessions, had mentioned a number of persons other than Holmes and Thurmond in incriminating or embarrassing light. Using his influence as a political insider, Jay McCabe had supposedly arranged to have the reports doctored, deleting all such references.

Miss McCabe said she was in possession of the original, unexpurgated documents, which she kept in a box under her bed, and she was willing to let Mrs. Smith examine them. But a few days later she withdrew the offer, explaining that the Harts were her good friends and on reflection she felt it would be better to squelch the matter.

Gertrude, who never married, was murdered in 1983, stabbed to death in her home. (The crime, which remains unsolved, was in no way connected to the matters under consideration here.) No documents of the type she had described were found among her effects.

If we have no credible evidence confirming the gambling-debt theory, we have considerable tending to refute it. When the kidnapping story broke, a large, talented, resourceful, and fiercely competitive press corps descended on San Jose. It is scarcely possible that if the crime had been rooted in Brooke's gambling, no reporter would have picked up the fact. Conceivably, the San Jose newspapers might have squelched it out of consideration for the Hart family and with an eye to their advertising revenues from Hart's store. But what would have impelled the out-of-town press, lacking such considerations, to sit on the story?

In 1933, San Jose had a handful of legal card rooms, several of which were on Post Street, literally at the back door of Hart's store. But Brooke did not frequent them; this we know from Joe Colla, the downtown shoeshine boy, who knew the denizens of every dive.

The community's illicit gambling took place mostly at Lo Curto's Gardens, a resort on Almaden Road, and at a hotel, so-called, in the easy-virtue enclave of Alviso. Johnny Lo Curto and most other San Jose gamblers were clients of Bill Foley, the underworld lawyer who spent the kidnapping night on the phone trying in vain to get a line on Brooke's abductors. In 1988 Foley's son, James, scoffed at the gambling-debt story; had it been true, he said, his father "would have known it in a minute."

The story also flies in the face of the FBI's findings. In a memo to J. Edgar Hoover, agent Vetterli wrote, "All speakeasies and gambling joints in the vicinity of San Jose were scrutinized carefully . . . but no information at all was received from anyone indicating any reason why the victim should have disappeared."

Chief Black's Strange Default

No puzzle in the Hart case is more baffling than the strangely subordinate role of San Jose Chief of Police John N. Black.

Brooke Hart was kidnapped in downtown San Jose, in the center of Black's jurisdiction, and the arrests of Thurmond and Holmes also took place there. The lynching occurred on city property, St. James Park. The Hart residence, on The Alameda, was in the city. Yet at every turn, Black let himself be upstaged by Sheriff Emig.

Very little of the criminal activity occurred within Emig's jurisdiction, which was primarily the unincorporated territory outside the city limits. Only the transfer of Brooke to Holmes's auto, in the Milpitas hills, and the kidnappers' rendezvous among the orchards took place on the sheriff's turf. (The murder site on the San Mateo Bridge was in Alameda County, outside the jurisdiction of either Emig or Black.)

From the outset Black demonstrated what almost seemed a deliberate lack of interest in the case. As the first officer to whom Brooke's disappearance was reported, he infuriated Miriam Hart with his casual attitude.

It was Emig, not Black, who secretly staked out a man in the Hart home to monitor every contact with the kidnappers. It was the sheriff, not the chief, who arrested Thurmond in the act of making the last ransom call—from a phone literally across the street from Black's office!

Black took part in the grilling of Thurmond, at Emig's invitation, but when Holmes was questioned in San Francisco the next day, the San Jose Police Department was not represented. It was the sheriff who enlisted Marshall Hall to undertake the waterborne search for Brooke's body, and it was Emig's deputies who, with the FBI, tracked down the key witnesses.

The Hart family saw a lot of Emig in the critical days after Brooke vanished; he was often in and out of the house. Black seldom if ever appeared, although he was a friend of the family. Finally, it was Emig who signed the complaint against the kidnappers.

The lynching was the most serious and violent insurrection against law and order in San Jose's history, but despite Emig's pleas for help, Black supplied only two San Jose policemen to help quell it (several others having been sent home earlier in the day).

From kidnapping to lynching, Black seemed to surrender every opportunity for public acclaim. From the first he may have sensed that the case was a no-win battleground; he would let Emig take the glory, but also the lumps.

"John Black was about as honest a guy as you would ever want to know," Jim Foley said in 1988. But the chief also had his detractors. The late Andy Anderson, one of the two San Jose policemen who defended the jail, considered Black a "do-nothing" and "strictly a politician," beholden to the city's boss, Charlie Bigley.

The deployment of only two men in the face of the mob was the equivalent of committing a single battalion to the overthrow of Saddam Hussein. When Black's failure to supply more officers is considered alongside the San Jose Fire Department's refusal to turn its hoses on the lynchers, another sinister conjecture becomes unavoidable. Was there a deliberate decision at San Jose City Hall to let the lynching go ahead unimpeded? If so, who made it? City Manager Goodwin? The councilmen, who were on record for "sure and swift justice"? Charlie Bigley, the city boss, who usually controlled at least four of the seven council votes? Nothing on the record hints at such a decision or remotely connects any of the foregoing persons with what happened in St. James Park. The question of their acquiescence will never be answered. But it must be asked.

The Jail Showdown: Desperate Stand or Sham Battle?

Addressing the San Jose Lions Club four days before the lynching, Bill Emig confidently declared, "We are determined that the kidnappers be dealt with for their crime under the law and in the courts of this county. . . . We are prepared to resist any attempt of those who may propose to take the law into their own hands." But ten hours later, the sheriff removed Jack Holmes and Harold Thurmond from the safety of the San Francisco City Prison and brought them back to San Jose.

"The return of the kidnappers," the *Chronicle* reported the next day in a story that proved squarely on the mark, "was expected to precipitate a crisis."

Four days after the lynching Emig declared in a signed story in the *News*, "With all my ability I tried to prevent it." Most of his constituents took him at his word. But the inconsistencies and absurdities of official actions led others to pose a question still troublesome: Was the stand against the mob a sham—a dramatization fashioned to legitimatize its end result?

Ray Blackmore later called the lynching "an execution," and his partner, Anderson, agreed. Whether or not the lost battle was a charade, it was costly in money, manpower, property damage, pain, blood, guilt, fear, and community esteem. In retrospect, three factors stand out as decisive to the outcome:

The return: When the kidnappers were arrested, as we know, Emig hustled them out of town within hours, fearing mob action. At that point the lynch-law potential was still vague. Why, then, did he bring them back to San Jose six days later, when the city was approaching the flash point of violence?

He ostensibly returned them for arraignment. That, however, could have been accomplished within minutes, and the prisoners could have been back in the safety of their San Francisco cells before the public knew it had happened. As it turned out, when they went to their deaths four nights later, they still had not been arraigned. *

The police line: Blackmore, little more than a rookie cop at the time ôf the lynching, was correct in his perception that the crowd was grossly mishandled. Twelve hours before the lynching the broad courthouse driveway, providing direct access to the jail from First Street, was already filling up with people.

"They should have roped it off, no one within a block of there," Blackmore said much later, after he had controlled many crowds himself as San Jose's chief of police. "But they let them all in, and it's just like a flood of water. After it's flooded, it's too late to plug up the holes."

When thinly manned barricades finally went up across the driveway, they were close to the jail, creating only a small no-man's-land outside its doors. Most of the driveway remained in possession of the lynchers, to become a staging area for their assaults.

Emig cannot be held wholly accountable for the thinness of his police line or the smallness of the area it enclosed. He commanded no more than nineteen deputies (including the jail matron), augmented by a handful of highway patrolmen and the two San Jose officers. To have thrown an effective cordon around the whole block, he would have needed a company of infantrymen with rifles, live ammunition, and fixed bayonets. Rolph had already turned him down on that score.

The "don't shoot" order: Although he said he did not realize it at the time, Emig sealed the fates of Holmes and Thurmond when he

---

* Ironically the arraignments had been postponed at the request of Thurmond's lawyer, J. Oscar Goldstein, who wanted more time to acquaint himself with the case.

forbade gunfire in the jail's defense and made his men lock up their weapons. His order to shed no blood suited the lynchers' plan. Yet later he took sole responsibility for the decision and never regretted it.

"Obviously we couldn't shoot and mow down innocent persons," he wrote. "We confidently thought tear gas would do the work. But tear gas had absolutely no effect on that crowd."

Knowing they would not be fired upon, the lynchers needed only stamina, patience, and strong stomachs.

The Long Shadow of Louis Oneal

Five years after the hangings, a profile of lawyer Louis Oneal entitled "The Battling Overlord of Santa Clara County" appeared in *Coast* magazine. Its author Richard V. Hyer, who had covered the lynching for the *San Francisco News*, wrote, "Oneal was the guiding genius of the successful manhunt for Thurmond and Holmes. . . . Whether Sheriff Emig, when the mob was battering down his jail doors, sought counsel or instructions from his political mentor is not known."

Now we know that Hyer's conjecture was on target. Oneal family lore has it that throughout the siege, the old boss had a phone line open from his ranch into the jail. And as we have seen, Oneal kept a finger on everything that happened in the Hart case from start to finish.

Emig was assuredly Oneal's political creature, elected with his encouragement, advice, endorsement, and money. Moreover, in the dynamics of the case, Oneal had an additional role as one of Governor Rolph's closest cronies. (To this day their families remain close; the boss's great-grandson is named James Rolph Oneal.)

Mystifyingly, the first appearance of the boss's name in the kidnapping episode was the *Examiner's* spurious report, less than thirty-six hours after Brooke was snatched, that Oneal had been proposed as a go-between in the ransom negotiations. Although wrong, the bogus story foreshadowed an immense role Oneal would play in the events ahead.

Why Emig invited Oneal to participate in the interrogation of Harold Thurmond on the night of the arrests, we do not know. Perhaps, having bagged the biggest game of his career, he felt the need for counsel. Another possibility, in keeping with subsequent events, is that Emig summoned Oneal because the old boss had so ordered.

Not only did Oneal sit in on the grilling; he had his whole team there: Belle Gallagher, the stenographer, was his dear friend; Marshall Hall, who held Holmes at bay with a simulated gun and later led the search for Brooke's body, was the newest member of his law firm; Skimp Letcher, who helped Emig spirit the kidnappers out of town in mechanics' clothes, was his pal in the Elks Club.

Among the sobriquets by which Oneal was known was "the Sphinx." In public affairs he normally shunned the spotlight in favor of the string puller's anonymity. We have little clue as to why, stepping out of character, he released the Thurmond confession transcript to the press from his own law office, rather than letting it come through usual channels at the courthouse. The procedure was highly irregular, and all manner of devious intent has been read into it. Was the confession in fact changed or censored before release? A tempting but unsupported conjecture.

Oneal was in a position to control the fate of Holmes and Thurmond if he wanted to. While researching this book, the author quizzed three of those who knew Oneal best—his son, his grandson, and Hall—about the likelihood of his collaboration with the governor in the decision to withhold the National Guard and give the lynchers free rein. All maintained that the old boss, far from abetting the mob's swift justice, was distressed by it. In separate interviews, widely spaced in time, all three cited precisely the same incident to support their contention, namely Hugh Stuart Center's quixotic efforts to halt the lynching by repeatedly yanking the rope down from the gallows tree. At that time, Center was an up-and-coming young lawyer in the Oneal firm.

"Hugh would never have done that if it hadn't had the approval of Louis Oneal," said Hall. Grandson Lou concurred. "Hugh always did my grandfather's bidding."

The surmise that Louis Oneal—boss of the courthouse, mentor of the sheriff, crony of the governor—was the éminence grise of all that happened in St. James Park is widely shared. But surmise is the operative word; it is a proposition that no hard evidence confirms.

Most of the actors of the seventeen-day drama of November 1933 lie silent in the grave, their secrets buried with them. Those who still live talk little. The full truth can never be known. There are more graves every year.

Epilogue

In human terms, the aftermath of the Hart case mingled tragedy with irony. Each of three families, all well-liked and respected, suffered the same bereavement, the loss of a cherished son. And each employed the same defenses—silence and denial—to cope with its agony.

In the Hart household, the crime against Brooke became a tacitly forbidden subject. It was something his brother and sisters seldom spoke of, with one another or with their parents.

"For years," Alex, Jr., recalled in 1988, "there was never a photo of my brother in the house, never a mention of his name, each parent trying to save the other from untold grief. It was just a situation that was private. After all these years I can't help becoming emotional about it. Talking about it is a difficult thing for me to do. It's like if you had your leg amputated: You always walk on a crutch; you know you're never going to grow the leg back. You know you're never going to forget it, and you just do the best you can."

For the surviving Hart children, the crime against their brother brought a curtailment of freedom and a circumscribed life-style as well as emotional devastation.

"We were very closely watched, and we had drivers take us everywhere we went, almost permanently," Alex, Jr., remembered. "It was a very difficult life for a youngster, to be constantly guarded, constantly watched, and constantly chaperoned."

Jane Hammond, Brooke's girlfriend and presumed fiancée, finished college and entered teaching, the career for which she trained. She married twice. Two sons by her first husband, Harvey Derne, live in California. Her second husband was Sir Leonard Usher, KBE, former mayor of Suva, the capital of Fiji, and ex-editor of the *Fiji Times*. In

1991 Sir Leonard said the horror of the Hart case haunted his wife until her death in 1984.

The trauma of 1933 still surfaces in odd, unexpected ways, as when Alex, Jr., was called for jury duty many years later: "The poor fellow, whatever he was doing, was found guilty, and he blamed that on me. I was never called back on jury duty again for a number of years."

As his family's sole surviving son, it fell to Alex, Jr., to carry on the retailing dynasty. At age twenty-two—the same age at which Brooke had died—he became head of the store in 1943, when his parents died within seven weeks of each other.

Alex, Sr., died first on June 23 at age seventy-three of a stroke following a heart attack. On August 9, after surgery, Nettie Hart at age fifty-one followed her husband in death. Both were entombed in crypts adjoining Brooke's in Oak Hill Mausoleum. The father left an estate appraised at $437,758, including more than 60 percent of the stock of L. Hart & Son Company.

The task of closing and selling the family home fell upon Alex, Jr., and Aleese. In the early 1950s they offered it to the City of San Jose at a bargain price, about $60,000, for a museum, but the plan never jelled. Finally the mansion, only a little more than three decades old, was razed. The Santa Clara Valley YMCA occupies the site today.

Five years after Brooke Hart's death, the department store underwent its last major expansion, though not on the six-story, landing-strip-on-the-roof scale that he had dreamed of. A third floor was added, and the bread-and-buttery old building was given a gleaming, modernistic exterior shell of stucco, steel, and glass bricks.

By the mid-1950s San Jose was well into a momentous but nonetheless painful transition from small town to metropolis. Its central core, with much of its rotting infrastructure dating from the nineteenth century, began to die, and one by one the big stores folded or moved out. Hart's stuck it out the longest, until 1968. The empty building at Market and Santa Clara fell to the wrecker's ball in 1973, clearing the site for an eight-story bank.

For a number of years the Hart firm continued with smaller stores in three suburban shopping centers, but by the mid-1970s they were suffering in the face of formidable new rivals that stampeded into what was beginning to be called Silicon Valley. When the last store closed in 1982, the *Mercury* headlined the story, "Broken Hart's."

* * *

Harold Thurmond's and Jack Holmes's survivors dealt with their tragedy in ways that curiously paralleled the Hart family's.

"I just put the whole thing out of my life," a member of the Thurmond family circle, who asked not to be identified, told the author. "I just never let it interfere with anything and never even thought about it. We have never talked about it ourselves, the family."

The same feeling pervades the remarks of David Holmes, Jack's son, who was six years old when his father died. The family was "shattered totally," he said in 1989, but, "Nobody talks about it. We avoided the issue. I've made myself disinterested all my life. . . . I was always brought up to believe that my father was not guilty. My grandfather, Maurice, bankrupted himself trying to prove it. He had two tailor shops; he lost both of them and ended up working for wages in order to support the lawyers."

Joyce Holmes, who was two weeks short of her fifth birthday when her father's life ended, was told first that he had gotten lost on a hunting trip. Later she was told he was dead, but that it was something she must never talk about, an admonition she accepted uncritically. For more than three decades that was all she knew. Then, when Joyce was thirty-six years old, her eighteen-year-old son learned the circumstances of his grandfather's death from other members of the family and asked her why he had never been told. The truthful answer she gave him was that until that moment, she had had no inkling of the secret herself.

Evelyn Holmes was twenty-nine when she fled with her children to her sister's home in Stockton after her husband's arrest. The ensuing days were a nightmare. She was hounded by the reporters for interviews she refused to grant. (Neither then nor later did Evelyn tell her story for publication until interviewed by the author in 1989. And strangely, neither before nor after the lynching was she questioned by the police, the sheriff's men, or the FBI.)

The family of Ira Langdon, the Stockton attorney retained for Holmes, became the target of ominous threats after the lynching.

"They got telephone calls at night, and the callers said that what happened to Jack could happen to their children," Evelyn recounted. Langdon was only too happy to turn her affairs over to Vincent Hallinan, who was already preparing to sue Governor Rolph and others on her behalf. Hallinan "had a lot of pictures of the mob—horrible pictures" and wanted her to identify any persons she recognized. He asked her to stick pins in their likenesses so he could put their names on the other side. She recognized no one.

Never would Evelyn return to live in her hometown of San Jose, and never again would she use Holmes as her surname. For both herself and her children, she reverted to her maiden name, Fleming. (David would resume using Holmes when he enlisted in the Navy during World War II.)

Facing the need to support herself and the children in the deepest trough of the Depression, Evelyn took a job as a knitting teacher with the Works Progress Administration, the centerpiece job agency of President Roosevelt's New Deal.

"I didn't intend to go on living, you know," she disclosed in 1989. "I spent a whole year deciding what I was going to do—more than a year actually. I was going to take Dave and Joyce with me, and we weren't going to face this thing through, that's all."

It was R. Stanley Kneeshaw, the San Jose family doctor who had delivered both her children, who dissuaded Evelyn from taking her own life and theirs. He was a common-sense man, a sometimes gruff but caring and skillful practitioner who would later become president of the California Medical Association.

"He really talked to me, yes," she remembered. "He told me that I had a right to bring life here but no right to take it away. He told me that I had no way of knowing how my children were going to turn out, and I should give them a chance to find out for themselves. Oh, I liked him. He was the only reason that I kept on living and why my children are alive today."

With her new will to live, Evelyn buckled down to her teaching job and so distinguished herself that she began to move up in the WPA hierarchy. Ultimately she was put in charge of all women's and white-collar programs in eight California counties. When the WPA was disbanded, she moved into a supervisorial position on the regular federal payroll.

Neither she nor her children have suffered derision, prejudice, or harassment because of their 1933 tragedy, but as with the Harts, unforeseen incidents freshen it in their consciousness from time to time. At Fresno State College a visiting professor lectured on the Hart case before David's history class, unaware that Jack Holmes's son was in the classroom. The visitor described the lynching in such vivid detail that David could only assume he had taken part in it. David did not identify himself, fearing that if he had confronted the lecturer, he "might have killed him."

Evelyn has had two other husbands since Jack's death, both now deceased. There are no children from either of her later marriages. In 1989, at age eighty-five, she lived alone in a spacious mobile home, tastefully furnished and neat as a pin, on the outskirts of a favored residential city. She still asserted her certain belief in Jack Holmes's innocence, insisting that he was at home with her during the hours when Brooke Hart was kidnapped and slain.

"I still dream that someday the truth will come out," she said, "but I don't know where or how or when."

By New Year's Day of 1934, Sunny Jim Rolph had weathered the worst of the storm he had created—or so he reckoned. The old campaigner's instincts told him he was ready to do battle for a second term in the governor's office.

His physicians were less sanguine. A bout with pneumonia a year earlier had weakened him, and his blood pressure was now chronically high. On February 28, while in Marysville on a "good will trip," Rolph collapsed and was taken by ambulance to San Francisco. He was on the "serious" list for several weeks, before collapsing again on May 3, from the third in a series of strokes. For his convalescence he accepted the hospitality of his friend, San Francisco attorney Walter Linforth, whose showplace Riverside Farm in the flatlands north of Santa Clara offered peaceful seclusion. Though gravely ill, Rolph retained a remnant of his feistiness. By his bedside he kept a pistol, and in his last days he summoned his nurses by firing blanks at the ceiling. He died on June 2.

Those who had strung up Jack Holmes and Harold Thurmond now had double reason for gratitude to the authorities who had decided not to prosecute them. Until Rolph's death, they had had his promise of pardon to fall back on. Now that was gone. And the re-election campaign which could have amounted to a voter referendum on the San Jose lynching would never be held. Was Sunny Jim a hero or an embarrassment to most Californians? The answer would remain forever imponderable.

Rolph's death doomed attorney Hallinan's efforts to obtain wrongful death damages for the Holmes family. On April 20 he had filed a $1 million damage suit against the governor and others in San Francisco Superior Court, taking advantage of the fact that San Francisco was Rolph's legal residence and therefore a proper venue. He followed up with two other actions, charging a wide range of defendants with inciting or condoning the lynching.

With Rolph gone, the remaining defendants won a change of venue to Santa Clara County, where Hallinan despaired of obtaining a

297

favorable verdict. One by one, the three lawsuits worked their way through the dockets to dead ends. The last was dismissed in 1937.

Although Emig's actions in the lynching crisis were controversial, he came through, overall, on a tide of public admiration and sympathy. Looking toward the 1934 elections, he saw little to fear. But early in the new year, for political reasons having nothing to do with the Hart case, he came to a parting of the ways with Louis Oneal. When he rebelled at orders, the boss told him coldly, "Well, then, you're going to lose the election." It was an accurate forecast; Emig lost to his old adversary, Lyle, by some 500 votes. "We figured that was about what Louis Oneal controlled," said his daughter, Florence Emig Wheeler, much later.

The estrangement of mentor and pupil was bitter, but not the end of the tale. In 1938 Emig recaptured the sheriff's office, defeating not only Lyle but another opponent backed by Oneal. The old cowboy's grip had slipped a little.

Oneal died of a heart attack on March 3, 1943, at age sixty-nine, and was entombed not far from Brooke Hart in the Oak Hill Mausoleum. Nearly half a century later his law firm remains, under the leadership of his grandson and namesake, one of the city's most prestigious.

Emig's re-election to a third term in 1942, amid rumors of corruption in his office, was the prelude to a tragic denouement. His career collapsed in 1945, when he and four others were charged with gambling conspiracy. Taken by surprise, Emig was arrested at his desk. He was convicted and sentenced to four months in the county jail farm, an extension of the jail where he had once stood off the mob. He was released after three months and ten days—twenty days having been lopped from his term for good behavior.

Eventually Emig settled in Palm Springs, working as a part-time process server. On the night of October 21, 1963, the seventy-two-year-old ex-cop set out to serve a summons and the next morning was found dead in a swimming pool, into which he had stumbled while crossing a yard in the dark. There was no suspicion of foul play.

Other officers prominent in the Hart case had widely varied careers thereafter. Chief of Police John Black remained in office for eleven more years, until his retirement was forced by a new-broom city council. He died in 1949. Boss Charlie Bigley, to whom Black had given fealty, died of cancer in 1946. Ray Blackmore, one of the two young San Jose cops who fired tear gas during the lynching battle, later became chief of police himself. He died in late 1988; his partner, E. D. "Andy" Anderson, survived him by six weeks.

Reed Vetterli, who headed the FBI investigation of the Hart case, resigned from the bureau in 1938 and returned to his native Utah, becoming chief of police in Salt Lake City. He later ran unsuccessfully for Congress and the Republican gubernatorial nomination. He died suddenly of a heart attack in 1949. William Ramsey, the FBI agent whose stakeout inside the Hart home led to the kidnappers' arrest, had only a few years left. In 1938, at age thirty-four, he was killed in a shootout with a suspected bank robber near Armstrong, Illinois.

Fred Thomas, the district attorney who was cheated of the chance to prosecute the kidnappers, was reelected in 1934, but in 1938 declined to seek another term. He died on December 29 of that year.

Earl Warren, the Alameda County district attorney, was elected California attorney general in 1938 and governor in 1942. In 1953 he was appointed by President Eisenhower as chief justice of the United States. He died in 1974.

The man identified in these pages as "Ray Sousa," who almost became a third victim of the mob, served out his manslaughter term and joined the army. He emerged from World War II in the grade of master sergeant. He still lived in San Jose, retired, in 1991.

Gertrude Estensen, the schoolteacher who had once been Jack Holmes' high school sweetheart and might have become his alibi witness, carried on with her private life and career intact. She eventually became a school principal. She and her husband, Leonard, had been wed fifty-five years when she died in 1986. Leonard died in 1991.

Anthony Cataldi, whose boastfulness made him the scapegoat for all the lynchers, later carved an impressive niche for himself in San Jose business and real estate. By the 1980s he owned several office buildings. He died in 1991.

Louis Rossi, the last Hart's employee to see Brooke alive, worked at the store until 1939 and opened his own large furniture store in 1946. As a veterans' affairs activist, he served as chairman of more than forty patriotic parades in San Jose. He died in 1990.

Marshall Hall, the newly minted attorney who led the search for Brooke Hart's body, went on to a distinguished career in the law, becoming a Superior Court judge in 1957. He died in 1990.

Another Hart drama player who more surprisingly attained the Superior Court bench is Joseph Karesh, the young rabbi. He left the rabbinate to become an attorney in 1939 and was elected a judge in 1960. He later presided at several high-visibility trials, including that of Black Panther leader Huey Newton. As this is written he is still on the bench in Oakland.

Vincent Hallinan, the San Francisco lawyer retained by the Holmes family, went on to a spectacular career as a defender of the innocent and the hopelessly guilty. He became, as well, a fiery champion of liberal and left-wing causes and was the Progressive Party's presidential candidate in 1952. At this writing he remains active.

Harold Thurmond's brother Roy, the Chico minister, became superintendent of the Northern California–Nevada District of the Assemblies of God, then returned to San Jose as pastor of the First Assembly of God in 1955. He died in 1972.

One of the hardiest myths about the Thurmond-Holmes hanging is that it was California's "last lynching." It was not. More than twenty months later, on August 3, 1935, a band of masked vigilantes surprised and overpowered the lone jailer at the Siskiyou County Jail in Yreka, near the Oregon line. They seized Clyde L. Johnson, the confessed slayer of F. R. Daw, the chief of police in Dunsmuir, and drove him about three miles south of town where they strung him up to a bull pine tree. Governor Frank Merriam, showing an attitude in sharp contrast to that of his predecessor, denounced the event as "a blot upon the fair name of California."

Another widely held misconception is that the San Jose lynching put an end to the kidnap epidemic of the 1930s. It did not. To the contrary, the incidence of the crime increased thereafter. Within the FBI's jurisdiction, there were ten major kidnappings in 1933, of which the Brooke Hart case was the ninth. The number jumped to eighteen in 1934, twenty-six in 1935, thirty-one in 1936, thirty in 1937, and thirty-seven in 1938.

Nationwide, there were twenty-eight lynchings in 1933, in which all but four of the victims—Holmes, Thurmond, and two others— were black. In 1934, at the behest of the NAACP, Senator Edward Costigan of Colorado introduced his measure (the Costigan-Wagner Bill) to make lynching a federal offense. It shared the fate of its predecessor, the Dyer Bill of 1922, dying in a Senate filibuster. To the present day, Congress has never enacted an antilynching law, but the civil rights legislation of the 1960s has partially filled the void, establishing a strong federal presence in any situation where rights of Americans—prisoners included—are denied or abused.

With the crimes of November 1933, tranquil San Jose took its place in the gazeteer of world infamy. A decade later during World War II, photographs of Holmes's and Thurmond's dangling corpses were used by Hitler's propagandists as depictions of American barbarism.

San Jose has grown thirteen-fold since 1933. The 1990 census counted its population at 782,242, making it California's third largest city—San Francisco having slipped into fourth position with 723,959. Shopping malls, subdivisions, and the temples of high-tech industry have replaced orchards and fields. The computer chip has supplanted the prune as the mainstay of the economy. What was once the "Valley of Heart's Delight" is now Silicon Valley.

The old jail is gone, succeeded by two others. The old courthouse suffered major structural damage in the earthquake that rocked the Bay Area in October 1989 and stands empty at this writing, awaiting a multimillion-dollar restoration.

A certain smugness about the lynching, once evinced by many San Joseans, has dissipated but not vanished. Among those unborn in 1933, attitudes range from curiosity to revulsion. To many newcomers, the names Hart, Holmes, and Thurmond mean nothing.

The fading of the events from community consciousness has come slowly. When young lawyer Melvin Hawley ran for sheriff in 1954, he found the episode still much on people's minds, but with attitudes changing. Repeatedly he was asked, "What would you do if a mob tried to storm the jail?"

"I'd shoot every one as he came through the door," Hawley responded.

He was elected, defeating five old-time cops, including the incumbent.

Selected Bibliography

Books

Arbuckle, Clyde. *Clyde Arbuckle's History of San Jose*. San Jose, Calif.: Smith & McKay Printing Company, 1985.

Boucher, Anthony, Mystery Writers of America. *The Quality of Murder*. New York: E. P. Dutton & Co., 1962.

Burrows, William E. *Vigilante!* New York: Harcourt Brace Jovanovich, 1976.

California State Text-Book Committee and State Board of Education. *Introductory History of the United States*. Sacramento: California State Printing Office, 1905.

Conot, Robert E. *Ministers of Vengeance*. Philadelphia and New York: J. B. Lippincott Company, 1964.

Farr, Finis. *Fair Enough—The Life of Westbrook Pegler*. New Rochelle, N.Y.: Arlington House, 1975.

Gentry, Curt. *Frame-up*. New York: W.W. Norton & Company, 1967.

Hallinan, Vincent. *A Lion in Court*. New York: G. P. Putnam's Sons, 1963.

Jordan, Frank C. *California Blue Book, 1932*. Sacramento: California State Printing Office, 1932.

Lamson, David. *We Who Are About to Die*. New York: Charles Scribner's Sons, 1935.

McKevitt, Gerald, S.J. *The University of Santa Clara, a History, 1851–1977*. Palo Alto, Calif.: Stanford University Press, 1979.

Melendy, H. Brett, and Benjamin F. Gilbert. *The Governors of California, Peter H. Burnett to Edmund G. Brown*. Georgetown, Calif.: The Talisman Press, 1965.

Mott, Frank Luther. *News Stories of 1933*. Iowa City, Iowa: Clio Press, 1934.

Pagano, Jo. *The Condemned*. New York: Prentice-Hall, 1947.

Powers, Richard Gid. *Secrecy and Power, The Life of J. Edgar Hoover*. New York: The Free Press, Macmillan, 1987.

Sawyer, Eugene T. *History of Santa Clara County, California*. Los Angeles: Historic Record Company, 1922.

Snyder, Louis L., and Richard B. Morris. *A Treasury of Great Reporting*. New York: Simon and Schuster, 1949.

Steinbeck, John. *The Long Valley*. New York: Viking Press, 1946.

Taylor, David Wooster. *The Life of James Rolph, Jr.* San Francisco: Recorder Printing & Publishing Company, 1934.

Walsh, James P. *San Francisco's Hallinan, Toughest Lawyer in Town*. Novato, Calif.: Presidio Press, 1982.

Warren, Earl. *The Memoirs of Earl Warren*. Garden City, N.Y.: Doubleday & Company, 1977.

Watkins, T. H. *California: An Illustrated History*. Palo Alto, Calif.: American West Publishing Company, 1973.

Watkins, T. H., and R. R. Olmsted. *Mirror of the Dream, An Illustrated History of San Francisco*. San Francisco: Scrimshaw Press, 1976.

White, G. Edward. *Earl Warren, a Public Life*. New York: Oxford University Press, 1982.

Young, John V. *Hot Type & Pony Wire*. Santa Cruz, Calif.: Western Tanager Press, 1980.

Articles and Documents

Bauerle, William. Term paper, "Nightmare in November." San Jose State University, 1978.

Brier, Royce. "Kidnappers Lynched—Mob Storms Jail, Hangs Slayers in San Jose Square." *San Francisco Chronicle*, November 27, 1933.

Carter, Leslie Stuart. "Last Lynching in California—1933." *Los Angeles Times* (View Section), December 4, 1983.

Chivers, Bill. "The Los Gatos Hangman's Bridge." *The Trailblazer*, quarterly bulletin of the California Pioneers of Santa Clara County, February 1985.

The Commonweal. Article, "The Lynching of Justice." December 8, 1933.

Copeland, George H. "Lynching Is Again a National Issue." *New York Times*, December 3, 1933.

Daley, Elizabeth W. Manuscript, "The Last of the California Vigilantes." 1957.

DeFord, Miriam Allen. "The Patriotic Justice of San Jose," from *The Quality of Murder*, Mystery Writers of America, edited by Anthony Boucher. New York: E. P. Dutton & Co., 1962.

Editor & Publisher. Article, "News Men Face Police Gas, Mob Guns To Cover California Lynchings." December 2, 1933.

Elliott, Lawrence. "The Day Judge Lynch Cried Hang!" *Coronet*, June 1956.

Giannecchini, Pamela. "1933: California's Last Lynching." *Highway Patrolman*, October 1975.

Gillard, John T. "Lynching and the Law." *The Commonweal*, December 15, 1933.

————. "Can We Stop Lynching." *The Commonweal*, December 29, 1933.

Greb, Gordon B. "The Golden Anniversary of Broadcasting." *Journal of Broadcasting*, Winter 1958–59.

Houston, James D. "Coming of Age with San Jose." *West*, Sunday magazine of the *San Jose Mercury News*, January 1, 1984.

Hyer, Richard. "The Battling Overlord of Santa Clara County." *Coast*, May 1938.

Jones, Ellis O. "Was An Innocent Man Lynched at San Jose?" *New Republic*, February 7, 1934.

Literary Digest. Article, "Curse of Lynching Agitates the Nation." December 9, 1933.

McGinty, Brian. "Shadows in St. James Park." *California History*, Winter 1978–79.

McLane, Tegan M. Term paper, "In Black and White." E. W. Scripps School of Journalism, Ohio University, Athens, Ohio, 1989.

Nation. Article, "The Terror in San Jose." August 8, 1934.

Nelson, Frank C. "The Last Lynching." *Cal Today*, Sunday magazine of the *San Jose Mercury News*, November 26, 1978.

New Republic. Article, "Mass Murder in America." December 13, 1933.

Peyton, Wes. "Ray Blackmore: Cop and 'Politician' for 42 Years." *San Jose Mercury and News*, January 23, 1980.

————. "The Lynching That San Joseans Wanted to Forget." *San Jose Mercury and News*, February 27, 1980.

Rischin, Moses. "Sunny Jim Rolph: The First 'Mayor of All the People.' " *California Historical Quarterly*, Summer 1974.

Rolph, James, Jr. "Rolph Restates His Attitude; Sees 'Criminals' Day at an End." *New York Times*, North American Newspaper Alliance, November 30, 1933.

Ruby, Matthew P. Term paper, "A City's Night of Shame—The San Jose Lynchings of November, 1933." Leland High School, San Jose, Calif., 1975.

Sullivan, Edward S. "The Brooke Hart Kidnap-Murder and the California Lynch Mob." *Master Detective*, May 1962.

Time. Article, "California Lesson." December 4, 1933.

————. Article, "Lesson Learned." December 11, 1933.

————. Article, "Parliament's Week." December 18, 1933.

Van Dyke, Karen. Term paper, "The Hart Kidnapping of November, 1933." Leland High School, San Jose, Calif., 1970–72.

Vetterli, Thelma F. "G-Man's Wife." *Salt Lake Tribune*, November 5, 1939.

Winslow, Ward. "San Jose's Night of Shame." *Peninsula Living* section of *Palo Alto Times*, June 9, 1956.

Winter, Ella. Article, "California's Little Hitlers." *New Republic*, December 27, 1933.

Documentary Tapes

KQED-FM, San Francisco. Documentary audio tape, "San Jose Lynching."
1988.

Whitman, Gary. Documentary audio tape, "The San Jose Lynching of
1933." San Jose State College, 1968.

Newspapers

Chicago Daily News. November 10, 1933.

Chicago Tribune. November 11–12, 1933.

Cincinnati Enquirer. November 11, 1933.

Los Angeles Evening Herald and Express. November 28, 1933.

Los Angeles Times. November 29, 1933, and December 4, 1983.

New York Herald Tribune. November 11, 1933.

New York Journal. November 11, 1933.

New York Post. January 18, 1934.

New York Sun. November 10, 11, and 16, 1933.

New York Times. November 11–30, 1933, December 1–13, 1933, January
12–28, 1934, and April 21, 1934.

Oakland Post-Enquirer. November 27, 1933.

Oakland Tribune. November 27, 1933.

Philadelphia Inquirer. November 17, 1933.

St. Joseph (Missouri) News Press. December 2, 1979.

Salt Lake Telegram. November 5–26, 1939.

San Francisco Call-Bulletin. November 17–27, 1933.

San Francisco Chronicle. November 10–29, 1933, August 4, 1935, January
13, 1940, July 11, 1946, October 24, 1946, and October 23, 1963.

San Francisco Examiner. November 11–27, 1933.

San Francisco News. November 27, 1933.

San Francisco Sunday Examiner and Chronicle. November 24, 1968, and
September 24, 1989.

San Jose Evening News. November 13–30, 1933, December 1–22, 1933,
January 18–27, 1934, June 23, 1943, September 12, 1945, October 4,
1945, March 31, 1975, and July 22, 1983.

San Jose Mercury. March 4, 1954, January 11, 1972, October 6, 1978, and
March 15, 1982.

San Jose Mercury Herald. May 26, 1922, March 4, 1926, May 13, 1926,
June 30, 1931, August 17, 1931, January 21, 1932, August 4, 1932,
September 19, 1933, November 4–30, 1933, December 1–31, 1933,
January 4, 1934, November 9, 1935, June 24, 1943, August 10, 1943,
and April 7, 1949.

San Jose Mercury News. March 16, 1975, April 20, 1975, November 26,
1978, October 10, 1983, November 28–30, 1983, and January 11, 1989.

San Juan Mission News. November 30, 1933.

The Santa Clara. November 23, 1933.

Washington Herald. November 11–28, 1933, and February 16, 1934.
Washington Post. November 11–29, 1933, December 4, 1933, and October 8, 1934.
Washington Star. November 10–20, 1933.
Washington Times. November 10–30, 1933.

Wire Services and Syndicates

Files of the Associated Press, International News Service, North American Newspaper Alliance, and United Press for November and December 1933.

Acknowledgments

In researching and writing the Hart case story, I have fallen into the debt of many persons for whose assistance, encouragement, information, and insights I am deeply grateful.

I have benefited immensely from the counsel of my agent, Maria Theresa Caen, and my editor at St. Martin's Press, Cal Morgan.

My former newspaper, the *San Jose Mercury News*, has given me greatly appreciated support in making its resources available to this project. I owe special thanks to Robert D. Ingle, executive editor, and to Gary Lance and his staff in the *Mercury News* library.

Each passing month thins the ranks of those who took part in the events of 1933. Many persons who have talked to me over the past several years are now gone.

By far, my greatest debt is to the exceptional corps of reporters and photographers who covered the story fifty-nine years ago. For seventeen punishing days, under round-the-clock deadline pressure, they labored to record the interplay of private tragedy, public fear and anger, politics, community frenzy, and violence. Their first rough draft of this history, in the yellowed newspapers of 1933, remains the best record of the matters with which they dealt. In a later era I was privileged to know and work with several of these fine journalists. I salute especially George Millard, Frank Lowery, and Len Kullmann of the *San Jose Evening News*; Bob Couchman and Loris Gardner of the *San Jose Mercury Herald*; Royce Brier, Carolyn Anspacher, Leo Raridan, Earl C. Behrens, Hale Shield, and Ted Pryor of the *San Francisco Chronicle*; Alvin D. Hyman and Reginald Clampett of the *San Francisco Examiner*; Rene Cazenave and Allan Campbell of the *San Francisco Call-Bulletin*; Dick Hyer and Baron Muller of the *San Francisco News*; H. R. Hill and Howard Robbins of the *Oakland Post-Enquirer*; Harry Lerner and Harold J. Fitzgerald of the *Oakland Tribune*; Ralph Heppe of the Associated Press;

Harry Sharpe of the United Press; Ralph Jordan of International News Service; and Acme photographer Melvin B. Meacham.

I especially appreciate the cooperation of the Hart family. The brother and sisters of Brooke Hart—Alex, Jr., Miriam, and Aleese—shared recollections that evoked great pain even after almost six decades, contributing immeasurably to the authenticity, scope, and human dimension of this work. I have also profited greatly from material supplied by the late Ray Renwick, whom Brooke Hart regarded as a brother-in-law.

The family and friends of the late Jane Hammond, Brooke's presumed fiancée, graciously assisted me with photographs and recollections. In particular I would mention her sons, Harvey and John Derne; her husband, Sir Leonard Usher, KBE; her sister-in-law, Delores Hammond; and her friend, Marge Pedder.

Special thanks go to Evelyn Holmes, the widow of Jack Holmes, for reminiscences of her husband and for the never-before-told story of her experiences after his arrest. David and Joyce Holmes, his son and daughter, were also most helpful.

I am in debt to Florence Emig Wheeler for her insights into the personality, life-style, thinking, and actions of her father, Sheriff William Emig.

Family survivors of FBI agent Reed E. Vetterli greatly aided my project. They include Annette Vetterli Kaye and Elaine Vetterli Brown, his daughters; Dora Trowbridge, his sister; and Richard Vetterli, his nephew.

Charles O'Brien, Jr., and the late Louis A. Rossi, Brooke's close friends who played important roles in the 1933 drama, gave generously of their time to tell me about it.

The late Duncan Oneal and Louis Oneal II, son and grandson respectively of the reputed political boss Louis Oneal, supplied fascinating recollections and knowledgeably sketched for me the political setting for the events herein set forth.

The two San Jose police officers at the center of the battle against the lynch mob, the late former chief of police Ray Blackmore and the late E. D. "Andy" Anderson, gave detail that brought the scene to life for me.

Judge Henry Rolph and Joseph A. Moore, Jr. provided interesting remembrances of their uncle, Governor James Rolph, Jr., as did George Christopher, a distinguished successor to the governor in his earlier office of mayor of San Francisco.

I had a stimulating interview with Judge Joseph Karesh who, as a young rabbi in 1933, was a friend and spiritual adviser to the Hart family and officiated at Brooke's funeral.

The FBI's file on the Hart case is the only official record of it that remains substantially intact. FBI personnel who assisted me in obtaining the file pursuant to the Freedom of Information Act, and who supplied other important background material, include Jack French, Milt Ahlerich, E. J. Porter, James K. Hall, Charles Monroe, Garland R. Schweikhardt, Mary Rose Hazzard, and Helen Ann Near.

Althea Simmons of the Washington, D.C., office of the National Association for the Advancement of Colored People provided helpful information on the history and status of antilynching legislation.

I had invaluable assistance, cheerfully given, from librarians, archivists, researchers, and officials of several institutions, both governmental and private. I would mention especially Clyde Arbuckle, San Jose city historian; Kathleen Muller, Mignon Gibson, Leslie Masunaga, and Diana Wix of the San Jose Historical Museum; the Rev. Gerald McKevitt, S.J., of the Santa Clara University history department; Julie O'Keefe and Cynthia Atmore of the Santa Clara University archives; Edith Smith, archivist of the Sourisseau Academy at San Jose State University; special collections archivist Gloria Henry at the San Jose State University library, Joanne Rife in the university's public information office, and James P. Walsh of the San Jose State history department; George Kobayashi, Carmen Newby, and the staff of the California Room at the Dr. Martin Luther King, Jr. Library of the City of San Jose; Steve Norman, head of reference at River Bluffs Regional Library, St. Joseph, Missouri; Cindy Vessey and Becky Dryden of the Somerset County Library System, Princess Anne, Maryland; Kathy Fueston, reference librarian of the Siskiyou County Public Library, Yreka, California; Nancy Zimmelman of the California State Archives in Sacramento; Janet Bombard-Pashin, Linda Coppens, and Arlene Hess of the Harrison Memorial Library in Carmel, California; Tom MacRostie of the San Jose City Planning Department; Barry Farris of the H. M. Gousha Company; the secretaries of the First Baptist and First Congregational churches in San Jose; and Kati Corsaut of the California Department of Justice.

Two grants from the Sourisseau Academy at San Jose State University defrayed a substantial part of my research and writing expense in connection with this book. I am most appreciative.

Numerous other persons who granted interviews or otherwise helped me deserve recognition. At the risk of inadvertently omitting some of them, I tip my hat to the following.

Jane Alexander, Richard F. Barrett, Richard Battin, Bill Bauerle, Robert D. Belshaw, Dwight Bentel, Ed Bernstein, Mildred Bolton, Dennis Britton, Halden Broaders, Bob Brown, Lurlene Bush, Eva Bustard, Cathie Calvert, Santina Pepitone Campagna, Bob Caya, Judge Gerald S. Chargin, Robert Cline, Joe Colla, Dominic J. Condensa, Robert E. Conot, Louise Cummins, Walter L. Cunningham, Leonard Dalve, Clarisse Day, Frank W. Doherty, George Dolfin, Louis Duino, Richard Ellefsen, the late Leonard Estensen, Frank Fielding, James Foley, Theron Fox, Fred H. Gardner, Charles Gates, Teresa Guerin Gates, Jeanne Gilbert, Joanne Grant, Gordon Greb, the late Judge Marshall Hall, Vincent Hallinan, Mike Harris, Melvin L. Hawley, Ron Hayes, Jeremiah G. Hickey, Bob Hill, Grace Hill, Charles Jellison, Mark Johnson, Wes Johnson, Al Jones, Shirley Katzander, Peter Kaye, Judge Jack Komar, Gloria LaLond, Edward Landels, Les Lantz, June Larson, James Leggate, Patricia Loomis, Mack Lundstrom, Al Magazu, Marjorie Mason, Sherman Millard, Alfred J. Montalbano, Hal Morris, Roland J. Narducci,

Dorothy Newell, Jennie Nielsen, the late Russell M. O'Brien, Roy Oleson, Carl W. Palmer, Janice Paull, Bob Payne, Manuel Pereira, Edward J. Perovich, Wes Peyton, Marjorie Pierce, Hope Raggett, Brooke Renwick, Matthew P. Ruby, Rod Rucker, the late Charles "Rocky" Santoro, Grace Sautter, Warren Scappettone, Isabel Silveria Schryver, Alton and Muriel Scott, Nancy Scott, John Sepulveda, Mrs. Martin E. Shaves, Alfred E. Smith, the late George Snell, the late Vince Strobel, Ray Tessler, Tony Traina, William and Leone Van Arsdale, Jill van de Velde, Helen Pabst Walsh, the late Philip J. Watson, Jack Webb, Lenore Wilkerson, Iola Williams, Francis Wyatt, and several persons who supplied information confidentially.

Index

319